De Chantigny

Hilaire Belloc's Prefaces:
Written for Fellow Authors

selected by J. A. De Chantigny
foreword by Christopher Hollis

Cloth, [34] + 347 pages, 1971
$14.95 T
ISBN 0-8294-0209-8
Library of Congress Catalog Card Number: 76-178120

All admirers of the prolific works of the late Hilaire Belloc will be grateful to De Chantigny for having hunted down the thirty-seven prefaces reproduced here in facsimile. Hollis maintains that these prefaces show "the extraordinary variety and versatility of his [Belloc's] genius" as fully as do his major works. The first preface was written in 1899, the last in 1938—four years before the stroke that ended Belloc's writing career but not his life.

It would indeed be a rare Belloc collector who had read all these prefaces since they were scattered both in time and place. Hollis' commentary on the prefaces is revealing; De Chantigny's "About Hilaire Belloc," a most informative review of Belloc's life and works.

For bibliophiles the facsimile reproductions indicate some now defunct printers' practices to identify signatures. Also evident in most prefaces is the unimaginative typographical design of older letterpress books. All the reproductions are actual size except #17 and #34. Anyone with a knowledge of repeated letterpress printings from the same type could gauge the popularity of certain books by the broken letters and heavy marginal type due to overworked, damaged metal—something rare today in lithographic or offset printing.

This unique volume reveals more than Belloc's versatility. It tells us something of the history of printing. Most of all, however, it proves that the vital Hilaire Belloc is still alive in the hearts of many readers, although he died July 16, 1953, in Guildford. The BBC that day, according to J. A. De Chantigny, "interrupted all its programmes to announce the passing away of one of England's greatest literary figures."

Hilaire Belloc's Prefaces

WRITTEN FOR FELLOW AUTHORS

selected by J. A. De Chantigny

with a foreword by Christopher Hollis

LOYOLA UNIVERSITY PRESS

Chicago   60657

© 1971 Loyola University Press

Printed in the United States of America
Library of Congress Catalog Card Number: 76-178120
ISBN 0-8294-0209-8
NOTE
For sale only in the United States and Canada

TO

MR. C. F. PETELLE

AND

DR. J. B. R. COSGROVE

WITHOUT WHOSE

HELP AND ENCOURAGEMENT

THIS VOLUME

WOULD NOT HAVE BEEN PRODUCED

CONTENTS / ACKNOWLEDGMENTS

Contents / Acknowledgments [9]

[10]   Contents / Acknowledgments

FOREWORD

In his amusing *Biographies for Beginners*, E. C. Bentley comments on Hilaire Belloc that,

> Mr. Hilaire Belloc
> Is a case for legislation ad hoc.
> He seems to think that nobody minds
> His books being all of different kinds.

Indeed this collection of his prefaces to other people's books shows as fully as is shown by his own works the extraordinary variety and versatility of his genius. There are here the introductions to works of Catholic apologetics, to an examination of Lourdes, to works of description on famous places such as Paris and London. There are essays of literary appreciation on the great Victorians—Froude, Carlyle, Freeman, Newman, and James Russell Lowell; Villon from the Renaissance; P. G. Wodehouse, Ruth Pitter, and Maurice Baring from his own time; his great favourite Kai Lung. He rides his hobbyhorses, brings the French Revolution and Napoleon to live at St. Helena, traces the influence of France on Ireland, denounces the plutocrats of the Reformation and the Prussians, as in the essay on Cecil Chesterton's *Perils of Peace*, praises the French and with characteristic aggressiveness turns to bay against the popular progressive liberal theses on Calas and the Inquisition. In some of the prefaces he takes the opportunity to enunciate his own views with not very much more than a nodding bow to the author whom he is introducing. Elsewhere he appreciates. One or two of the prefaces—such for instance, as that on the Catholic parishes of Guildford and Farnham or the parliamentary history of Horsham, are but tributes of requested courtesy to another's works.

Over all the prefaces, as over all his writing, the first mark is that of the consistent excellence of his English prose—an excellence which was universally recognised in his great days in the first decade of this century but is now less recalled—whether because he himself cared less in his closing years or because men had come to care less about good prose. In those early years of his enormous energy, when he was the candidate for Salford in the 1906 election, in the evening after his own campaigning was finished he used to go over into the neighbouring constituency to listen to the speeches of the candidate there, the young Winston Churchill. He heard him say one evening of his opponents, "They shall be forgiven. In this world a man should be forgiven everything save the writing of bad prose," and he said to himself, "This young man will amount to something." In those years young men who had no especial sympathy with his opinions, such as, for instance, Sir Alan Herbert, would unhesitatingly acclaim him as "the greatest living English prose writer."

In these prefaces it is interesting to turn to, for instance, his preface to Froude's *Essays in Literature and History* and to note the amount of space that he gives there to a most careful analysis of the construction and defects of Froude's sentences. He wrote this preface in 1906. One must wonder whether later in life he would have thought it worthwhile to have gone into such detailed linguistic analysis. The preface on Villon shows his sympathy with the expression of what he called "the bitterness of reality" that faces the world and its suffering without illusion but at the end preserves, but only just preserves, the consolations of religion.

"I challenged and I kept the Faith./The bleeding path alone I trod," he wrote in "The Prophet Lost in the Hills at Evening." The pseudo-Chinese of Kai Lung exactly suited with its ironic interrogations his refusal of the easy speeches that comfort cruel men.

One of the most interesting of the prefaces is the second of them—written in 1899, the preface to the *Extracts from the Diaries and Letters of Hubert Howard with a Recollection by a Friend* of his Balliol friend, Hubert Howard, who was killed in Egypt at the age of twenty-eight. Whatever Howard's achievements might have been had he lived to a full span, he died before he had time to win any distinction or to show himself more than a good friend, a man of adventurous disposition and high spirits. The *Diaries and Letters* even at the time of their publication cannot have been of interest to more than a small circle of friends and relatives, and even in his family circle Hubert Howard must today be quite forgotten. It was in the Victorian tradition to publish such memoirs. Today, in our age of the telephone, there would not have been enough letters to make a volume and his achievement would not have been thought to rate more than a few obituary notices. But one of Belloc's most lovable characteristics was his deep devotion to his friends, and his preface is typical and attractive in its generosity. But what is most interesting in it to us who know nothing of Howard is his almost unqualified eulogy of imperialism and of Howard's devotion of himself to the cause of Empire as a cause to which honour should properly call a young Englishman of aristocratic family. For this preface was of course written immediately before the Boer War and therefore gives to us important evidence how it was the experience of the Boer War which turned Belloc to bitter cynicism of the imperialist gospel. He praises Howard in phrases which are often curiously evocative of phrases of most bitter cynicism which he was afterwards to incorporate into his *Modern Traveller*. There was indeed a curious ambivalence in Belloc's attitude toward imperialism. Belloc was not, like Chesterton, a man who gave all his affection and loyalty to small units simply because they were small. He would never himself have written the lines which Chesterton wrote in his dedication to him of *The Napoleon of Notting Hill*: "For every tiny town or place/God made the stars especially."

Belloc disliked British imperialism—not because it was imperialism but because it was a false imperialism—because, as he alleged, under the pretence of imposing an imperial rule, alien and unscrupulous adventurers were exploiting the subject peoples whom they ruled.

> I have said it before, and I say it again,
> There was treason done and a false word spoken.
> And England under the dregs of men,
> And bribes about and a treaty broken.

But of course the imperialism of Rome—the mark of Rome which civilized all those upon whom it was imposed and left those outside its borders irreclaimable barbarians—was never absent from his mind. He recounted with relish and all that love of physical detail in which he so much reveled the passage of the roads that radiated from Rome. When he spoke of cities—Paris and London, for instance, in these prefaces—it was in their Roman origins that he was first interested. The battles of Charlemagne and Roland in the Pyrenees were battles for the defence of the Roman thing. He praised Arles in one of his essays because Rome was more alive there than in any other town. Whereas in the mouth of Hobbes it was as a denigration of the Catholic Church that he described it as the ghost of the Roman Empire sitting on its tomb, to Belloc that was its glory. The Roman Empire had not died and would never die. It lived on in the Church and of course the centre of Christian civilization was to his mind France. France was Christian because of its Roman origin even in spite of itself and at times even beyond its own desire. Thus, at any rate in his youth, he combined his Catholicism with an ardent championship of the Revolution. The Revolution, he sweepingly asserted in agreement with the great Bishop Dupanloup, was in no way in essential conflict with Catholic doctrine. "We accept," wrote Dupanloup, "we invoke the principles and the liberties proclaimed in '89. . . . You made the Revolution of 1789 without us and against us, but for us, God willing it so, in spite of you." It deprived, he one day boldly asserted in the Balliol Senior Common Room, no one of anything which he had a right to possess. Nor was the torrent of his rhetoric at all checked when a quiet little man in the corner of the room was heard to murmur, "Heads?" The years of the first decade of this century when Belloc was most vigorously writing were years when the French government was conducting a most savage campaign against the Church. The religious orders were all being driven into exile. But Belloc was little disturbed in his thesis by such happenings. The total rejection of the Christian claim by a skeptic was a mood that was always intelligible to him.

"Loud cries for Author—but he doesn't come," was the conclusion of his sonnet of meditation on the world as a stage, and he always acclaimed that it was an essential part of Catholic culture to respect its anticlerical opponents whom he inevitably found in all Latin countries. Such men, in his view, were to be preferred to the men of half culture that one found in Protestant countries. He never pretended to any understanding of the Protestant mind. Even Catholics who lived in Protestant countries could in his opinion enjoy no more than half a faith. "Comme les autres Anglais—même plus bête," he said one day in Belgium when asked what the English Catholics were like.

There is here a preface to Newman's *Apologia Pro Vita Sua* but in truth, for all his eulogy, Belloc did not wholly understand Newman, the most English of Englishmen. He had been a boy under Newman at the Oratory School and he knew something of what Newman's name had come to mean in England and the world. He wrote of him fine and conventional formal eulogies of the high privilege for a boy to have sat under that great man, but in his private conversation he confessed that what the boys really used to say to one another when they heard that Newman was preaching was, "There's old Jack booming away again." Belloc was essentially a Manningite in the great battle between Newman and Manning. He preferred the sundering and absolute clash and as a consequence his preface to the *Apologia* is in some ways the least satisfactory of these prefaces, for Belloc really misunderstood—or at any rate misstated—Newman's achievement there. He wrote as if Newman in his *Apologia* reestablished there his domination within the Catholic community. Newman indeed wrote the *Apologia* to refute Kingsley's charge that he was a man indifferent to truth. But, sensitive though Newman was, his objection to Kingsley was not that Kingsley had made a personal charge against him so much as that he had not only accused Newman of untruthfulness but accused him of being representative of the Catholic priesthood in his lack of regard for truth, and the blow was wounding to Newman precisely because at that time he was so widely distrusted within the

Catholic community. Nor is it true, as Belloc thought, that the *Apologia* reestablished Newman's position within the Catholic community. On the contrary, he was still distrusted, at any rate in the dominant Catholic circles in which Manning moved, for another twelve years until Pius IX died and Leo XIII, by making him a cardinal, lifted the cloud forever. But what it did do was to reestablish Newman's friendship with his old Anglican friends, such as Church and Rogers—to win for him a position in the general English and Protestant world such as no other English Catholic had ever come near to achieving. This has been of immense importance in the ecumenical developments but these were not developments which it was natural for Belloc to appreciate. To him Newman was a heroic man who had shaken off the Protestant influences of Oxford and found refuge in the Catholic Church. But, as he used to say, Newman was "too much of a Don" and he never appreciated that Newman had brought to the Church lessons which Oxford had taught him.

Belloc's belief that civilization was confined within the boundaries of the Roman Empire which, except for England, corresponded with such surprising exactitude with the boundaries that were retained for Catholicism at the Reformation, caused him to write in his *Europe and the Faith*, "The Faith is Europe and Europe is the Faith." This belief caused him to exaggerate the alien nature of the new countries of America and Australia—to the latter of which he was almost insanely antipathetic—and to constitute himself without compunction the unflagging enemy of Prussia, the alien country that had arisen outside the boundaries of Europe and was threatening Europe's essential civilization. "It is already half-mad," he wrote of the Prussian character.

Before long we shall see it run amuck. And if we do not kill it it will kill us. Prussia can no longer think widely, she cannot paint. She cannot write. And most of what Germany had patiently learnt from the civilised west and south, through centuries of industrious pupillage, Prussia has tarnished and got rid of in no long interval of time.

So, for instance, his prefaces to Cecil Chesterton's *Perils of Peace* and John Lewis Griffiths' *The Greater Patriotism* teach the same lesson.

There will be some who dismiss as obsession both his detestation of Prussia and his too facile dichotomy which saw the Germans divided into the good Catholics of the south and the bad Protestants of the north. Hitler, it will be said, and a very large proportion of the Nazi leaders, were men of Catholic origins and from the south. As we can see from his preface to Eyre Crowe's book (not reproduced in this volume), he much too easily ascribed all Germany's evils to the Prussian General Staff and was absurdly in error when Hitler came to power in mocking at him as no more than a creature of that Staff, and indeed I do not think that even those who defend his general thesis could deny that he overpitched and that his history was selective.

"I partly write to give you pain," he wrote in one of his poems, and his whole manner was certainly tinged with a calculated aggressiveness. The pacifist case seemed to him merely ridiculous, man was born to fight.

"Pale Ebenezer thought it wrong to fight,/But Roaring Bill who killed him thought it right," he wrote, and imagined that he had thus dismissed the case for nonresistance. He did not even consider the possibility that Pale Ebenezer might think it right to sacrifice his own life and fancy that he would win a truer victory by such conduct. The love of conflict was in his blood. He used to tell the story how his grandfather once beat an insolent Parisian cabman who had overcharged him and concluded the anecdote with, "We Bellocs have always had guts."

It was his belief, right or wrong, that English Protestant complacency could only be punctured by a most deliberate offensive. Take for instance the opening sentences to the preface on Father Bévenot's *Pagan and Christian Rule.*

It is sufficiently clear to those who survey Europe in the mass and follow the full outline of their time, that our civilization must return to the Faith or be destroyed.

It is a conclusion arrived at in a hundred ways by observation, by instinct, by history. There stands in support of it the evident formation, insistent throughout the West, of growing intellectual superiority upon the Catholic side: so that to-day no-one is worthy to stand as an equal against the Catholic controversialist save that rare being, the pure sceptic. We have to-day against the full and convincing system which Catholicism permanently presents, opponents, who, for the most part, do not know what they are attacking, and, therefore, in their attack can do little more than abuse. The moral and the intellectual tide of the *moment* is clearly with the return of that philosophy which is more than a philosophy.

Who can doubt that here Belloc asserts that a number of propositions are clear, which he was well aware that the great majority of so-called intellectuals vigorously repudiated and that he very deliberately said this in order to annoy them?

Belloc when he wrote on religious topics wrote always of the Church, and of the Church as an institution—as a political body to be defended against its attackers. Take for instance his defence of the Inquisition, in his preface to Mr. Hoffman Nickerson's book. He writes of the campaign against the Albigensians as a purely military campaign. Naturally enough, he is no advocate of unnecessary violence or suppression. Nevertheless he takes it for granted that the Church was an institution which had the right to defend itself with arms against heretics who attacked it, nor does he at all avert to even the possibility that the authority might itself be corrupted by its exercise of repression.

Many people would, of course, either deny that the Church which Christ founded was an institution at all in any political sense, or, say that, if it was such an institution, its institutional nature was of subsidiary importance, and its formal unity should not be defended by action that was inevitably damaging to its essential spiritual nature. Its survival was a matter that could be safely left with the divine promises of almighty God. The action of men should be concerned with obedience to the moral law rather than calculation of results. The Second Vatican Council has told us that much Christian practice is to be found outside as well as inside the formal Catholic Church, but such language would have seemed strange to Belloc.

"Caritas non conturbat me," as he said in one of his songs, only half in jest, and nothing but the vigour of his faith and his humility could have brought him to accept the Council's rulings, had he survived into our more ecumenical days. Outside the Catholic Church he found, as he wrote in an open letter to Dean Inge, nothing but "the puerilities and the despairs." To Chesterton, who was a very different sort of man from Belloc, however frequently they may have been linked together, political and social questions, though of importance, were of only secondary importance. Chesterton was more at home in the company of St. Francis and in the mysteries of the interior life. Belloc would of course as an obedient Catholic never have dreamed of speaking disrespectfully of the mystical life. But it was not a field on which he felt in the least at home. He would never have written of it, or, as he once said, had he done so, not under his own name. It is curious that in all the volumes of his writings about religion he never in any place speaks of the stories of the Gospels. His talk is all of the Church and little of Christ—a few pious little childlike verses about our Lord and that is all—and he dismisses with too impatient a contempt the anxieties of the souls of prayerful seekers for the truth outside the Church. The first decade of the century was a decade of modernism and of its condemnation by Pius X. Belloc accepted the rulings of the pope as a soldier accepts the orders of his commanding officer. He never greatly attempted to understand the subtleties of the controversy. One of the leading English modernists of the day was Miss Maud Petre and Belloc was content to dismiss the modernist claim by parodying our Lord's promises as interpreted by them as, "Thou art Maud Petre and on this rock will I build my Church." His curiosity did not carry him to inquire much beyond this excellent witticism. What he would have thought had he lived to see the Mass in the vernacular, the exchange of pulpits between Catholics and ministers of other denominations, traditional rulings on such matters as birth control brought into debate, one hesitates to think. It is not that he treated the detailed regulations of the Church with ridiculous respect. I remember one Friday on which he found himself at breakfast in a Catholic company. "We're all Catholics here, aren't we?" he said with joviality. "Then I'll have a slice of ham." As has been said, the appeal of skepticism was always strong in him. He could understand a person who rejected altogether the Catholic promise, or who defied it knowing that he sinned in doing so. He had little patience with those who sought to play fast and loose with it; who sought, as he would have put it, to rewrite it in order to suit their own convenience.

It was the greatest disappointment of his life that at the conclusion of his Balliol years he was not elected to a Fellowship of All Souls' at Oxford. Why he minded as much as all that —allowed it indeed, almost to poison his life and to be largely responsible for all the bitter contempt with which he ever afterwards spoke of the Dons and academic history—so evident in his criticism of Freeman in the preface to Nickerson's book on the Inquisition—it is indeed something of a mystery. We can surely see today that even if he had been elected, his restless disposition would never have allowed him to spend a lifetime in the quiet of an Oxford College. He would have quarreled with the academic historians whether he had himself been technically one of them or not. Yet he certainly felt it, particularly in his closing years, as a bitter affront both to his exquisite feeling for prose and his vivid sense of the past that he was compelled by the needs of bread and butter to turn out historical works at so excessive a pace. Whether he would, in fact, have done otherwise had circumstances been different, whether any power could have prevented him from expounding versions of history that were aggressive, whether he did not to a large extent himself invent the pressure under which he wrote and lived is an open question. He was essentially a fighter.

England, to me that never have malingered,
    Nor spoken falsely, nor false flattery used,
Nor even in my rightful garden lingered,
    What have you not refused?

he wrote in his "Stanzas Written on Battersea Bridge during a Southwesterly Gale." The love of conflict was in his blood and would have come out one way or another, Dons or no Dons, Protestants or no Protestants. So, too, would his restlessness. It is an amusing curiosity that while he praised the virtue of a stable and settled peasantry as the necessary cement of society, his own life was essentially the life of Peter Wanderwide.

When Peter Wanderwide was thrown
    By death himself beyond Auxerre,
He chanted in heroic tones
    To priest and people gathered there.

Hilaire Belloc was essentially an extrovert, a lover of achievement. We have already noticed the meticulous care with which he analysed the structure of Froude's sentences. His verse was always restrained, classical, and most strict in obedience to its scheme of metre. He admired Ruth Pitter for her regularity and restraint of form. Readers of *The Cruise of the Nona* will know all about his love of the sea and of the boat that sailed on it—the strict rules for arranging the tackle which he laid down, though he confessed that he did not obey them. Some have regretted that he did not impose on his opinions a similar discipline of restraint to that which he imposed on his form. Such criticism, I think, misunderstands the contribution that Belloc had to make to English Catholic thought. It is true that we have now moved into an ecumenical age in which it is the fashion to speak with all courtesy of those who differ from us and in which we can with confidence look for fair-mindedness from them in return. All that is to be welcomed, but, if we feel inclined to criticise Belloc for not writing in that manner, it is necessary to remember what was the confidently Protestant English mentality of Victorian times, what was the language in which it was then the fashion to speak of Catholic beliefs, and we may then understand how it was perhaps necessary to challenge that world with a gesture of bravado in order to break down its self-confidence. If the modern Catholic writers can write to an audience from which they can confidently expect to receive fair play and can address it in moderate terms, it is largely because Belloc in his time breached for them the wall through which they can enter as perfect gentlemen and without a ruffle to the parting of their hair. . . . He remains, if not considered a very great historian, at the least and beyond challenge a very great artist—great in spite of the fact that, French in so many other ways, he had in him no trace of that French reverence for the writer as the cher maître—an attitude which he always found as ridiculous as it was contemptible.

CHRISTOPHER HOLLIS

March 1969

ABOUT HILAIRE BELLOC

In 1929 a collection of thirty-seven introductions by Gilbert Keith Chesterton entitled *G. K. C. as M. C.* was brought out by his friend and admirer, J. P. de Fonseka. It was this compilation of Chesterton's fascinating forewords that first gave me the idea of editing a similar volume of prefatory pieces for his dear and lifelong friend, Hilaire Belloc.

As far as I have been able to ascertain to date, Belloc wrote introductions to more than fifty books published by a striking variety of authors. These introductions provide a panoramic view of the wide range of Belloc's interests, as well as an echo of his brilliant conversation. Indeed, any discourse of Belloc's, written or spoken, reveals the clarity, the order, and the integrative quality of a philosophic mind to whose generous holism, no subject is alien. These introductions further exemplify Belloc's mastery as a writer of English prose; that gift of expression of his, which, in spite of the shifts of fashion, will ensure him of lasting literary fame.

By the timeless relevance of the reflections they embody, as well as by the exact justness of their style, these miniature essays, almost *On Everything*, and here for the first time, between the covers of a single book, should, on their respective and aggregate merits, recall Belloc's militant mind and challenging art to a younger generation that has all but forgotten him. Nor would it be exorbitant to count upon these incidental, but not fugitive, pieces to incite both the lay and the scholarly reader to turn for further inspiration and sustenance to the vast and varied corpus of Belloc's output. Those who do so will find it teeming with life.

Joseph Hilaire Pierre Belloc has been described as a Frenchman, an Englishman, an Oxford man, a country gentleman, a soldier, a democrat, a satirist, a novelist, a poet, and a practical journalist. He was born near Paris at La Celle, St. Cloud on July 27, 1870. Eight of his great-uncles had served as generals under Napoleon. His father, Louis Belloc, was a French lawyer; his mother, Bessie Parkes, was an English woman who participated in the feminist movement which eventually secured votes for women. His paternal grandfather was the celebrated artist, Hilaire Belloc, whose paintings still hang in the Louvre. His maternal grandfather, Joseph Parkes, was a scholarly Liberal solicitor, remembered as a founder of the Birmingham Reform Club, as an active protagonist of various Reform bills, and as the historian of the Chancery Bar. Thus Belloc became the heir of a truly bicultural background with roots in two fatherlands, for both of which he had a great affection and devotion.

Belloc commenced his primary education when he enrolled in 1880 at the Oratory School at Edgbaston near Birmingham, which was still under the aegis of its celebrated founder, Cardinal Newman. The boy became proficient in mathematics and the Classics, having done some drama under the tutelage of the headmaster, Father John Norris. He graduated in 1887 with high distinction, carrying away most of the prizes for his distinguished performance, as illustrated by what his mother could write of him on his birthday:

> On Friday, 18, dear, my lad of 14 carried off the Second Norfolk Prize, the First English Prize of the whole school, the Prize of his own form, was second in mathematical marks, and within the running zone, as it were, of two other prizes. The Duke of Norfolk stood by Cardinal Newman and gave him the books all the time.

Leaving the Oratory, armed with testimonials from the cardinal and Father Norris, he entered the Naval Course at the Collège Stanislas in Paris in October 1887. After a brief period at this institution, from which he was glad to get away, he returned to England, worked at a few inconsequential employments and then, as joint editor with Arthur Pollen, Belloc received his first experience as editor in 1890 when, for six months, they published *The Paternoster Review*.

In 1891, being still a French citizen, he served as a gunner in the Eighth Regiment of Artillery at Toul. Having served the minimum period with the French army, he went back to England where he enrolled at Balliol College and received a Brackenbury scholarship in history and later took first-class honours in this subject in 1895. While at Oxford he distinguished himself as an orator at the Oxford Union and became president of the Union in his senior year. His speeches here have often been referred to and praised since. Years later, in February 1924, Belloc spoke as a guest of honour at the Oxford Union Centenary Banquet, replying to a "Toast of Letters" proposed by Mr. Christopher Hollis, a president of this august debating society for its centenary year. And as late as 1955, a record for physical vigour set by Belloc and the Honourable A. M. Henley when students at Oxford, remained unbroken: this was their great walk from Carfax to Marble Arch in eleven and a half hours.

In 1896 Belloc married an Irish-American girl, Elodie Hogan, in her distant home in Napa, California. The young bride proved to be an exceptional wife and a powerful influence in establishing her gifted husband more deeply in his faith. Five children blessed this union. Elodie was destined not to live long, for she died following a severe illness in February 1914. It was thus as a widower that Belloc cared and provided for his family.

In 1902 Belloc became a naturalized British subject; his papers were cosigned by his very good friend, E. C. Bentley. Four years later he entered the House of Commons, as Liberal member for South Salford; he was a member of Parliament from 1906 to 1910.

On leaving Oxford Belloc commenced his literary career in 1895 with the publication of a small volume entitled, *Sonnets and Verse*. This was a book of sixty-four pages, printed on cardboard paper. Of this book Maurice Baring wrote in his *Puppet Show of Memory* in 1922:

> I do not think that this book excited a ripple of attention at the time, and yet some of the poems in it have lived, and are now found in many anthologies, whereas the verse which at this time was received with a clamour of applause is nearly all of it not only dead but buried and completely forgotten.

Besides other multifarious activities, Belloc was the author by 1942 of over one hundred fifty books. These books range the whole gamut of literature, from travel sketches to essays significantly entitled *On Nothing and Kindred Subjects* (1908), *On Everything* (1909), *On Anything* and *On Something* (1910), to simply *On* in 1923; from *The Bad Child's Book of Beasts* (1896) to *A History of England*, four volumes of which were published by 1929. He wrote several books of satirical fiction, the greatest of which was *Mr. Clutterbuck's Election* in 1908, where he delights to expose British underground politics in his most hilarious manner.

In 1902 Belloc published his *The Path to Rome*, which is a unique book in the literature of England. It is a highly spirited travel book which brings back to the reader the full tradition of Europe and the Catholic faith—themes he expounded more scientifically in so many of his historical writings. In this book we come to know something of the character of Belloc. In 1925 he published his *Cruise of the Nona*, a book which may be considered as the reflections of a man in middle age. This book is less ardently written than *The Path to Rome*; there is considerably less joy in it, but from it we acquire a greater insight into Belloc's philosophy.

His historical studies and biographies, *Danton* (1899), *Robespierre* (1901), and *Marie Antoinette* (1909), are classics of their kind and from these volumes we see Belloc's intellectual grasp of the French story. In these he attempted what he and Michelet considered essential to effective historical writing, that of resurrecting the past and making it live. With equal vividness and acumen, he recorded the English story anew in a sequence of biographies: *Charles the First* (1933), *Cromwell* (1934), *Charles II, The Last Rally* (1940), *James the Second* (1928), and *Elizabethan Commentary* (1942). We get from all of these a very luminous perspective of the history of England since the Reformation.

His *Nonsense Rhymes, Cautionary Tales for Children, The Bad Child's Book of Beasts,* and *More Beasts for Worse Children* are comparable to Edward Lears'. Although Belloc wished to be remembered as a poet, his poetry is very engaging, but here, he is somewhat less original. His humorous and burlesque stanzas are always refreshing, but he is most himself when he writes of malt liquor and wine and his beloved Sussex. The "Lines to a Don"—any don Belloc explained—in defence of his friend and fellow-poet, Chesterton, and "The South Country" are the most persuasive of his earnest poems. "Tarantella," with its internal rhymes and shifting rhythms, is a skillful approximation of the dance which gives this poem its name. His heroic poem, "The Praise of Wine," of which Duff Cooper tells us he was very proud that Belloc should have dedicated it to him, will rank, for its epic qualities, as one of the greatest poems in the language and comparable to some of the best lines in Milton's "Paradise Lost."

Contrary to the widely held opinion that Belloc was an arrogant and condescending man, is the testimony of his friends and his biographer about his attitude toward honours and titles. Public recognitions were certainly due to him and he did accept a few of them, but this he did with great scruple and reluctance. In 1920 he was made an honorary doctor of law at Glasgow University. This degree he accepted because his close friend, John Phillimore, professor of Greek at this institution, had acted to secure him this distinction and in 1929 he accepted the ribbon of an officer of the Légion d'Honneur. He was, also, made a Knight of the Order of Saint Gregory the Great by Pope Pius XI in 1934, along with G. K. Chesterton. In 1943 Winston Churchill offered to him the medal of the Companion of Honour, a distinction he might have accepted with dignity but which he begged to decline.

In 1941 his son, Peter, a captain in the Royal Marines, died while on active service. This was a very heavy blow to the aging Belloc who had lost his oldest son, Louis, in World War I. He now suffered a stroke which, midway through 1942, left him incapable of further writing and thus marked the end of over fifty years of exuberant literary output. This was followed by twelve years of inactivity, during which declining health was accompanied by the vicissitudes of clear and cloudy periods of the mind until a fatal fall, while attending to his fireplace on the twelfth of July, 1953. He died on July 16 at the Mount Alvernia

Nursing Home of the Franciscan Missionaries in Guildford. At the hour of death the British Broadcasting Corporation interrupted all its programmes to announce the passing away of one of England's greatest literary figures. In the following days the English press paid tribute to the greatness of Hilaire Belloc, remarking that he had gained an assured place in English literature, and that he had defended the faith he held most vigorously.

J. A. DE CHANTIGNY

Loyola College
Montreal
May 1971

PARIS.

CHAPTER I.

INTRODUCTION.

WHEN a man looks eastward from the western heights that dominate the city, especially from that great hill of Valerian (round which so many memories from Ste. Geneviève to the last war accumulate), a sight presents itself which shall be the modern starting-point of our study.

Let us suppose an autumn day, clear, with wind following rain, and with a gray sky of rapid clouds against which the picture may be set. In such a weather and from such a spot the whole of the vast town lies clearly before you, and the impression is one that you will not match nor approach in any of the views that have grown famous; for what you see is unique in something that is neither the north nor the south; something which contains little of scenic interest and nothing of dramatic grandeur; something which men have forborne to describe because when they have known Paris well enough to compre-

1 (1)

hend that horizon, why then her people, her history, her life from within, have dominated every other interest and have occupied all their powers. Nevertheless this sight, caught from the hill-top, shall be our first introduction to the city; for I know of no other which so profoundly stirs the mind of one to whom the story and even the modern nature of the place is unknown.

There lies at your feet—its fortifications some two miles away—a great plain of houses. Its inequalities are lost in the superior height from which you gaze, save where in the north the isolated summit of Montmartre, crowned with the scaffolding of its half-finished church, looks over the city and answers the hill of Valerian.

This plain of houses fills the eye and the mind, yet it is not so vast but that, dimly, on the clearest days the heights beyond it to the east can be just perceived, while to the north the suburbs and the open country appear, and to the south the hills. Whiter than are the northern towns of Europe, yet standing under a northern sky, it strikes with the force of sharp contrast, and half explains in that one feature its Latin origin and destiny. It is veiled by no cloud of smoke, for industry, and more especially the industry of our day, has not been the motive of its growth. The fantastic and even grandiose effects which are the joy of London will never be discovered here. It does not fill by a kind of gravitation this or that group of arteries; it forms no line along the water-course, nor does it lose itself in those vague contours which the necessity of exchange frequently determines, for Paris was not made by commerce; nor will any theory of material conditions and environment read you the riddle of its growth and form. It is not the mind of the on-looker that lends it unity, nor the emotions of travel that make it, for those who see it thus, one thing. Paris, as it lies before you from those old hills that have watched her for two thousand years, has the effect and character of personal life. Not in a metaphor nor for the sake of phrasing, but in fact; as truly as in the case of Rome, though in a manner less familiar, a separate existence with a soul of its own appeals to you. Its voice is no reflection of your own mind; on the contrary, it is a troubling thing, like an insistent demand spoken in a foreign tongue. Its corporate life is not an abstraction drawn from books or from things one has heard. There, visibly before you, is the compound of the modern and the middle ages, whose unity convinces merely by being seen.

And, above all, this thing upon which you are looking is alive. It needs no recollection of what has been taught in youth, nor any of those reveries which arise at the identification of things seen with names remembered. The antiquarian passion, in its best form pedantic and in its worst maudlin, finds little room in the first aspect of Paris. Later, it takes its proper rank in all the mass of what we may learn, but the town, as you see it, recalls history only by speaking to you in a living voice. Its past is still alive, because the city itself is still instinct with a vigorous growth, and you feel with regard to Paris what you would feel with regard to a young man full of memories; not at all the quiet interest which lies in the recollections of age; still less that happy memory of things dead which is a fortune for so many of the most famous cities of the world.

Whence proceeds this impression, and what is the secret of its origin? Why, that in all this immense extent an obvious unity of design appears; not in one quarter alone, but over the whole circumference stand the evidences of this creative spirit. It is not the rich building for themselves in their own quarter, nor the officials concentrating the common wealth upon their own buildings; it is Paris, creating and re-creating her own adornment, realizing her own dreams upon every side, insisting on her own vagaries, committing follies which are her own and not that of a section of her people, even here and there chiselling out something as durable as Europe.

Look at the great line before you and note these evidences of a mind at work. Here, on your right, monstrous, grotesque and dramatic in the extreme rises that great ladder of iron, the Eiffel, to its thousand feet, meant to be merely engineering, and therefore christened at its birth by all the bad fairies, but

managing (as though the spirit of the city had
laughed at its own folly) to assume something of
grace, and losing in a very delicate grey, in a good
curve, and in a film of fine lines, the grossness which
its builders intended. It stands up, close to our
western standpoint, foolishly. It is twice as high as
this hill of Valerian from which we are looking; its
top is covered often in hurrying clouds, and it seems
to be saying perpetually : " I am the end of the nineteenth century; I am glad they built me of iron ; let
me rust." It is far on the outskirts of the town,
where all the rest of the things that Paris has made
can look at it and laugh contentedly. It is like a
passing fool in a crowd of the University, a buffoon
in the hall; for of all the things that Paris has made,
it alone has neither wits nor soul.

But just behind it and somewhat to the left the
dome you see gilded is the Invalides, the last and,
perhaps, the best relic of seventeenth century taste,
and with that you touch ground and have to do with
Paris again ; for just beneath it is Napoleon, and in
the short roof to the left of it, in the chapel, the flags
of all the nations. Behind that, again, almost the
last thing the eighteenth century left us, is the other
dome of the Pantheon. How great a space in ideas
between it and the Invalides ! Between Mansard
and Soufflot ! Its dome is in a false proportion; a
great hulking colonnade deforms its middle; its sides
and its decorations are cold and bare. The gulf

between these two, compared, is the gulf between
Louis XIV. and the last years of decay that made
necessary the Revolution.   It stands, grey, ugly and
without meaning, the relic of a grey and ugly time.
But you note that it caps a little eminence, or what
seems, from our height and distance, to be a little
eminence.   That hill is the hill of Ste. Genevieve,
" Mons Lucotetius," Mont Parnasse.   On its sides
and summit the University grew, and at its base the
Revolution was born in the club of the Cordeliers.

It will repay one well to look, on this clear day,
and to strain the eyes in watching that hummock—a
grey and confused mass of houses, with the ugly
dome we. spoke of, on its summit.   A lump, a little
higher than the rest, half-way up the hill, is the Sor-
bonne; upon the slopes towards us two unequal
square towers mark St. Sulpice—a heap of stones.
Yet all this confusion of unlovely things, which the distance turns into a blotch wherein the Pantheon alone
can be distinguished, is a very noteworthy square
mile of ground; for at its foot Julian the Apostate
held his little pagan circle; at its summit are the
relics of Ste. Genevieve.   Here Abelard awoke the
" great curiosity " from its long sleep, and here St.
Bernard answered him in the name of all the mystics.
Here Dante studied, and here Innocent III. was
formed.   Here is the unique arena where Catholicism
and the Rationalists meet, and where a great struggle is never completed.   Here, as in symbol of that

wrestling, the cross is perpetually rising above and falling from the Pantheon—now torn down, now reinstated. Beneath that ugly dome lie Voltaire and Rousseau; in one of the gloomy buildings on that hill Robespierre was taught the stoicism of the ancients and sat on the bench with Desmoulins; at its flank, in the Cordeliers, Danton forged out the scheme of the Republic; it was thence that the fire spread in '92 which overthrew the old *régime;* here, again, the students met and laughed and plotted against the latest despotism. It was from the steps of that unlovely Pantheon, with "To the great men of France" carved above him, that Gambetta declared the third Republic. It was the 4th of September, 1870, and it rained.

There is, however, in the view before you another spot, touching almost the hill which we have been noting, and of yet more importance in the story of the city, though it may not be so in the story of the world,—I mean the Island of the Cité.

From this distance we cannot see the gleam of the water on either side of it; moreover, the houses hide the river and the bridges. Nevertheless, knowing what lies there, we can make out the group of buildings which is the historic centre of Paris, and from whence the town has radiated outwards during the last fourteen centuries.

We are five miles away, and catch only its most evident marks. We see the square mass of the

Palais, whence, uninterruptedly, for eighteen hundred years the government has held its courts and its share in the administration of the town.   Perhaps, if it is very clear, the conical roofs of the twin towers of the Conciergerie can be made out; and, certainly, to the right of them we see the high-pitched roof and the thin spire of the Sainte Chapelle, which St. Louis built to cover the Holy Lance and the Crown of Thorns.   But the most striking feature of the Island and the true middle of the whole of Paris will be clear always even at this distance,—I mean the Cathedral of Notre Dame.

The distance and the larger aspect of nearer things make exiguous the far towers as they stand above the houses.   You look, apparently, at a little thing, but even from here it has about it the reverence of the middle ages.   In that distance all is subdued; but these towers, which are grey to a man at their very feet, seem to possess to a watcher from Valerian the quality of a thin horizon cloud.

I know not how to describe this model of the middle ages—built into the modern town, standing (from whichever way you look) in its very centre, so small, so distant, and yet so majestic.   Amiens and Rheims, Strasburg, Chartres and Rouen—all the great houses of the Gothic, as they pass before our minds, have something at once less pathetic and less dignified. They are no larger than Notre Dame; they have not —even Rheims has not—her force of repose, of height and of design. But they stand in provincial cities. The modern world affects, without transforming, their surroundings. Amiens stands head and shoulders above the town; Rheims, as you see it coming in from camp, looks like a great sphinx brooding over the champaign and always gazing out to the west and the hills of the Tourdenoise; Strasburg is almost theatrical in its assertion; Chartres is the largest thing in a rural place, and is the natural mother of the Beauce, the patroness and protectress of endless fields of corn; and even Rouen, though it stands in the hum of machinery and in the centre of countless industries, is so placed that, come from whichever way you will, it is the dominant fact in the town.

But Notre Dame is always one of many things and not the greatest. She was built for a little Gothic town and a huge metropolis has outgrown her. The town was once, so to speak, the fringe of her garment ; now she is but the centre of a circle miles around. There are but three spots in Paris from which the old church alone takes up the mind, as do the churches of the provincial towns; I mean from the Quai de la Tournelle, from the Parvis, and from the Place de Grève. And yet she gradually becomes more to the spirit of those who see her than do any of these other churches, for the very anomaly of her position leads to close observance, and she touches the mind at last like a woman who has been continually silent in a strange company. To a man who loves and knows the city, there soon comes a desire to constantly communicate with the memories of the Cathedral. And this desire, if he is wise, grows into a habit of coming close against the towers at evening, or of waiting under the great height of the nave for the voices of the middle ages.

Notre Dame thus lost in distance, central and remote, is like a lady grown old in a great house, about whose age new phrases and strange habits have arisen, who is surrounded with the youth of her own lineage and yet is content to hear and understand without replying to their speech. She is silent in the midst of energy, and forgotten in the many activities of the household, yet she is the centre of the estate, and but for her the family would be broken up and the home grow desolate. And to me at least, when I see in that famous view her square towers draped and veiled by distance, it has something of the effect made by a single small harbor-light which shines when one is coming in at the dead of a night, and with sweeps from lack of wind, while all about one, in a high port-city and in the great black landscape of cliffs, no other beacon is showing.

There stands, then, in the midst of our view this little group of the Island of the Cité, the old Roman town with which so much of our history will deal. As the eye turns to the left, that is to the northern half of the town, it is passing over the place of its great expansion. It is here that Paris has worked and has grown, while Paris of the centre governed and Paris of the south thought and studied. It is in this half of the city that we shall note her greatest theatres, her most famous modern streets, her houses of rich men, her palaces, even her industries.

But this northern half has little to distinguish it in a general panorama; here and there a spire or tower or a column, but as a rule only a mass of high houses in which even the distant Louvre seems to possess no special prominence, and in which the Palais Royal, the Madeleine, the Bourse are so many roofs only, conspicuous in nothing but their surface. The old world makes but little effect from the distance at which we stand, and indeed is less apparent in the northern half of the city even to a spectator who is placed within its streets. Close against the Island you may perhaps catch the fine square tower of St. Jacques, the last of the Gothic; but with that exception the view of the left side is modern. If we may connect it with any one period or man rather than another, it is Napoleon that its few prominent points recall. Between us and the heart of the city is the ridge of Passy; less than a mile from the fortifications and on the summit of this ridge the great Triumphal Arch full of his battles and his generals' names.

You may see beyond it, towards the more central parts of the town, a line here and there of those straight streets so many of which he planned, and nearly all of which are due to his influence upon Paris.   Thus opening straight before you, but miles away, running to the Louvre and on to the Hotel de Ville, is that Rue de Rivoli which is so characteristically his, obliterating, as did his own career, the memories of the Revolution.   Running over the spot where the riding-school stood, and where Mirabeau helped to found a new world, draining the Rue St. Honorè (that republican gulf) of half its traffic, it strikes the note of the new Paris which the nineteenth century has designed.

Just off the line of this street you may catch the bronze column, the Vendôme, which again perpetuates Napoleon; it stands well above the houses and rivals the other column which distance scarcely permits us to discern, and which overlooks the site of the Bastille.

But when we have noted these few points, have tried to make out the new Hotel de Ville (as distant and less clear than Notre Dame), and have marked the great mass of the opera roof, the general aspect of the northern bank is told.   There is nothing on which the eye rests as a central point.   Only in itself, and without the aid of monuments, the great expanse of wealth and of energy fringing off into the industries of the northern and western roads shows us at once the modern Paris that works and enjoys.

One last feature remains to be spoken of while we are still looking upon the view at our feet, and before we go down into the city to notice the closer aspect of its streets and buildings. I mean the hill of Montmartre. It lies on the extreme left as we gaze, that is in the northernmost part of the city, just within the fortifications, and rises isolated and curiously steep above the whole plain of the northern quarter. No city has so admirable a place of vantage, and in no other is the position so unspoiled as here. For centuries, from the time when it was far outside the mediæval walls, Montmartre has been the habitation of bohemians and chance poor men. Luckily it has remained undisturbed to this day. And if you climb it you look right down upon the town from the best and most congenial of surroundings. Nothing there reminds you of a municipality forcing you to acknowledge the site and the view. There is not a park or statue, not even a square. A ramshackle café with dirty plaster statues, a half-finished church, a panorama of the true Jerusalem (the same all falling to pieces with old age and neglect), a number of little houses and second-rate villas, a few dusty studios; this is the furniture of the platform beneath which all Paris lies like a map.

Long may it remain so untouched. For the hill is now truly Parisian. The tourist does not hear of it, even the systematic traveller avoids it. But it is dear to the student, and to that type in which Paris is so prolific. I mean the careless and disreputable young men who grow up to be bourgeois and pillars

of society. For them the slopes of the hill are almost sacred ground. Half the minor verse of Paris
has been born here, and that other hill of the Latin
quarter has arranged, as it were, for its play-ground
in this forsaken and neglected place. Paris inspires
you well as you look down upon it from such surroundings, and for one who understands the race
there is a peculiar pleasure in noting that officialism,
which is one product or rather aspect of the national
character, has spared Montmartre to the carelessness
and excess which is its paradoxical second half. Not
so long ago a crazy windmill marked the summit.
It has disappeared, but it is characteristic of the hill
that it should have lingered to so late a date. Not
another square yard of Paris, perhaps, has been so
left to chance as this admirable opportunity for the
interference of official effect.

Such, imperfectly described, is Paris when you
see it first from the highest of the western hills. But
our insistence upon this or that particular point must
not misrepresent to the reader the general effect.
These domes, arches, towers, spires—even the hills,
are but incidents in the vast plain of houses with
which our summary began, and which is the note of
the whole scene. What is this plain, seen from within? What is the character of its life, its architecture, its monuments? Above all, what surmise
gradually rises in us as we pass through its streets

and try to discover the historic foundations upon which all this modern society rests? To answer these questions let us go in to the city by one of the western gates and gain close at hand an impression of her buildings and streets.

This is what you will notice as you pass through the thoroughfares of Paris. Two kinds of streets, and, to match them, two kinds of public buildings; and yet neither clearly defined, but merging into one another in a fashion which, as will be seen later, gives the characteristic of continuity to the modern town.

As an example of the first, take the Rue St. Honoré; as an example of the second, its immediate neighbor the Boulevard des Italians. The Rue St. Honoré is narrow, paved with square stones, sounding like a gorge on the sea-coast. Its houses are high, and with hardly a pretence of decoration. Their stone or plastered walls run grey and have black streaks with age. Commonly an old iron balcony will run along one or more of the upper stories. They are covered with green-grey Mansard roofs, high in proportion to the buildings. From these look the small windows of attics, where, in the time these houses were built, the apprentices and servants of the bourgeois householders were lodged. The ground floor, as everywhere in Paris, is a line of shops. The street is not only narrow and high, but sombre in effect. Here and there (but rarely) an open court,

looking almost like a well, lets in more light. The
street is not straight, but follows the curves of the old
mediæval artery upon which it was built. You would
look in vain for the Gothic in such streets as these.
Even the Renaissance has hardly remained. Their
churches and their public buildings date from much
the same time as the houses. They are uniformly
of the seventeenth or early eighteenth centuries. It
was in such surroundings that the grand siècle moved,
and in such hotels lived the dramatists and the orators
of the Augustan age of literature. These streets, all of
much the same type, are the old Paris. They are
least disturbed, perhaps, in the Latin quarter. They
are, of course, not to be found in all that outer ring
of the city which has been the creation of our own
time, and in fine they still make up a good proportion of the circle within the boulevards, which is the
heart of Paris. It is in them that you will note the
famous sites of the last two hundred years almost
unchanged, and waiting under their influence the
student can at last reproduce the scenes and the
spirit of the Revolution.

Whole sections of the town—the Ile St. Louis, for
example—show no architecture but this, and the
high, sad houses, the narrow, sombre streets, the age-
marked grey walls are still the impression left most
vividly on one who knows a little more of Paris than
the Grand Hotel.

Through these old quarters, cutting them up, as it

were, into isolated sections, run like a gigantic web of straight lines the modern streets. The foundation of the system is the ring of internal boulevards. Here and there great supplementary avenues cut through the heart of the city within their limits, and finally the inner and the outer boulevards are similarly connected with a series of broad streets lined with trees. Thus the new Paris holds the old, as a framework of timbers may hold an old wall, or as the veins of a leaf hold its substance.

And what is to be said of these new streets and of the new quarters about the interior of the city? It is the fashion to belittle their effect, and more especially do foreigners, whose foreign pleasures are catered for in the newest of the new streets, compare unfavorably this modern Paris with the old. They are heard to regret the rookeries of the Boucherie. They would not have the tower St. Jacques stand in a public square, and some, I dare say, have found hard words even for the great space in front of Notre Dame and for its statue of Charlemagne.

This attitude with regard to the new Paris seems to me a false one. Certainly its architecture suffers from uniformity. Light rather than mystery, comfort rather than beauty, has been the object of its design. They are to be regretted, but they are the characters of our generation. And Paris being a living and a young city, not a thing for a museum, nor certainly a place for fads and make-believes, it is well that our

2

century should confess itself even in the Haussman-
ized streets, in the wide, shaded avenues of three or
even five-carriage roads side by side, and the perpetual repetition of one type of modern house.

Moreover, Paris is here very true to the character
she has maintained in each one of her rebuildings.
She shows the whole spirit of the time. If she gives
us, in a certain monotony and scientific precision and
an over-cleanliness, the faults of the new spirit, she certainly has all its virtues. Her taste is excellent. These
open spaces and broad streets make, for the monuments, vistas or approaches of an admirable balance.
You will see them lead either to the best that is left
of her past or to the more congruous designs of her
modern public buildings, and the effect, never sinking to the secondary, often rises to the magnificent.
Take (for example) the present treatment of the
Tuileries. The Commune burnt that old palace,
leaving the three sides of the Louvre surrounding a
gaping space. It has been harmonized with the Tuileries gardens by planting, and the whole great sweep
down from the Arc de l'Etoile, though the Tuileries
gardens to the court of the Louvre is, as it were, an
approach to the palace. The grandeur of that scene
has the demerit of being obvious, but it has also the
singular value of obtruding nothing that can offend
or distract the eye.

Even the Avenue de l'Opera, with the huge
building at the end of it, will bear praise. If it lacks

meaning yet it does not lack greatness, and the Opera itself has something in it of the fantastic which avoids the grotesque. It is a " Palais du Diable," and it is not a little to say for a modern building that it holds the statuary well and harmoniously, especially when there are such groups in that statuary as " La Danse."

Moreover, if you will notice, Paris does not so announce her failures; no great avenue leads up to and frames, for instance the Trocadero.

As to the silly reasoning that any rebuilding was an error, it is fit only for a club of antiquarians. Paris has rebuilt herself three separate times, and had she not done so we should have none of those architectural glories which are her pride to-day. The Revolution was not the first profound change of ideas that the city experienced. The great awakening that made the University turned Paris into a Gothic city almost in a generation. The " Grand Siècle " swept away that Gothic city and replaced it by the tall houses that yet mark all her older quarters. In this last expansion Paris is but following a well-known road of hers, and the people who will come long after us will find it a good thing that she did so.

This also is to be noted: that if Paris is somewhat negligent of what is curious, yet she is careful of what is monumental. As we shall see in this book, the twelfth and even the sixth centuries—the fourth also in one spot—come against one in the midst of a modern street. Much that has been destroyed was not destroyed by the iconoclasm of the nineteenth, but by the sheer lack of taste of the eighteenth century—a time that could add the horrible false-Renaissance portico to the exquisite Cathedral of Metz and that was capable of the Pantheon, pulled down without mercy. We suffer from it yet.

There is one feature which is perhaps not over-obvious in the buildings of Paris and which it is well to point out in this connection, especially as it is the modern parallel of a spirit which we shall find in all the history of the town. I mean a remarkable historical continuity.

Paris to the stranger is new. Or at least where it evidently dates from the last or even from the seventeenth century, it yet seems poor in those groups of the middle ages which are the characteristic of so many European towns, and one would say at first sight that it was entirely lacking in many relics of still earlier times. This impression is erroneous, not only as to the actual buildings of the city, but especially as to its history and spirit. But it is not without an ample excuse. There is nothing in Paris so old but that its surroundings give it a false aspect of modernity, nor is there any monument so venerable but that some part of it (often some part connected with the identity of the main building) dates from our own time.

The reason for this is twofold. First, Paris has

never been checked in its development. You find no relics because it has never felt old age, and that species of forgetfulness which is necessary to the preservation of old things untouched has never fallen upon her. For, if you will consider, it is never the period *just past* which we revere and with which we forbear to meddle; it is always something separated by a century at least from our own time. It needs, therefore, for the growth of ruins, and even for the preservation of old things absolutely unchanged, a certain period of indifference in which they are neither repaired nor pulled down, but merely neglected. Thus we owe Roman ruins to the dark ages, much of the English Gothic to the indifference of the seventeenth and eighteenth centuries. Such periods of indifference Paris has never experienced. Each age in her history, at least for the last six hundred years, has been "modern," has thought itself excellent, has designed in its own fashion. And on this account the conductor of Cook's tourists can find in the whole place but little matter for that phrase so dear to his flock: "It might have stepped out of the middle ages."

Secondly, Her buildings are at the present moment, and have been from the time of the Revolution, kept to a use, repaired and made to enter into the present life of the city. The modern era in Paris has had no sympathy with that point of view so common in Europe, which would have a church or a

palace suffer no sacrilegious hand, but remain a kind of
sacred toy, until it positively falls with old age, and
has to be rebuilt entirely. The misfortune (for example) which gives us in Oxford the monstrosity
of Balliol new buildings in the place of the exquisite fourteenth century architecture of which one
corner yet remains to shame us; or, again, the condition of the west front of Peterborough Cathedral,
which (apparently) must either be rebuilt or allowed
to fall down—such accidents to the monuments of
the past Paris has carefully avoided. She was
taught the necessity of this by the eighteenth century conservatism, and if she is too continually re-
pairing and replacing, it is a reaction from a time
when the stones of the capital, like the institutions of
the state, had been permitted to rot in decay.

There are one or two points of view in Paris from
which this character is especially notable. We shall
see it best, of course, where the oldest monuments
naturally remain,—I mean in the oldest quarter of
the city. Stand on the northern quay that faces the
Conciergerie and the Palais de Justice, and look at
their walls as they rise above the opposite bank of
the stream. What part of this is old and what new?
Unacquainted with the nature of the city, it would
be impossible to reply. That Gothic archway might
have been pierced in this century; the clock-tower,
with its fresh paint and the carefully repaired mouldings on its corners, might be fifty years old. Those

twin towers of the Conciergerie might be of any age,
for all the signs they give of it. Part of that building was destroyed in the Commune, and has been
rebuilt. Which part? There is nothing to tell. It
is only when we know that it is against the whole
genius of the people to imitate the styles of a dead
age,—when we are told (for example) that such things
as "the Gothic Revival," under which we groan in
England to-day, and which is the curse of Oxford
and Hampstead, has not touched Paris,—it is only
when we appreciate that the French either create or
restore, but never copy, that we can see how great a
work has been done on this one building.

The wall and the towers before you are not a
curiosity or a show; decay has not been permitted to
touch them; they are in actual service to-day in the
working of the law-courts. Yet that corner clock-
tower was the delight of Philippe le Bel. It was
Philippe the Conqueror who built those two towers,
with their conical roofs, and from one of their windows
he would sit looking at the Seine flowing by, as his
biographer describes him; through that pointed archway St. Louis went daily to hear the pleas in the
Palace gardens; from such and such a window the
last defense of Danton was caught by the mob that
stretched along the quay and over the Pont Neuf.

Or, again, take a contrasting case—one where a
spectator would believe all to be old, and yet where
the moderns have restored and strengthened. As you

stand on the quays that flank the Latin quarter and look northward to the Island and the whole southern side of Notre Dame, it is not only the thirteenth century at which you gaze; at point upon point Viollet le Duc rebuilt and refaced many of the stories—some, even, of the carvings are his work; yet you could never distinguish in it all what aid the present time had given to the work of St. Louis.

As for the Sainte Chapelle, it is at this day so exactly what it was when St. Louis first heard Mass in it,—and that has been done at the expense of so much blue and gold, just such color as he used,—that the traveller will turn from it under the impression that he is suffering at the hands of the third Republic, and will say, "How gaudy!" It is only when you note that the stained glass is the gaudiest thing in the place that you begin to feel that here alone, perhaps, in Europe, the men who designed the early Gothic would feel at home.

And if this continuity in her buildings is so striking a mark of modern Paris, and goes so far to explain her newness, you will find something yet more remarkable in the preservation of her sites. To take but three. The place of the administration, of the central worship and of the markets are as old as the Roman occupation. The Louvre has grown steadily from similar use to similar use through more than a thousand years; the Hotel de Ville, through more than seven hundred. And a man may go over the

Petit Pont from the southern bank, cross the Island, and come over to the northern side by the Pont Notre Dame, and be following step by step the road that so spanned the two branches of the stream centuries and centuries ago,—not the road of Roman times, but one earlier yet,—back in the vague time when the Cité was a group of round Gaulish huts, and when two rough wooden bridges led the traveller across the Seine on his way to the sea-coast.

And this continuity in buildings and in places is matched by one spirit running all through the action of Paris for fifteen hundred years. This is the fixed interest of her history, and it is this which so many men have felt who in the studios, or up on the hill of the University, though they had learned nothing of the past of the city, yet feel about them a secular experience and a troubling message difficult to understand—that seems to sum up in a confused sound the long changes of Christendom and of the West.

Well, what is the peculiar spirit, the historical meaning, of the town whose outer aspect we have hitherto been describing? No history can have value—it would perhaps be truer to say that no history can exist unless while it describes it also explains. Here we will have to deal with a city many of whose actions have been unique, much of whose life has been dismissed in phrases of wonder, of fear, or of equally impotent anger. If this is all that a book can do for Paris, it had better not have been written. To stand aghast at her excesses, to lift up the hands at her audacity, or to lose control over one's pen in expressing abhorrence for her success, is to do what any scholar might accomplish, but it would be to fail as an historian. *Why* has Paris so acted? The answer to that question, and a sufficient answer, alone can give such a story value. What is her nature? What is, if we may use a term properly applicable only to human beings, her mind?

You will not perceive the drift towards the true reply by following any of those laborious methods which stultify so much of modern analysis. You will not interpret Paris by any examination of her physical environment, nor comprehend her by one of those cheap racial generalizations that are the bane of popular study. In all the great truths spoken by Michelet, one is perhaps pre-eminent, because it seems to include all the others. He says: "La France a fait la France;" and if this be true (as it is) of the nation, it is more especially true of the town. There is within the lives of individuals—as we know by experience—a something formative that helps to build up the whole man and that has a share in the result quite as large as the grosser part for which science can account. So it is with states, and so, sometimes, with cities. A destiny runs through their development which is allied in nature to the human soul, and which material circumstance may bound or may modify, but which certainly it cannot originate.

In the first place Paris is, and has known itself to be, the city-state of modern Europe. What is the importance of that character? Why that certain habits of thought, certain results in politics which we can observe in the history of antiquity, are to be noted repeating themselves in the actions and in the opinions of Paris. It is a phenomenon strange to the industrial nations of to-day yet one with which society will always have to deal, perhaps at bottom the most durable thing of all, that men will associate and act by neighborhood rather than by political definitions. And this influence of neighborhood, which (with the single important exception of tribal society) is the greatest factor in social history, has formed the village community and the walled town whose contrast and whose coexistence are almost the whole history of Europe. When great Empires arise, a fictitious veil is thrown over these radical things. Men are attached to a wide and general patriotism covering hundreds of leagues, and even in the last stages of decay and just before the final cataclysm, Rhetoricians love to talk of a federation of all peoples, and merchants ardently describe the advent of a universal peace. But even in such exceptional periods in the history of mankind, the village community and its parallel the city are the real facts in political life; and when, in the inevitable fall and the subsequent reconstruction of society, the fictions are destroyed and the phrases lose themselves in realities, these fundamental and original units re-emerge in all their ruggedness and strength.

Upon the recognition of such units the healthy life of the middle ages reposed; in the satisfactory and human conditions of such societies the arts and the enthusiasms of Greece took life. It is in the autonomous cities of Italy that our civilization reappeared, and the aristocratic conceptions upon which the social order of Europe is still founded sprang from the isolation and local politics of the manor.

In a time when the facility of communication has been so greatly augmented, and when therefore the larger units of political society should be at their strongest, Paris proves to the modern world how enduring the ultimate instincts of our political nature may be.

The unit that can practically see, understand and act at once and together; the " city that hears the voice of one herald," is living there in the midst of modern Europe. By a paradox which is but one of many in French politics, the centre which first gave out to other societies the creed of the large self-governing state, the power whence radiated the enthusiasm even for a federal humanity, " the capital of the Republic of mankind" from which poor Clootz, the amiable but mad German Baron, dated his correspondence—this very town is itself an example of an intense local patriotism, peculiar, narrow and exclusive.

Paris acts together, its citizens think of it perpetually as of a kind of native country, and it has established for itself a definition which makes it the brain of that great sluggish body, the peasantry of France. In that definition the bulk of the nation has for centuries aquiesced, and the birthplace of government by majority is also the spot where distinction of political quality and the right of the head to rule all the members is most imperiously asserted.

It is from this standpoint that so much of her history assumes perspective. By recognizing this feature the chaos of a hundred revolts assumes historical order. You will perceive from it the Parisian mob, with all the faults of a mob, yet organizing, creating and succeeding; you will learn why an apparently causeless outburst of anger has been fruitful, and why so much violence and so much disturbance should have aided rather than retarded the development of France.

It is as the city-state (and the metropolis at that) that Paris has been the self-appointed guardian of the French idea. Throughout the middle ages you will see her anxious with a kind of prevision to safeguard the unity of the nation. For this she watches the diplomacy of the Capetians and fights upon their side, for this she ceaselessly stands watch with the King over feudalism and doubles his strength in every

blow that is dealt against the nobles. It is this feature that explains her attitude as the ally of Philip
the Conqueror, her leaning later on the Burgundian
house, her hatred of the southerner in the person of
the Armagnac.

You will find it, without interruption, guiding her
conduct in the history which links the middle ages
to our own time. She is the faithful servant of
Louis XI. ; she is the bitter fanatic for religious unity
in the religious wars. Thus you see her withstanding Henry IV. to the last point of starvation, and
thus a population, careless of religion, yet forces a
religious formula upon the Huguenot leader; and
when the first Bourbon accepted the mass with a jest,
it was Paris which had exacted, even from a conqueror, the pledge of keeping the nation one.

In the Revolution all this character appears in
especial relief. She claims to think for and to govern
France; she asserts the right by her energy and
initiative to defend the whole people and their new
institutions from the invader, and she ratifies that
assertion by success. With this leading thought
she first captures, then imprisons and finally over-
throws the King; lays (on the 2d of June) violent
hands upon the Parliament, directs the terror, and
then, when her system is no longer needed, permits in Thermidor the overthrow of her own spokes-
man.

If the condition of the city is considered, the

causes of this strong local unity will become apparent. Paris is a microcosm. She contains all the parts proper to a little nation, and by the reaction of her own attitude this complete character is intensified; for since she is the head of a highly organized state all is to be found there. Here is at once the national and the urban government; the schools for every branch of technical training. Here is the centre of the arts—not by a kind of accident such as will make the London artists live in Fitz-Johns Avenue, nor by the natural attraction of the great schools of the past, nor through peculiar collections such as cause the congeries at Munich, at Venice, or at Florence or at Rome, but by a deliberate purpose: by the placing within the walls of the city of all the best teaching that the concentrated effort of the nation can secure.

Within her walls are all the opposing factors of a vigorous life. She is not wholly student nor wholly industrial nor wholly mercantile, but something of all three. Even the noble is present to add his little different note to the harmonious discord of competing interests; and, alone of the great capitals of the world, she is the seat of the old University of the nation. Here, running wild through a whole quarter of the city, is that vigorous youth, undiscoverable in London or in Berlin; I mean the follies, the loves and the generous ideals of the students. They keep it fresh with a laughter that is lacking in the cen-

tres of the modern world, and they supply it with a
frank criticism bordering on intellectual revolt, which
the self-satisfaction of less fortunate capitals, mere
seaports, or simple military centres, fatally ignores.
They, from their high attic windows on the Hill, interpret her horizons; and, as they grow to fill the
ranks of her art and science, help to keep the city
worthy of the impressions with which she delighted
their twentieth year.

And Paris has also the last necessary quality for
the formation of a city-state. I mean that her stories
are so many memories of action which she has undertaken unaided, and that her view of the past is
one in which she continually stands alone. It is a
record of great sieges, in which no outer help availed
her, and in which she fell through isolation or succeeded by her own powers. More than one of her
monuments is a record of action that she undertook
before the nation which depends upon her was willing
to move; and she records herself, from the Column
of July to the Arsenal of the Invalides, the successful
leader in movements that the general people applauded
but could not design.

Her history has finally produced in her what was
in the middle ages but a promise or perhaps a thing
in germ,—I mean the sentiment and the expression of
individuality. The story of her growth from the dim
origins of her political position under the early Capetians, through the episode of Etienne Marcel to the

definite action of the seventeenth century and finally of the Revolution, is the story of a personality growing from mere sensation to self-recognition, and to functions determinate and understood. It is a transition from instinct to reason, and at its close you have, as was expressed at the opening of this chapter, a true and living unit, not in metaphor but in fact, with a memory, a will, a voice, and an expression of its own.

Such is the first great mark of Paris, and with that clue alone in one's hand the maze is almost solved.

But, if Paris has these characteristics of continuity and of being the city-state, she has also a third, which, while it is less noticeable to her own citizens, is yet more interesting to the foreigner than the other two. She is the typical city, at least of the western civilization,—I mean, her history at any moment is always a reflection peculiarly vivid of the spirit which runs through western Europe at the time. To say that she leads and originates, which is a commonplace with her historians, is not strictly true; it is more accurate to say that she mirrors. It cannot be denied that her action at such and such a crisis has differed from the general action of the European cities; nor can it be forgotten that her course has more than once produced a sense of sharp and sometimes painful contrast in the minds of her neighbors. Paris has not been typical in the sense of being the average. That character would have produced a

3

history devoid of features, whereas all the world knows that the history of Paris is a series of strong pictures too often overdrawn. If she has been the typical city of the west, it is rather in this sense, that on her have been focussed the various rays of European energy; that she has been the stage upon which the contemporary emotions of Europe have been given their *Personæ*, through whose lips they found expression; that she has time and time again been the laboratory wherein the problems that perplexed our civilization have always been analyzed and sometimes solved.

It may be urged that every city partakes of this character, and that the civilization which has grown up upon the ruins of Rome is so much of a unity that its principal cities have always reflected the spirit of their time. This is true. But Paris has reflected that spirit with a peculiar fidelity. While it has, of course, been filled with her own strong bias of race and of local character, yet her treatment of this or that time has been remarkable for proportion; you feel, in reading of her past action, that not the north or the south, not this people or that, but all Europe is (so to speak) being " played" before your eyes. The actors are French and, commonly, Parisian; the language they speak is strange and the action local, yet the subject-matter is something which concerns the whole of our world, and the place given to each part of the movement is that which, on looking over the surrounding nations, we should assign to it were we charged with drawing up an accurate balance of the time.

Before pointing out the historical examples which show how constantly Paris has been destined to play this international rôle, it is well to appreciate the causes of such a position. First among these comes the feature which has been discussed above. The fact that she contains within her walls all the parts of a state fits her for the character of representative, and makes her action more complete than is the case with another European city. The interests of exchange and of commerce, of finance (which in this age may almost be called a separate thing); the struggle between the proletariat and capital; the unsatisfied quarrel between dogmatic authority and the inductive method; militarism, and the reaction it creates; even the direction which literature and discussion may give to these energies,—all these are found within the city, and the general result is a picture of Europe. But this quality of hers is not the only cause of her typical character. Geographical position explains not a little of its origin. She is of Latin origin and of Latin tradition; her law and much of her social custom is an inheritance from Rome, yet the basis of the race is not Latin, and among those in the studios who almost reproduce the Greek, there is hardly a southern face to be found. Her lawyers and orators will model themselves upon Latin phrases, but you

would not match their expression among the Roman
busts ; and it has been truly said that the Italian profile was more often met with in England than in
northern France.   Even the insular civilization of
England, which has had so great an effect upon the
politics, if not the society, of the world, is to be found
strongly represented in this medley.   For England
looks south (or, at least, the England which once
possessed so great an influence did so), and Paris is
the centre of those northern provinces upon whom
the British influence has been strong.   Though this
part of her thought is of less importance than some
others, yet it is worth carefully noting, for it has been
neglected to a remarkable degree.   It is from this
that you obtain in Parisian history the attempts at a
democracy based upon representation ; it is from this,
again, that the principal modern changes in her judicial methods are drawn ; and so curiously strong has
been the attraction of English systems for a certain
kind of mind in Paris, that even the experiment of
aristocracy and of its mask—a limited monarchy—has
been tried in these uncongenial surroundings.   The
greatest of the men of '93 regret the English alliance.
Mirabeau bases half his public action upon his memories of the English whigs.   Lamartine delights in
calling England the Marvellous Island.

   And, if we go a little deeper than historical facts
and examine those subtle influences of climatic condition (which, as they are more mysterious, are also

of greater import than obvious things), we shall find
Paris balanced between the two great zones of
Europe. It is hard to say whether she is within or
without the belt of vineyards; a little way to the
south and to the east you find the grapes; a little
way to the north and west, to drink wine is a luxury,
and the peasants think it a mark of the southerner.
There are days in Chevreuse, in the summer, when a
man might believe himself to be in a Mediterranean
valley, and, again, the autumn and the winter of the
great forest of Marly are impressions purely of the
north. The Seine is a river that has time and again
frozen over, and the city itself is continually silent under heavy falls of snow. Yet she has half the custom
of the south, her life is in the open air, her houses are
designed for warmth and for sunlight; she has the
gesture and the rapidity of a warmer climate.

For one period of her history you might have
called her a great northern city, when she was all
Gothic and deeply carved, suited to long winter
nights and to weak daylight. But in the course of
time she has seemed partly to regain the traditions
of the Mediterranean, so that you have shallow
mouldings, white stone and open streets, standing
most often under a grey sky, which should rather
demand pointed gables and old deep thoroughfares.
The truth is that she is neither northern nor southern,
but, in either climate (they meet in her latitude) an
exile, satisfying neither, and yet containing both of

the ends between which Europe swings; so that, in all that is done within Paris, you are at a loss whether to look for influence coming up from the Mediterranean, or to listen for the steep waves and heavy sweeping tides of the Channel and the North Sea. Only with one part of Europe—a part which may later transform or destroy the west—she has no sympathy,—I mean that which lies to the east of the Elbe. She was a town of the Empire, and the darker and newer part of Europe is as much a mystery to her as to the nations which are her neighbors.

If you will notice her first prominence, you will discover that Paris rises upon Europe just where the modern period begins. It is as a town of the lower Empire, of the decline, of the barbarian invasions, of the advent of Christianity. Paris first becomes a great city just as the civilization to which we belong starts out upon its adventures, and her history at once assumes that character upon which these paragraphs insist. She receives the barbarian; the mingled language is talked in her streets; her palace is the centre of the Teutonic monarchy, which has carved its province from the Empire; of the two extremes, she seems to combine either experience. She does not lose her language (like the Rhine valley), nor her religion and customs (like Britain); but, on the other hand, she is strongly influenced by the conquest, and knows nothing of that lingering Roman civilization, almost untouched by the invader, which left to Nimes,

Arles and the southern cities a municipal organization lasting to our own day. At the outset of her history she includes the experience of the south and of the north.

During the Carlovingian epoch she loses her place for a time; but, with the rise of the nationalities that followed it, and with the invasions, she is not only intimately concerned but again furnishes the example of which we have been speaking. She sustains siege after siege; like the Europe of which she is the type, she finally, but with great pain, beats off the pirates, and in her walls rises the first and what is destined to be the most complete type of the national kingships. The Robertian House was neither feudal nor a reminiscence of imperial power; it was a mixture of both those elements. It was founded by a local leader who had defended his subjects in the " dark century," and in so much it attaches closely to the feudal character; on the other hand, its members are consecrated kings; they have the aim of a united and centralized power, and in this they hold even more than do the Ottos to the Imperial memory.

Note how, as Europe develops, the experience of Paris sums up that of the surrounding peoples. The Roman law finds her an eager listener, but it does not produce in her case the rapid effect which you may notice in some of the Italian cities. Custom weighs hard in the northern town, and Philip Augustus, after all his conquests, could never hear the language which the professors of Bologna used to Barbarossa just before his defeat. On the other hand, the power of the king which that law was such a powerful agent to increase, was not destined to suffer from repeated reaction as it did in England, and the kings of Paris never fell beneath a direct victory of aristocracy such as that which crushed John at Runnymede, and centuries later destroyed the Stuarts.

The struggle between government and feudalism was destined to last much longer in France than it did in the neighboring countries, and as it goes on, Paris sees all its principal features, and the crown finally triumphs only in that same generation of the seventeenth century which saw the complete success of the aristocracy in England and in the Empire.

In the religious world the experience of Paris has been equally typical. She heard the first changes of the twelfth century; the schoolmen discussed in her University; Thomas Aquinas sat at table with her king. When the sixteenth century shook and split the unity of Christendom, its treble aspect was vividly reflected in Paris. The evangelical, the Catholic and the Humanist are represented distinctly and in profusion there; for it is in Paris that Calvin dedicates his book, that Rabelais is read, and, finally, that the St. Bartholomew is seen. She does not change her creed at the word of a dynasty, nor is she swept by the same purely religious zeal for reform that covers Geneva and so much of Holland; nor does she stamp out the new movement with the ease of the Italian or the Spaniard; but all the powers of the time seem to concentrate in her, and, as she has always done, she pays heavily for being the centre of European discussion. The appeal with her (as elsewhere) is to arms, and the struggle is still continuing under Louis XIV., when its importance wanes before the rise of a rationalism around which the future battles of her religious world will be fought.

This is always the lesson of her history and the way we should read it if we wish to understand. We are looking down into a little space where all our society is working out its solutions. Whether we dwell upon the Gothic Paris of Louis XI., fixing nationality and centralized government, or upon the Paris of '93,—cutting once for all the knot of eighteenth century theories,—or the Paris of '48, where the old political and the new economic problems met; or upon the Paris of 1871, where the older social forces and the love of country just managed to defeat the revolt of the new proletariat; in whatever aspect or at whatever time, she is always the picture of Europe, catching, in a bright and perhaps highly colored mirror, the figures which are struggling in the nations around her. And it is in this character that her history will be most easy of comprehension and will leave with us an impression of greatest meaning.   But whenever we think of the city we do well to remember Mirabeau: "Paris is a Sphinx." He added, "I will drag her secret from her;" but in this neither he nor any other man has succeeded.

A RECOLLECTION

WHEN Hubert Howard fell in his twenty-
eighth year at the very close of the
Campaign in Egypt, the last to be sacrificed
in a final and decisive success, we lost
suddenly a man of such a kind as makes us
know why history is necessary to us ; history
and the fixing of things past. There passed
in a moment from our lives a character upon
whose continued presence we had counted as
a certain thing : his future was not in that
vague promise with which we connect whatever is young, active and of great opportunities :
it was rather a part taken for granted in all
that we knew or guessed concerning the fate
of our society. He could not fail ; and the
kinds of actions in which he would have led
and succeeded, the movements whose character
he would have determined, the doubts in which

B 2

he would have influenced rather than have
guided—the nature of all these was as clear
and as definite as the lines of his face and
as the few and simple forces that made up
the power of his spirit.

With the violence of a blow, in one
moment and in the reading a dozen words
the whole of this certitude disappeared. For
some I know a foundation failed without
warning ; for all who had been near him
there vanished from between the hands something that had been held, if not for support,
at least for sustenance ; grasped close rather
than observed.

Now in this disaster there is a necessity
of preserving whatever remains, although
these are only memories. Had he lived but
a few years the society around us would
easily have fulfilled such a task, and he
would have been safe in the observation and
recollections of a great number of men ; but
this natural fate which seemed predestined
and which is so surely reserved for contemporaries of less parts or value, has made

default. He died just at the moment when such men pass from the domestic to the public sphere, having been for a small number what he was later to have become for many.

This being so, it is the best that one can do to write down accurately whatever impressions are vivid at the moment, and thus perpetuate as much as is possible the lines which a long process of time is certain to fade : to do for his character and his memory what our rough sketches of a great thing just seen do for the answering of our questions long after : our memory tells us this or that event or person filled the mind, but a few lines of pencil build it up for us freshly after many years and tell us how and why we wondered.

So what I am going to attempt is the picture of Hubert Howard. It will be very difficult because we can least describe what we most intimately admire, and because he was known in different circumstances by such different men. Also I knew nothing of him

outside our friendship, so that there will be
a great deal lacking; but if I write down an
exact account of what I saw and knew, why
then any one who also saw and knew him
can build in the rest, for his strength con-
sisted in simplicity, and everything he did
was part of a spirit perfectly united.

The story of who he was by birth, what
he did and what happened to him, is very
short.   There is hardly anything of moment
save in the three adventures which his daring
called him into; one in Cuba, one in South
Africa, and this last upon the Nile.   These
are best told in his own letters and diaries
which, pieced together and noted, are the
matter of this.   The rest is very quickly told.
It is what he was that is difficult to tell.

The second son of Lord and Lady Carlisle,
he was born at their house in Palace Green
on the third of April, 1871.   As a little boy
he was delicate, and some of the first part
of his life was spent in the south of France
and in Italy for the sake of his health.   This
passage, as he grew up, certainly influenced

those vivid though confused memories which
men inherit from their early childhood, for
I remember him speaking of the South with
more appreciation than can come from later
experience ; and while his home would account for much of it, there may yet have
partly proceeded from these journeys the
excellent and familiar French which he spoke ;
for he was in this point an heir of older
traditions : his constant use and perfect knowledge of that tongue reminded me not of his
own generation, but of the conversation which
remains to us of the early century when the
intercourse of Europe was based upon such
an acquaintance.

As he grew up his health returned to him,
and the later years of his boyhood and
adolescence developed the vigour that we
knew, a vigour full of the North country
from whose stock he was drawn, suited to
the sports he found there as he became a
man in Cumberland, and instinct with the
very spirit which should by right fall upon
the godson of Charles Kingsley.

In these years between his boyhood and his manhood he was taught at home: he never passed through a public school, and in the place of the formative routine, strength, follies and traditions with which a public school would have made him familiar, he took all his manner from his home and all his knowledge from a tuition particular and widespread. He therefore, on entering the larger world, had less to unlearn in habit than have most men, but more to acquire in direction. His originality and personal power which would always have made him remarkable, were emphasised: but the way to use them and how they fitted into general surroundings were less known to him.

He spent his nineteenth year studying in the house of Mr. A. L. Smith of Balliol, and matriculated himself from that College in October, 1889. From that moment he came into a life with which all our memories of him are associated. It was in the four years of his residence at Oxford that he formed the group of friends in whose affection he

will always chiefly reside.   He there found
himself in the many-sided companionship for
which his character seemed to be especially
designed, and in an association where impressions, rapidly made, are yet most permanent.
He was there surrounded by those to whom
his qualities would most immediately appeal.
Great daring and great generosity, a bodily
energy always seeking action, and these united
with excellence in the mind, have no place
in the world, perhaps, where they show more
clearly than at Oxford, and, of all her colleges,
his college is best fitted for such things.

At the University he was three years my
senior, and the account which I am drawing
up must from this point become the notes
upon things that I have myself observed.
I met him first at the invitation of Mr.
Urquhart of Balliol and in his rooms.   It
was in the autumn just before my matricula-
tion.   In the hour we spent together a friendship was struck which a certain lapse of time—
fatally short—neither emphasised nor altered
because it was graven.   For it was in the

nature of his open gesture, his keen interests, and his rapid manner that his character was, not slowly, but at once comprehended; and that the impression made, deep and endurable beyond any I have known, was also immediate.

In this undergraduate time he was an air and an influence, like the change of season. For he affected men without exactly leading, and, one of a body of friends, he was their soul more than they knew. I look back to that time and remember him always as one of a group, but the groups change and he is always there: he is always there where the life of very young men is strongest: it is his figure that comes up when one recalls the fresh winds in the river valleys, the races on the February floods, the canoes on the Cher, and those glorious runs. across country which he continually led with laughter and with a kind of enthusiasm for hazard and for danger. He is there also in his room, smoking before his fire and turning with eagerness and not without dogmatism to discussion; our

work also was associated with him, because
he took the good average of things, and his
degree was the result of a very careful and
a very industrious energy in a department
that would hardly naturally have interested or
pleased him.   He would speak sometimes at
the Clubs, but their administration absorbed
him more than their debates; he was eager
to get a new man for his own society, to argue
a rule or to assert a point much more than to
make a speech in the ordinary fashion.

There was not noticeable while he was at
Oxford that interest in politics which later
showed itself in him.   Nothing was much to
him unless he could touch and know it by
personal contact; things distant or abstract
soon wearied a nature intense upon ideals
but never sufficiently tenacious of a mere
idea.   Yet even in politics I remember more
of what he, than of what others, said.

I cannot tell how it is, but all who were
with him will bear me out in this: that he
seems universally present when we put ourselves back into that good time: we at Balliol

knew more of what he did in the Balliol boat
than of what another man did in the University Eight.

He took his degree in the second class of
the Modern History School in June, 1893,
and after that date three main adventures
and a little work at the parliamentary Bar
fill up the rest of what is to be told. All
these are put forth in detail later and need
only be mentioned here.

He left Balliol with that readiness, or rather
appetite, for adventure which, as it was the
first to be noticed, was also the most characteristic of his qualities. Its first satisfaction
was in a short, picturesque, dangerous and
unfruitful expedition to Cuba during the
insurrection. He left England in August,
1895, and returned in three months: he had
passed the Spanish lines, risked more than
most of the combatants, seen the danger that
he desired to see, and returned rather disappointed than otherwise at the paucity of
fighting. His journey and what he wrote on
his return have also this interest, that he was

the first man who came from the outside to
see the problems in the island for himself;
he made, moreover, in this adventure some
acquaintance with America, and drew, as was
his custom, rapid and definite conclusions
from what he had seen. When later the
rebellion ended in a conflict whose effects are
still moving the world, he took a clear and
definite position based upon a considerable
knowledge; he weighed his judgment, but
defended it with enthusiasm, and applauded
the results of the war.

It was shortly after this, in the autumn of
1896, that a second expedition led to an
experience, which should have moulded the
course of his life. It formed his politics, gave
him a chief interest and remained the starting-
point of what could not have failed to become
a definite line of action for his future. He
sailed for South Africa to join in the repression of the revolt in Rhodesia.

It is with this passage that we have the
most familiarity from his letters and diaries;
he stayed in this business longer than in any

other, and I believe he returned from it with more durable impressions than he had received in any other kind of action.

He first fought as an officer in one of the native levies that were raised for the purpose of the war. Then, after sustaining a slight but troublesome wound in action, he received the offer of being secretary to Lord Grey. In this office he found a very complete and vigorous interest, his letters are full of the instinct which has so greatly increased the power of England, and he found in this work and in what preceded it the trade for which he was meant and to which he would, I think, in time have returned. To see new things and take pleasure in wonderful horizons, to find danger and risk, to govern, to administer —all those things entered into his life and found there a right place. The enthusiasm with which we had seen him turn to a man or to a passing idea, we now saw concentrated upon a permanent object, and one in which he found himself well in sympathy with a great amount of the thought around him.

From that moment he became, as all young Englishmen of worth at last become, political. He thought of the State. The domestic problems which had wearied him or which he had hardly noticed, now became part of a larger scheme. The Empire absorbed him: and his new care did not diminish or change but strengthen. All his deep sentiments were enduring, but in this alone they were public, and in this alone he found the general and active interest which a personal devotion, a friendship or an academic pursuit can never give.

He returned, then, from Africa in the early summer of 1897 ready for action when the time should come. His conversation from that time onwards was more and more full of the ideas he had there received.

He was called to the Bar and joined the North-Eastern circuit. In this work he was interested, and he did well. But I doubt whether it would ever have become a permanent career for him; he had inherited a certain capacity for the legal profession, and he had certainly shown in part of his South African work the qualities necessary to success in a court. But he would not have found in the Law a passion, and unless he was taken altogether, possessed permanently by some strong ideal, unless his heart was in a swing together with his intellect, his nature tended to abandon effort and to cast one work aside for another.

With the advance upon Khartoum his opportunity returned. But the circumstances were not those of South Africa. He could march with the army only under conditions less active than those which had permitted his career in Rhodesia. The writing he had done after his expedition to Cuba, coupled with a certain knowledge of literary work, decided him to obtain a post as correspondent which might give him some place in an advance where every unit not necessary to the military plan was rigorously excluded. He was sent with such a mission by the *Times*, for which paper Colonel Rhodes was also writing, so that he and Howard were thrown together

during the whole of the war; the one was
wounded and the other fell upon the same day.

In this capacity he wrote the notes and
despatched the letters which will be found
in the later pages of this Memorial, but the
work lacked body until they came in touch
with the enemy. In those very few days
the action and danger which were almost
a necessity to him refreshed his interest: they
were perhaps, as he said to a friend in the
excitement of the battle, the happiest of his
life. The adventures into which he threw
himself and which were those rather of
soldiering than of the part he had undertaken will be told in the place to which they
belong; it is enough to say here that he
found the same delight in the chances and in
the joy of fighting, that he had discovered in
Rhodesia. He took part in more than one of
the smaller actions of the first day, and when
the Battle of Omdurman was over, he rode
with the Lancers into the charge that was the
occasion of so much courage and applause.

It was on the evening of the same day

C

that he entered the city with the Sirdar's staff. He was still eager and alert with the great event through which they had just passed, seeming, as he always did in a moment of excitement, to see, hear and do all that the place and time permitted—or more. The narrow lanes still held some few and scattered defenders making for such cover as they find ; a last and futile effort against the conquerors. These it was necessary to clear; and by a misunderstanding, the shells from one of the batteries were still bursting over the city.

Two companies of Egyptian soldiers had been sent through the great open square, or " Mosque," to clear the city beyond of certain stragglers—who were (though it was not then known) the rearguard of the escaping Khalifa. Hubert Howard went with them, bringing a small camera. Just as they reached the further side of the great square it was noticed that shells were falling on the Khalifa's house, which bordered it, and the officer in command ordered the men to fall back: they did so in small bodies, Howard himself a little behind the officer in command and a little in front of the soldiers. As you leave the great open square there is a small sheltered court-yard before the Khalifa's house. Into this he had just passed when a shell was seen to burst above it, and immediately after he was found by an officer who had followed him, lying on the ground before the door. He had been suddenly killed.

The general opinion has been, and is, that he was killed by the shell. But it is possible also that he may have been shot at close quarters by a straggler. A Dervish is said to have been seen bending over the body, and to have made his escape immediately as the officers who followed came up. It is a matter that cannot be finally decided.

The hour and day of his death was about 6 o'clock of the afternoon on September 2nd, 1898 ; he was the last man to fall.

——————

This, very shortly, is the history of his life. But his character and his look and his manner were more important things.

C 2

His head and the lines of his face were singularly clear; the outline of his head was of that rare kind which may be expressed at once in the curve made by the quick sweep of a pencil, for it was very even. His hair lay closely about his head in curls that strongly defined its shape; they had been dark brown and abundant in all his early youth, but they were very rapidly turning to a hard grey as he neared thirty, and they grew thinner. The character of his face was best seen in its profile, and, of such portraits as remain of him, he is more vividly brought back to me by those which show him thus, especially looking downwards. This profile was very exact in its proportions and remarkable for the definition of its parts. Thus his forehead was straight and not high; and it lay in a straight line with the nose, as you may see in old Greek pictures of men. His mouth was firm, and he was one of those who kept his lips habitually closed as an expression. There lay upon them when he was not speaking a slight curve that was almost a smile, as though the things of which he was thinking appeared to him in their complexity rather than in any other light.

It was a face made for repose and to which repose alone gave its full meaning. But this the eagerness and unrest of his mind rarely permitted.

There had appeared about his mouth, since I first knew him, that is within the last five years, the two strong lines that so often come with maturity ; his brows also were marked very slightly by the contraction of permanent thought. But with these exceptions his face was smooth-set. You could see in it what people mean by such words as "chiselled" or "clear cut," for every feature was defined in itself with perfection ; all this appeared the better because he was clean shaven. Indeed though it is difficult to describe these things in writing, perhaps I shall put the whole thing best by saying that when one had once seen his face it remained with peculiar permanence in the memory, and this quite apart from the way in which one had dwelt upon it. So that I make no doubt that many to whom he was but a passing stranger can see him in their minds almost as clearly as I do now, who was his friend.

In complexion he was dark; and this, which might not have been remarkable in a face less determined, lent him a special appearance which I can only express in the rather vague phrase that it was Southern: such a tone also strongly marked by contrast the character and light of his eyes. For these were of great beauty, clear and grey, and by nature untroubled, having the vividness and translucency which is the sign of a vigorous health. They were not, however, vivacious, and this was remarkable in one whose energies prompted rapid gesture and quick expression, and they alone lent to his general bearing a character which all felt in him. That which so much reminds me of him in the lines that run:

> ... "Oh! Anima Lombarda ...
> .   .   .   .
> ... muover degli occhi onesta e tarda."

In stature he was short, a little over five foot eight, and in build sturdy, though the squareness of his shoulders and the strength of his limbs did not strike one as they so often do in men of that height. This was because of his activity, an activity that showed itself in a certain ease of carriage and rapidity of gesture. With such movements he possessed more grace than is customary in men of his build.

His walk was on the whole rapid, and he carried his head higher than most men, as though the things which he desired to see were above the level of his eyes. It was part of this general carriage that he was neat and close in his dress as he was in the mould of his limbs, and altogether the effect he gave was one of an energy never completely stilled, but either somewhat unquiet and ill at ease, or enjoying the full satisfaction of active employment.

His hands were peculiar in a man who felt no attraction towards the arts, for their gestures were far more plastic than you will

usually find among Englishmen. Thus he
would emphasise a point in speaking by that
half opening of the fingers which gives to
a period the effect of grasping with the hand.
Then, when he was pleased or was saying
something indicative of light praise, he had
an upward gesture of the fingers, very noticeable, and rather the characteristic of an artist
than of a man of action. I do not know
that he ever employed this quickness of touch,
but it would not surprise me to learn that
it was valuable to him in matters such as
shooting or rapid draughtsmanship of maps
outside of the arts which I knew he did not
cultivate.

The movements of his head were sudden,
and indicative rather of gesture to be expressed than of an observation to be taken.
He was one of those who on turning to
speak or to observe, move the whole body,
facing round upon the feet; thus if he were
in an argument he would often turn on the
heels squarely to look at the man whom he
was addressing. But he had, as I have said,

especially the movements of interest and of appreciation.

For a modern man he was singularly lacking in constraint ; he would throw his head back to laugh, laughing also loudly and heartily. He would put the hand and arm forward on the table in speaking, he would strike the table to emphasise enjoyment at, or disagreement with, or his belief in the accuracy of, a phrase which he had heard.

In fine, the instinctive movements of his body, his walk, gesture, glance, laugh, everything, was what would have been expected of a great energy seeking outlet.

But were I to leave this impression it would be false, because though true of many moments it was profoundly modified by his action at others. I do not believe that I or any other one have seen him in an attitude of lassitude, but I have seen him more frequently than any other man of similar energy in repose, not without melancholy and even in reverie.

He also delighted in this, the discussion of

matters which can only be debated by the aid of analysis. Thus he would compare writers and policies, when neither the style of the one nor the direction of the other were determined, and he would follow out with pleasure those useless and enchanting debates that have always interested active minds because their solution is known to be impossible. He also had this quality, which is surely rare in active men, that he loved a general interest and a general knowledge. He had acquired all those first steps in a hundred matters where so many men to-day desire to be specialists or nothing. He had the old and excellent familiarity with the things of major interest in life, the beginnings of the sciences and of the arts : that reasonable wideness which diffuses without dissipating an education. In this admirable result some praise should be given to his college and much to his tutor, a man with whom, as all who have known him will say, the general interests are always put before the special. But Hubert Howard was well fitted to take advantage of the breadth and many-sidedness which has been the peculiar glory of Balliol ; and this was due to the long and sustained influences of his home, where, before he came to the University, he had read widely and of those books which a child as he grows chooses for himself in his father's house.

As to art he seemed to care little ; he felt strong antipathies and had reactions against sadness, but I have not myself heard him express any strong emotion of pleasure at a building or a picture. He was not without the fear that such things might lead to his being taken for a critic, or even for a professional appreciator—for one of the men who can never do nor produce. These characters were so abhorrent to his own, that he went, as I think, out of his way, in order to avoid any resemblance to them, and as it seems to me he wasted in this, even with his intimate friends, a great power which was apparent throughout his intelligence and which would have been like a gift from him had he been willing to betray it. I could wish for instance to have known how he, in whom the power of England worked with the effect of a great artistic presentation, had been affected by the sceneries and by the immense distances of her empire, or by the effects of London. I remember him in Cumberland full of interest and eager to show me the marks that Roman soldiers had left upon a rock, but refusing to express anything at the sudden sight of the hills round Skiddaw, which we saw from horse-back as we came to the top of a steep grass field. I believe he had for the expression of these emotions, which have been so much abused by affectation, a kind of fear, as some writers have of the platitude and others of what has grown false by usage.

There is one other very characteristic thing with regard to matters of the intelligence or the sense of beauty, without mention of which I could not complete even so short a passage as this. Just as he would fall suddenly into reveries, so for all his suddenness and determination he would fall sometimes into a diffidence with regard to these matters. There was a particular tone of doubt which of course written words will fail to express, but which I can best indicate by saying that it was the result of giving to an affirmation the tone and manner of a question. It was not without a certain pathos to see him seeking the opinion of men whose judgment was entirely inferior to his own, and I have heard him say as a confidence with regard to things undoubtedly beautiful that they had pleased him ; telling me secretly, as though in this he had done something which he feared might be out of the common. There was not in all he said or did anything greater or more beautiful than this occasional or accidental trait, because it was the direct result of that simplicity which I am certain to have been the cardinal virtue from whence his nobility proceeded.

To speak too much, however, of his habit of mind or of his conversation would be to give an impression of him other than that

which we who saw him received. His interests worked outwardly ; it was in sports and
in bodily activity that he chiefly showed
himself. Our memory of him is in these,
and that especially because there was no
transition in which we might have seen his
vigour failing ; it is the picture of him in
full life that remains.

There was no special part of English
athletics nor any particular sport to which
he attached himself exclusively. He might
perhaps, had he taken one alone, have been
preëminent, for he was very skilful, quick
and strong ; but to choose and keep but one
interest in such a matter as amusement was
not in his nature. The college life at Oxford,
the chances and fellowship which such an
exercise gives there, turned him chiefly to
Rowing. He was the life of our own Eight,
but he did not reach the University crew.
I do not remember his keeping to this as
a habit after leaving the University; I think
it appealed to him more because it was of
a piece with the common life of Balliol than

for its own sake. After his degree he would row on occasions, when he came up to visit, but I never knew him do anything more.

He was on the contrary naturally attracted to particular feats which contained the elements of risk, difficulty, or the necessity for endurance. It was he who would propose the impossible to us in long runs across country or in canoeing through the floods or in the achievement of a hard athletic task in a limited time. While he was at Oxford he gave to Balliol a particular character for these things. It was he who attempted to break the record in walking between the University and London ; to paddle the forty miles of the Cherwell from Banbury between sunset and sunrise of a February day ; and he continually led us in hunts over the fields after nothing, taking jumps that led nowhere, and swimming rivers that were well bridged for those who took life easier.

Now as I write I know that the ten or fifteen of us who were nearest to Hubert Howard are thinking continually of those races over the winter grass. No one can remember him, without his figure suggesting the flat meadows down to Sandford, the hedges and walls by Marston, and the risks of taking the Cherwell or of jumping the bank below the Kennington willows. One might almost say that these days had no purpose in them, yet it is difficult or impossible to convey their fulness : they had no purpose except to feel the open air in the best of good companionship, the desire to run risks in the presence of others, to lead and to be led and to be boys. Hubert Howard made them, and I can only think of them and him together—they are the clearest days in our lives.

Among other sports he was fond of fishing, as one should be if one comes from the Eden and the small rivers that feed it from the fells. He shot with a good average skill, and was fond of that sport also. His horsemanship was of the kind that comes from a great delight in the exercise without any remarkable keenness or aptitude for the management of one's horse. Like many men of his build he sat his horse firmly and with a good seat, and showed well against the sky; but he rode roughly. He seemed to need in this matter some animal that would have felt as he did; something short, strong, and untiring. Nor did he suit his actions to the needs of his mount; he rode hard in the exercise of his own energy, and there was a point where he forgot the fatigue of his servant, whether animal or man.

In the letters and diaries that follow there will be found this pleasure in the outdoor life which marked him; there will also be found, I think, that lack of specialisation to which I have alluded. He speaks of the Veldt with enthusiasm, its great distances inspire him; he makes a particular note of the effect produced by Egypt, and there are sentences, though rare, in his notes on service which display the same feeling. But there is also a lack in them of particular remark and object, there is no one attitude, not even the military, that takes up his mind altogether in his Cuban, or in his South African, or in his Egyptian experiences. What he loved was action; the

D

way it came to him was little, save that in later years it pleased him best when it had something to do with the purpose of the Empire, and that it always pleased him best in proportion to its hazard.

And speaking of this it becomes necessary to emphasise that side of him in which the love of danger played so great a part. There are many men who are brave, there are not so many who are daring, and there are still less in whom daring furnishes a motive. Now with Hubert Howard daring was the one and leading thing that, given his virtues, moulded his character. He dared continually and always; to find an occasion for daring was so to speak his business, to take action where action involved danger was a recreation to him; and perhaps I can best express this quality by saying that whereas with many men whom we admire courage is a kind of passive thing, latent but ready to be used when occasion requires it, with him it was active and always seeking an opportunity rather than waiting for a necessity.

It was this I think which gave him his principal power over the young men who knew him ; it was irresistibly attractive. It produced an effect like beauty, so that one admired, and was certain that one would continue to admire, everything he did ; and yet it was also unconscious, so that those things for which we ought chiefly to reverence his memory were in some way separate from it ; for this splendid quality which he brought into a time that has forgotten such things was an intimate part of his nature, depending upon no necessity of control and calling for no restriction and for no effort.

To complete this picture one must talk of something more even than courage ; I mean that he was steadfast. I suppose it has always been seen that while some men keep a good general average of truth and of loyalty yet those do not make idols or anchors of particular points, while others changeful and easily wearied yet do cling with an astounding perseverance to one or two things : and this perseverance forms a nucleus for the whole

D 2

character.   Well, this was to me not the most
striking nor the most beautiful, but the deepest
sign of the kind of man that he was.   There
were one or two things upon which he would
admit of no compromise.   Not only would he
refuse to abandon them, but they became so
clearly an understood part of his usual habits
that one would not have attempted for a
moment, I do not say to have moved him, but
even to have talked to him upon such matters.
Of several that might be mentioned, I will
take one that was sufficiently familiar.   It
was his determination never to take either
spirits or wine or any form of intoxicant.   He
maintained this as an ordinary habit of life
without the minutest change under every kind
of circumstance.   This temperance was with
Hubert Howard a matter so dependent upon
general strength of purpose that when we
thought or spoke of him his teetotalism never
entered our heads ; and yet that when he was
with us it never entered our heads either to
offer him a glass of wine.   I mean that he
was capable of making a principle, to which

he was profoundly attached but in which he differed from the bulk of his society, so far forgotten as to lead to no kind of emphasis or irritation, and yet so far remembered as to leave him always entirely free. Now this is precisely the quality which distinguishes a steadfast man ; the quality of keeping to this or to that with so silent, so permanent, and so strong a current of emotion, as makes it a part, not only of what is known but also of what is felt about them. Of many things this one is the easiest for me to give as an example.

Here then is all that I remember save those particular things with which the latter part of his memorial must deal. Let me sum up as far as I can the general picture which remains in the mind, and which, if I make it permanent, will be my most sacred possession.

A figure strong, active, short, well built and expressive in its gesture : a habit always sufficiently restrained to suggest descent, never so much as to suggest concealment; a face of the most peculiar impress, clear, straight, and

with equal proportions, not untouched by sadness but with vivacity in everything except in
the slow movement of the eyes. A carriage
erect and determined, but also unrestful, and
the laugh which comes only from full companionship with every kind of man.

This figure and these features when they
come back to me are associated with a character which would in any circumstance have
remained remarkable, which in our own time
was suited to a special kind of criticism and
of praise. From the point of view of the time
in which he lived it was a character whose
faults of over-eagerness and of a desire for
action pushed to an extreme, unfitted him for
certain of the liberal professions to which our
civilisation calls its first men in great numbers ;
but its virtues of great bravery, of steadfast-
ness and of permanent sympathy gave it a
value that our time also could use well: because our time is full of dangers, and we run
the risk of falling into the hands of men who
are neither brave nor steadfast nor possessed
of principle.

In the special matter that most concerns
the English people at this moment he found
himself particularly apt for service ; by the
combination of his birth, of his love of adventure and of the form which his idealism
took, the Empire stood before him as a career.
Nor must these words be taken as too vague
and wide ; if the Empire has one quality more
than another that distinguishes it among the
nations it is this, that it chooses and can find
from a comparatively small circle the energy,
the devotion and the ability without which its
whole character would be changed. Now it
is not an exaggeration nor a set of words
made for the occasion, but a truth which will
be borne witness to by all who knew him and
were fitted to judge, that in the circle of
younger men from which England chooses he
was conspicuous in possessing the qualities
that make up the defenders and perpetuators
of her foreign rule. And to these qualities he
added, more than any of the younger men of
our own time and more than most of those
of whom we read in the past, a distinct idea of

what his first pleasure was in the matter; it
lay entirely outside the considerations that in
the case of other men produce apathy, or
hesitation, or excess. So that one may say
with perfect justice that when he fell the
State suffered a great loss. He would have
done very wonderful things for England.

To all this we must add the things, that,
had he fallen upon times less suited to his
nature, would still have distinguished him and
made him stand alone: that of himself without effort he could group men as friends, that
he was ready always to do and desirous to
find difficulty in doing, that the struggle which
some men avoid and which others endure he
rather sought and loved.

Finally, in this figure of my friend there
will remain to me, more conspicuous than the
rest, the personal quality which a public life
would not have developed, but which a few
years of his youth had emphasised for us all.
In the most remote and the most obscure of
circumstances he would have been loved; but
what this is, or how it is to be defined, I do

not think any man has yet known. Certainly
it cannot be done in words, though there are
lines of verse which suggest it and pictures
which almost give it in the full. I will not
attempt a thing that would fail even in an
effort of art, and of which a mere description
can never be master; it has the force and the
elusiveness of sacred things.

All this was not permitted. It is our custom
when such losses fall upon us to look among
the greatest works for a parallel and to describe, partially, in the words of others what
we cannot describe at all in our own. There
is a place I think in the literature of Europe
where you may find Hubert Howard. It is
a passage which I read and re-read in the
desire to discover some foothold when I heard
of his death; I mean that passage in the song
of Roland wherein the simplicity and the
directness of the great epic of chivalry gives
the effect of such losses as these and ennobles
an emotion that without some such support
would be intolerable. It was from the blood
of these men that he was descended. His

virtues and his faults were the faults and
virtues of that early time which is also the
greatest that our civilisation has known.

> "Ami Roland, de toi ait Dieu mercy.
> Onques nul homme tel chevalier ne vit
> Pour grandes batailles juster et definir.
> Là mon honneur est tournée en declin.
>
>   .   .   .   .
>
> Ami Roland, Dieu mette ton âme en fleurs
> En Paradis entre les glorieux.
> Comme en Espagne venu à mal, Seigneur !
> Jamais n'est jours que je n'en ai douleur.
> Comme decarrat ma force et ma baldur !
>
>   .   .   .   .
>
> Ami Roland, preud'homme, juvente belle !
> Viendront li hommes ; demanderont nouvelles :
> Je leur dirai et merveilleuses et pesmes :
> Mort est mis nies qui tant sut conquerir.
> L'ame de mon corps quand sera departie
> Entre la tienne soit apportée et mise
> Et ma chair soit portée pres de ta chair."

This is the end of all that can be said with
accuracy or with any purpose, the rest would
be only a repetition. Further detail would
confuse and further praises weary, or begin to
exaggerate what above all should be kept
distinct and true.

There is no purpose in the reiteration of

mourning. The hopes that relieve it and even the aspect that makes it endurable are to-day only personal and have no public place. But this much is allowed. We have lost Hubert Howard. With men that go away suddenly like this there are two things to be said, the manner of their going and its effect. I dare to find relief in both.

There were among those who most loved him many different kinds of men, some who were distant from the Pride of Empire and the love of England which inspired his generous enthusiasm ; others who had by birth no right to share in such great feelings, though they shared all with him. I say that to all who knew him nearly it is an enduring relief that he died in the circumstances which his patriotism would have desired. There was no one of us about him who did not—for most part openly —cherish and defend some ideal: nor could any man to whom the appetite of a great goal was lacking have long associated with his energy. Each then would, I think, have chosen that particular end which should come

from the enemies of his effort, and a death
not too late for a kind of glory nor too early
to have robbed him of a complete success.

Now with Hubert Howard, as I have said,
it was the power of England active, aggressive if you will, moving under a destiny, that
absorbed his mind. Her success in this effort
was his continual desire, her mission his peculiar faith. Therefore it seems to me that
the evil fate waited (as it were) with blind
kindness; was he to die then? at least he
died at the close of a great day, during all of
which his ears had been filled with the noise
of an unquestioned victory, and his eyes bright
with the one light which action alone could
bring into them. There had been taken with
him present and under arms, one of those
irrevocable steps in the advance of England
which he and his leaders demanded. He
must in that evening have seen a new horizon,
and there can be no better place to turn in a
journey than the crest of a hill from which
the view so long sought suddenly appears to
satisfy and fulfil the eyes. And when, years

hence, my mind can go back to his story in painful pilgrimage I shall find in this thought a place of repose.

And as for the effect of his death this is certain, that men either disappear to grow less and, when once they have gone, soon become the letters of a name, or else (a rare and exceptional thing) they remain. Hubert Howard was such and such a thing to such and such men who have, themselves young, outlived his own more powerful and splendid youth. Some of these will take influence and public action : this is certain, because he consorted only with what was best. He will therefore not decay but increase.

H. BELLOC.

INTRODUCTION

FROUDE had this merit—a merit he shared with Huxley alone of his contemporaries—that he imposed his convictions. He fought against resistance. He excited (and still excites) a violent animosity. He exasperated the surface of his time and was yet too strong for that surface to reject him. This combative and aggressive quality in him, which was successful in that it was permanent and never suffered a final defeat, should arrest any one who may make a general survey of the last generation in letters.

It was a period with a vice of its own which yet remains to be detected and chastised. In one epoch lubricity, in another fanaticism, in a third dulness and a dead-alive copying of the past, are the faults which criticism finds to attack. None of these affected the Victorian era. It was pure—though tainted with a profound hypocrisy; it was singularly free from violence in its judgments; it was certainly alive and new : but it had this grievous defect (a defect under which we still labour heavily), that thought was restrained upon every side. Never in the history of European letters was it so difficult for a man to say what he would and to be heard. A sort of cohesive public spirit (which was but one aspect of the admirable homogeneity of the nation) glued and immobilised all individual expression. One could float imprisoned as in a stream of thick substance : one could not swim against it.

It is to be carefully discerned how many apparent exceptions to this truth are, if they be closely examined, no exceptions at all. A whole series of national defects were exposed and ridiculed in the literature as in the oratory of that day; but they were defects which the mass of men secretly delighted to hear denounced and of which each believed himself to be free.

ix   *a 2*

86   Froude / *Literature and History*

They loved to be told that they were of a gross taste in art, for they connected such a taste vaguely with high morals and with successful commerce. There was no surer way to a large sale than to start a revolution in appreciation every five years, and from Ruskin to Oscar Wilde a whole series of Prophets attained eminence and fortune by telling men how something new and as yet unknown was Beauty and something just past was to be rejected, and how they alone saw truth while the herd around them were blind. But no one showed us how to model, nor did any one remark that we alone of all Europe had preserved a school of water-colour.

So in politics our blunders were a constant theme ; but no one marked with citation, document, and proof the glaring progress of corruption, or that, for all our enthusiasm, we never once in that generation defended the oppressed against the oppressor. There was a vast if unrecognised conspiracy, by which whatever might have prevented those extreme evils from which we now suffer was destroyed as it appeared. Efforts at a thorough purge were dull, were libellous, were not of the "form" which the Universities and the public schools taught to be sacred. They were rejected as un-readable, or if printed, were unread. The results are with us to-day.

In such a time Froude maintained an opposing force, which was not reforming nor constructive in any way, but which will obtain the attention of the future historian, simply be-cause it *was* an opposition.

It was an opposition of manner rather than of matter. The matter of it was common enough even in Froude's chief decade of power. The cause to which he gave alle-giance was already winning when he proceeded to champion it, and many a better man, one or two greater men, were saying the same things as he ; but *they* said such things in a fashion that suggested no violent effort nor any demand for resistance : it was the peculiar virtue of Froude that he touched nothing without the virile note of a challenge sound-ing throughout his prose. On this account, though he will convince our posterity even less than he does ourselves, the words of persuasion, the writings themselves will remain : for he chose the hardest wood in which to chisel, knowing the strength of his hand.

What was it in him which gave him that strength, and which permitted him, in an age that would tolerate no formative grasp upon itself, to achieve a permanent fame? I will not reply to this question by pointing to the popularity of his History of England; the essays that follow will afford sufficient material to answer it. He produced the effect he did and remained in the eminence to which he had climbed, first because his manner of thought was rigid and of a hard edge; secondly, because he could use that steel tool of a brain in a fashion that was general; he could use it upon subjects and with a handling that was comprehensible to great masses of his fellow-countrymen.

It is not certain that such a man with such interests would have made his voice heard in any other society. It is doubtful whether he will be translated with profit. His field was very small, the points of his attack might all be found contained in one suburban villa. But in our society his grip and his intensity did fall, and fall of choice, upon such matters as his contemporaries either debated or were ready to debate. He therefore did the considerable thing we know him to have done.

I say that his mind was rigid and of a close fibre: it was a mind (to repeat the metaphor) out of which a strong graving-tool could be forged. Its blade would not be blunted: it could deal with its material. Of this character, which I take to be the first essential in his achievement, the few essays before us preserve an ample evidence.

Thus you will find throughout their pages the presence of that dogmatic assertion which invariably proceeds from such a mind, and coupled with such assertion is a continual consciousness that his dogmas *are* dogmas: that he is asserting unprovable things and laying down his axioms before he begins his process of reasoning.

The contrary might be objected by some foreign observer, or by some one who had a larger acquaintance with European history than had he. I can imagine a French or an Irish critic pointing to a mass of assertion with no corresponding

admission that it is assertion only : such a critic might quote
even from these few pages phrase after phrase in which
Froude poses as certain what are still largely matters of
debate. Thus upon page 144 he takes it for granted that
no miracles have been worked by contact with the bodies
of saints. He takes it for granted on page 161 that the
checking of monastic disorders, and the use of strong language in connection with them, was peculiar to the generation which saw at its close the dissolution of the monasteries.
He takes it for granted on page 125 that what we call
"manifestations" or what not,—spirit rappings, table-turnings,
and the rest—are deceptions of the senses to which superstition alone would give credence.

He ridicules (upon p. 128) the tradition of St. Patrick which
all modern research has come to accept. He says downright
(upon pp. 186–187) that the Ancient world did not inquire
into the problem of evil. On p. 214 he will have it that the
ordinary man rejects, "without hesitation," the interference
of will with material causes. In other words, he asserts that
the ordinary man is a fatalist—for Froude knew very well
that between the fatalist and the believer in a possibility of
miracle there is no conceivable position. He will have it (on
p. 216) that a modern doctor always regards a "vision" as
an hallucination. On p. 217 he denies by implication the
stigmata of St. Francis—and so forth—one might multiply
the instances indefinitely. All Froude's works are full of
them, they are part and parcel of his method—but their
number is to no purport. One example may stand for all,
and their special value to our purpose is not that they are
mere assertions, but that they are assertions which Froude
must have known to be personal, disputable, and dogmatic.

He knew very well that the vast majority of mankind
accepted the virtue of relics, that intellects the equals of his
own rejected that determinism to which he was bound, and
that the Pagan world might be presented in a fashion very
different from his own. And in that perpetual—often gratuit-
ous—affirmation you have no sign of limitation in him but
rather of eagerness for battle.

It is an admirable fault or perhaps no fault at all, or if a fault an appendage to the most considerable virtue a writer of his day could have had : the virtue of courage.

See how he thrusts when he comes to lay down the law, not upon what the narrow experience of readers understands and agrees with him about, but upon some matter which he knows them to have decided in a manner opposed to his own. See how definite, how downright, and how clean are the sentences in which he asserts that Christianity is Catholic or nothing :—

" . . . This was the body of death which philosophy detected but could not explain, and from which *Catholicism* now came forward with its magnificent promise of deliverance.

"The carnal doctrine of the sacraments, which they are compelled to acknowledge to have been taught as fully in the early Church as it is now taught by the Roman Catholics, has long been the stumbling-block to Protestants. It was the very essence of Christianity itself. Unless the body could be purified, the soul could not be saved ; or, rather, as from the beginning, soul and flesh were one man and inseparable, without his flesh, man was lost, or would cease to be. But the natural organization of the flesh was infected, and unless organization could begin again from a new original, no pure material substance could exist at all. He, therefore, by whom God had first made the world, entered into the womb of the Virgin in the form (so to speak) of a new organic cell, and around it, through the virtue of His creative energy, a material body grew again of the substance of His mother, pure of taint and clean as the first body of the first man when it passed out under His hand in the beginning of all things."

Throughout his essay on the Philosophy of Christianity, where he was maintaining a thesis odious to the majority of his readers, he rings as hard as ever. The philosophy of Christianity is frankly declared to be Catholicism and Catholicism alone; the truth of Christianity is denied. It is called a thing "worn and old" even in Luther's time (upon page 194), and he definitely prophesies a period when " our posterity" shall learn " to despise the miserable fabric which Luther stitched together out of its tatters."

His judgments are short, violent, compressed. They are

not the judgments of balance. They are final not as a goal reached is final, but as a death-wound delivered. He throws out sentences which all the world can see to be insufficient and thin, but whose sharpness is the sharpness of conviction and of a striving determination to achieve conviction in others —or if he fails in that, at least to leave an enemy smarting. Everywhere you have up and down his prose those short parentheses, those side sentences, which are strokes of offence. Thus on page 199, "We hear—or we used to hear *when the High Church party were more formidable than they are*," &c. ; or again, on page 210, "The Bishop of Natal" (Colenso) has done such and such things, "coupled with certain arithmetical calculations *for which he has a special aptitude.*" There are dozens of these in every book he wrote. They wounded, and were intended to wound.

His intellect may therefore be compared, as I have compared it, to an instrument or a weapon of steel, to a chisel or a sword. It was hard, polished, keen, stronger than what it bit into, and of its nature enduring. This was the first of the characters that gave him his secure place in English letters.

The second is his universality—the word is not over-exact, but I can find no other. I mean that Froude was the exact opposite of the sciolist and was even other than the student. He was kneaded right into his own time and his own people. The arena in which he fought was small, the ideas he combated were few. He was not universal as those are universal who appeal to any man in any country. But he was eager upon these problems which his contemporaries wrangled over. He was in tune with, even when he directly opposed, the class from which he sprang, the mass of well-to-do Protestant Englishmen of Queen Victoria's reign. Their furniture had nothing shocking for him nor their steel engravings. He took for granted their probity, their common sense, and their reading. He knew what they were thinking about, and therefore all he did to praise or blame their convictions, to soothe or to exasperate them, told. He could see the target.

Perpetually this looking at the world from the standpoint

of the men around him makes him say things that irritate more particular and more acute minds than his own, but I will maintain that in his case the fault was a necessary fault and went with a power which permitted him to achieve the sympathy which he did achieve. He talks of the "Celt" and the "Saxon," and ascribes what he calls "our failures in Ireland" to the "incongruity of character" between these two imaginaries. He takes it for granted that "we are something which divides us from mediæval Christianity by an impassable gulf." When he speaks of asceticism he must quote "the hair shirt of Thomas à Becket." If he is speaking of Oxford undergraduates one has "pleasant faces, cheerful voices, and animal spirits," and at the end of the fine but partial essay on Spinoza we have six lines which might come bodily from a leader in the *Daily Telegraph*, or from any copy of the *Spectator* picked up at random.

These are grave faults, but, I repeat, they are the faults of those great qualities which gave him his position.

And side by side with such faults go an exceptional lucidity, a good order within the paragraph and in the succession of the paragraphs. A choice of subject suited to his audience, an excision of that which would have bored or bewildered it, a vividness of description wherewith to amuse and a directness of conclusion wherewith to arrest his readers —all these he had, beyond perhaps any of his contemporaries.

Occasionally that brotherhood in him leads him to faults more serious. You get gross commonplace and utterly false commonplace, of which when he came back to them (if indeed he was a man who read his own works) he must have been ashamed :—

"Persecutions come, and martyrdoms, and religious wars ; and, at last, the old faith, like the phœnix, expires upon its altar, and the new rises out of the ashes.

"Such, in briefest outline, has been the history of religions, natural and moral."

Or again, of poor old Oxford :—

"The increase of knowledge, and consequently of morality, is the great aim of such a noble establishment as this ; and the rewards and honours dispensed there are bestowed in proportion to the industry and good conduct of those who receive them."

But the interesting point about these very lapses is that they remain purely exceptional. They do not affect either the tone of his writing or the value and intricacy of his argument. They may be compared to those undignified and valueless chips of conversational English that pop up in the best rhetoric if it be the rhetoric of an enthusiastic and wide man.

While, however, one is in the mood of criticism it is not unjust to show what other lapses in him are connected with this common sympathy of his and this very comprehension of his class to which he owed his opportunity and his effect.

Thus he is either so careless or so hurried as to use— much too commonly—words which have lost all vitality, and which are for the most part meaningless, but which go the rounds still like shining flat sixpences worn smooth. The word "practical" drops from his pen ; he quotes "in a glass darkly," and speaks of "a picture of human life"; the walls of Oxford are "time-hallowed"; he enters a church and finds in it "a dim religious light"; a man of Froude's capacity has no right to find such a thing there. If he writes the word "sin" the word "shame" comes tripping after. It may be that he was a man readily caught by fatigue, or it may be, it is more probable, that he thought it small millinery to "travailler le verbe." At any rate the result as a whole hangs to his identity of spirit with the thousands for whom he wrote.

To this character of universality attach also faults not only in his occasional choice of words but in his general style.

The word "style" has been so grossly abused during the last thirty years that one mentions it with diffidence. Matthew Arnold well said that when people came to him and asked to be told how to write a good style he was unable to reply ; for indeed it is not a thing to be taught. It is a by-product, though a necessary by-product, of good thinking. But when Matthew Arnold went on to say that there was no such thing as style except knowing clearly what you wanted to say, and

saying it as clearly as you could, he was talking nonsense.
There is such a thing as style. It is that combination of
rhythm, lucidity, and emphasis, which certainly must not
be consciously produced, but which if it arise naturally from
a man's pen and from his method of thought makes all the
difference between what is readable and what is not readable.
If any one doubt this let him compare the French Bible
with the English—both literal and lucid translations of the
same original ; or again let him contrast the prose phrases of
Milton when he is dealing with the claims of the Church
in the Middle Ages with those of Mr. Bryce in the same
connection.

Now I say that just as the excellences of Froude's prose
proceeded from this universality of his so did the errors into
which that prose fell, and it is remarkable that these errors
are slips of detail. They proceed undoubtedly from rapid
writing and from coupling his scholarship with a very general
and ephemeral reading.

A few examples drawn from these essays will prove what
I mean. On the very first page, in the first line of the
second paragraph we have the word "often" coming after the
word "experience," instead of before it. He had written
"experience," he desired to qualify it, and he did not go back
to do what should always be done in plain English, and what
indeed distinguishes plain English from almost every other
language—to put the qualification before the thing qualified ;
a peculiarly English mark in this, that it presupposes one's
having thought the whole thing out before writing it down.

On page 3 we have exactly the same thing; "A legend
not known unfortunately to general English readers." He
means of course, "unfortunately not known," but as the
sentence stands it reads as though he had meant to say,
somewhat clumsily, that the method in which English readers
knew the legend was not unfortunate.

He is again careless in the matter of repetitions, both of
the same word, and (what is a better test of ear) of rhymes
within the sentence : we have in one place "which seemed *to*
give a soul *to* those splendid donations *to* learning," and
further on in the same page "a priority in mortality."

On pages 34 and 35 you have "an intensely *real* conviction." You are then told that "the most lawless men did
then *really* believe." Then that the American tribes were
in the eyes of the colonists "*real* worshippers" of the Devil,
and a few lines later we hear of "the *real* awfulness of the
world."

The position of the relative is often as slipshod as the
position of the qualicative; thus you will find upon page 37
that the pioneers "graved out the channels, and at last paved
them with their bones, through which the commerce and
enterprise of England *has* flowed out of all the world." This
sentence is quite deplorable; it has a singular verb after two
nominatives, and is so framed that one might imagine the
commerce and enterprise of our beloved country to have flown
through those hollow interior channels, with which, I believe,
our larger bones are provided, and in which is to be discovered that very excellent substance, marrow.

It is singular that, while these obvious errors have excited
so little comment, Froude should have been blamed so often
and by such different authorities for weaknesses of the pen
from which he did not suffer, or which, if he did suffer from
them, at least he had in common with every other writer
of our time and perhaps less than most.

Thus, as an historian he has been accused of two faults
which have been supposed by those who are ill acquainted
with the history of letters to be correlative: a straining
for effect and an inaccuracy of detail. There is not one of
his contemporaries who less forced himself in description
than Froude. Often in Green, very often in Freeman and
always in Carlyle you feel that your author is deliberately
exciting his mind and your own. Violent colours are chosen
and peculiar emphasis—from this Froude was free. He was
an historian.

To the end Froude remained an historian, and an historian
he was born. If we regret that his history was not general,
and that he turned his powers upon such a restricted set of
phenomena, still we must rejoice that there was once in
modern England a man who could sum up the nature of
a great movement. He lacked the power of integration.

He was not an artist. But he possessed to an extraordinary degree the power of synthesis. He was a craftsman, as the modern jargon goes. There is not in the whole range of English literature as excellent a summary of the way in which the Divinity of our Lord fought its way into the leading brains of Europe, as appears upon page 192 of this book. It is as good as Boissier; there runs all through it knowledge, proportion, and something which, had he been granted a little more light, or been nurtured in an intellectual climate a little more sunny, would have been vision itself :—

"The being who accomplished a work so vast, a work compared to which the first creation appears but a trifling difficulty, what could He be but God? Who but God could have wrested His prize from a power which half the thinking world believed to be His coequal and co-eternal adversary? He was God. He was man also, for He was the second Adam—the second starting-point of human growth. He was virgin born, that no original impurity might infect the substance which He assumed; and being Himself sinless, He showed in the nature of His person after His resurrection, what the material body would have been in all of us except for sin, and what it will be when, after feeding on it in its purity, the bodies of each of us are transfigured after its likeness."

There's a piece of historical prose which summarises, teaches, and stamps itself finally upon the mind! Froude saw that the Faith was the summit and the completion of Rome. Had he written us a summary of the fourth and fifth centuries—and had he written it just after reading some dull fellow on the other side—what books we should have had to show to the rival schools of the Continent!

Consider the sharp and almost unique judgment passed upon Tacitus at the bottom of page 133 and the top of page 134, or again, the excellent sub-ironic passages in which he expresses the vast advantage of metaphysical debate: which has all these qualities, that it is true, sober, exact, and yet a piece of laughter and a contradiction of itself. It is prose in three dimensions.

That pedantic charge of inaccuracy, with which I have

already dealt in another place, in connection with another and perhaps a greater man, is not applicable to Froude. He was hasty, and in his historical work the result certainly was that he put down things upon insufficient evidence, or upon evidence but half read ; but even in his historical work (which dealt, remember, with the most highly controversial part of English history) he is as accurate as anybody else, except perhaps Lingard. That the man was by nature accurate, well read and of a good memory, appears continually throughout this book, and the more widely one has read one's self, the more one appreciates this truth.

For instance, there is often set down to Disraeli the remark that his religion was "the religion of all sensible men," and upon being asked what this religion might be, that Oriental is said to have replied, " All sensible men keep that to themselves." Now Disraeli could no more have made such a witticism than he could have flown through the air; his mind was far too extravagant for such pointed phrases. Froude quotes the story (page 205 of this book) but rightly ascribes it to Rogers, a very different man from Disraeli— an Englishman with a mastery of the English language.

Look again at this remark upon page 20, " The happy allusion of Quevedo to the Tiber was not out of place here : ' the fugitive is alone permanent.' " How many Englishmen know that Du Bellay's immortal sonnet was but a translation of Quevedo? You could drag all Oxford and Cambridge to-day and not find a single man who knew it.

Note the care he has shown in quoting one of those hackneyed phrases which almost all the world misquotes, " Que mon nom soit flétri, *pourvu* que la France soit libre." Of a hundred times that you may see those words of Danton's written down, you will perhaps not see them once written down exactly as they were said.

So it is throughout his work. Men still living in the Universities accuse him vaguely of inexactitude as they will accuse Jowett of ignorance, and these men, when one examines them closely, are found to be ignorant of the French language, to have read no philosophy between Aristotle and Hobbes, and to issue above their signatures such errors of

plain dates and names as make one blush for English scholarship and be glad that no foreigner takes our historical school
seriously.

. . . . . .

There is always left to any man who deals with the writings
of Froude, a task impossible to complete but necessarily to be
attempted. He put himself forward, in a set attitude, to
combat and to destroy what he conceived to be—in the
moment of his attack—the creed of his countrymen. He was
so literary a man that he did this as much by accepting as by
denying, as much by dating from Elizabeth all we are as by
affirming unalterable material sequence and the falsity of
every transcendental acceptation. His time smelt him out
even when he flattered it most. Even when he wrote of the
Revenge the England of his day—luckily for him—thought
him an enemy.

Upon the main discussion of his life it is impossible to
pass a judgment, for the elements of that discussion are now
destroyed ; the universities no longer pretend to believe.
And "free discussion" has become so free that the main
doctrines he assailed are no longer presented or read without
weariness in the class to which he appealed and from which
he sprang.

The sects, then, against which he set himself are dead :
but upon a much larger question which is permanent, and
which in a sort of groping way he sometimes handled,
something should be said here, which I think has never been
said before. He was perpetually upon the borderland of the
Catholic Church.

Between him and the Faith there stood no distance of space,
but rather a high thin wall ; the high thin wall of his own
desperate conviction. If you will turn to page 209 of this
book you will see it said of the denial of the Sacrament
by the Reformers and of Ridley's dogma that it was bread
only "the commonsense of the country was of the same
opinion, and *the illusion was at an end.*" Froude knew that
the illusion was not at an end. He *probably* knew (for we
must continue to repeat that he was a most excellent historian)
that the "commonsense of the country" was, by the time

Ridley and the New English Church began denying the real presence, and turning that denial into a dogma, profoundly indifferent to all dogmas whatsoever. What "the common-sense of the country" wanted was to keep out swarthy men, chivalrous indeed but imperialists full of gold who owned nearly all the earth, but who, they were determined, should not own England.

Froude was fond of such assertions, his book is full of them, and they are more than mere violence framed for combat ; they are in their curious way definite expressions of the man's soul ; for Froude was fond of that high thin wall, and liked to build it higher.   He was a dogmatic rationalist—one hesitates to use a word which has been so portentously misused.   Renan before dying came out with one of his last dogmas ; it was to this effect, that there was not in the Universe an intelligent power higher than the human mind. Froude, had he lived in an atmosphere of perfectly free discussion as Renan did, would have heartily subscribed to that dogma.

Why then do I say that he was perpetually on the border-land of the Catholic Church?   Because when he leaves for a moment the phraseology and the material of his youth and of his neighbourhood, he is perpetually striking that note of interest, of wonder, and of intellectual freedom which is the note of Catholicism.

Let any man who knows what Catholicism may be read carefully the Essay on the Dissolution of the Monasteries, and the Essay on the Philosophy of Christianity which succeeds it in this book, but which was written six years before. Let him remember that nothing Froude ever wrote was written without the desire to combat some enemy, and, having made allowance for that desire, let him decide whether one shock, one experience, one revelation would not have whirled him into the Church.   He was, I think, like a man who has felt the hands of a woman and heard her voice, who knows them so thoroughly well that he can love, criticise, or despise according to his mood ; but who has never seen her face.

And he was especially near to the Church in this : that having discussed a truth he was compelled to fight for it and

to wound actively in fighting. He was an agent. He did.
He saw that the mass of stuff clinging round the mind
of wealthy England was decaying. He turned with regret
towards the healthy visions of Europe and called them
illusions because they were not provable, and because all
provable things showed a face other than that of the creed
and were true in another manner. He despised the cowardice
—for it is cowardice—that pretends to intellectual conviction
and to temporal evidence of the things of the soul. He saw
and said, and he was right in saying, that the City of God is
built upon things incredible.

"*Incredibilia : nec crederim, nisi me compelleret ecclesiae
auctoritas.*"

H. BELLOC.

INTRODUCTION

THE position of Carlyle in English Literature will necessarily be twofold, for he chose to add to his general survey of thought the particular task of the historian.

The number of men who have chosen the field of letters in general, and who have added to it in any important degree the department of History, is very small. Dickens cannot be said to have done it seriously in his little history, nor Thackeray in his Essay on the Georges, and if we consider the literature of other nations the same holds good.

Conversely, though the historian properly so called who has dipped into general letters is common enough, yet there have been very few historians, whether in England, France, or Germany, who did not profess to stand upon their history rather than upon their other work.

Two men, however, have particularly chosen to combine the functions of philosopher and of historian, and to express their philosophy in many works as serious and as profound as their historical writings ; these two men are Taine and Carlyle.

It must be clearly recognised in any approach to an appreciation of their position, that a man who so attempts the double function stands under a sharper light than can any other sort of writer. And that for this reason : that the work of the historian is justly recognised by men to be one of supreme importance, and to be one that, while it requires literary power for its fulfilment, requires also twenty other qualities as rarely possessed or as difficult of attainment. It is of supreme importance, because upon a just presentation of the past depends all our concrete judgment of the present. History is the object-lesson of politics, and unless history is presented to us truly, it had better not be presented to us at all ; upon History is based our judgment of men so far as long experience can inform it, and if the picture is false, rather than receive it we had better be left to our instinct and to the little circle of exact knowledge conveyed to us by our own experience.

It is, therefore, principally as an historian that Carlyle in England (as Taine in France) will be judged. His position as a writer is secure ; his wisdom in entering the field of history is one upon which debate can still be fruitful, and criticism of value.

What motive was it which moved such men, and Carlyle especially, to enter that field? It was the great expansion of historical knowledge which coincided with the moment when his own powers were at the fullest, coupled with the fact that all the reaction which Carlyle himself represented could find its best arguments in the domain of human actions.

If a thesis has to be maintained which purports to be " practical," and to chastise the tendency to abstraction, that thesis is best maintained by a continual appeal to fact. The vague and generous ideals of the young are combated in this way by the old, and it is generally true that anyone who quarrels with a deductive and ideal system bases his quarrel upon direct, concrete, and personal experience. History is but such experience enlarged.

It is remarkable that with so incisive and so rebellious a mind Carlyle should have fallen so easily, where history was concerned, into the general current of his generation. Indeed, the further we are separated in time from the men of that generation, the more shall we wonder that such doubtful and ill-supported theories should have obtained not only an universal recognition, but a sort of ' passive obedience' from the men who filled what is called the 'Victorian Era' in literature. For example—the whole of that group was filled with " Teutonians." To study the ' Teutonic Race,' as it was called—that is, to study North Germany, and to confirm the cousinship between the English and the North German peoples— was nearly all the task of history. There went with this a strong appetite for the romantic in history as in every other department of letters. Violent action, characters in high light and in deep shadow were compelled to appear in chronicles as much as in novels ; in rhetoric as in poetry, and indeed throughout the whole literary effort of the time. To both these tendencies Carlyle easily succumbed.

It might be advanced that he was not a disciple but an originator, and that but for him neither would the English of the middle nineteenth century have developed that passion of theirs for things German, nor would the picturesque, vivid and romantic history which Green, Freeman, and even Kinglake wrote, have come into existence. It is certain that but for Carlyle the double current would not have become so strong as it did become. It is equally certain that but for him the two influences of admiration

for the German and the romantic would hardly have coalesced.
Yet it is true that he did not originate either the one tendency or
the other; the one proceeded from the natural religious sympathy
between all Protestant peoples; the other, upon the contrary, from
the maturing of French influence upon England, and that enormously increasing power which the Revolution bequeathed to the
Latins, and which is only now beginning to bear fruit.

The romantic movement began not with Byron or with Wordsworth, but with Rousseau; the natural alliance of the Protestant
peoples began not with Waterloo, but with that treaty between
Austria and France in the middle of the eighteenth century, which
is perhaps the greatest turning-point in the story of European
relations.

It must also be remembered that in England there were separate
causes all making both for the Teutonic sentiment and for the
romantic. England had never possessed a continuous classical
tradition. What Milton had begun and Dryden continued
withered long before the first of them had been dead a hundred
years. In England, again, the romantic spirit had received no
chastisement from the facts of war. England alone of European
nations had not suffered invasion, dynastic change or serious
internal disorder, and it is in peace and in leisure that the
romantic illusion flourishes best. England was passing also
through a period of abnormal expansion; all her energies were
strained to the utmost; there was a vast growth everywhere. As
for the German influence, a German dynasty, German allies, the
momentary eclipse of the Italian spirit throughout Europe, and
the crude beginnings of philology, all helped to foster it and to
maintain it.

All this is passing to-day; much of it has already passed. The
theories of race based on Max Müller's researches are doubted;
they have certainly failed at the test. The rudimentary anthro-
pology of our grandfathers has been corrected by innumerable
experiments and by a vastly extended research. Catholicism has
organised a full defensive system, and has proceeded from that to
carry the war into Africa, and though we have not had in England
itself an experience of disaster, yet the pleasing and somewhat
virile illusions of romanticism have been so bled out of Europe in
general that we ourselves can hardly maintain them.

In a word, we are in a position to look steadily back at the whole
historical work of Carlyle and to judge it, as yet, without undue
lack of sympathy, but already with sufficient detachment. We are

b

able to present to ourselves and to answer without passion (and with a considerable certainty) the great question which must be asked of all historians, Did he make dead men live again? There are many who call up phantoms, and many who can present the corpse of the past; there are few who can cause it to rise and act before you with its own body and its own soul. To what extent was he of these few?

In order to answer that question the very first thing to be done is to consider the defects which have been noted in his writings.

It has been said (we will see in a moment with how much or how little justice) that Carlyle could not sympathise with things separate from the conditions of his own birth. He was a peasant and a Calvinist, and it is maintained that to things of which the peasant or the Calvinist are incapable he had no avenue of approach, and therefore that he had no understanding of them.

If that be so, his book upon the French Revolution must be the very best test which we could apply to his powers, for the French Revolution was essentially the work of leisured men, of highly trained intelligences, and of men whom the process of academic education had removed as far as possible from the peasant-life of Europe. Again, it was distinctly the product of a Catholic nation— of a nation, that is, with a contempt for fatalism, an adherence to abstract dogmas, and a military hatred of mere force and of the religions of fear.

It is secondly objected to Carlyle that he could not justly deal with history on account of a constant preoccupation of his: the desire to excite the emotions of his readers.

It has been thirdly objected to him that in the particular case of the French Revolution he could not properly delineate the French character, because he had a most imperfect acquaintance with the language of France, and no acquaintance whatever with its people.

Added to these criticisms, another of some weight has often been heard. It is the criticism which all can make against the few historians of modern times: the accusation of inaccuracy.

Now if Carlyle's work be examined upon such lines, it is not difficult to conclude that the main part of the charge against him is false.

Every man is something; if he is not a Calvinist he is a Catholic, an Agnostic or a Mohammedan; if he is not a peasant, he is a shop-keeper or a noble or a soldier. Every man that writes History must therefore have an initial difficulty in comprehending some, and probably most of the characters he sets out to portray. The

measure of his power is not to be found in the extent of this difficulty, but in his success in overcoming it. For instance, the best
monograph on Robert Burns has been written by a quiet, wealthy
man, a foreigner, and a Picard at that, writing in Paris and in the
French tongue; and success of that sort, precisely because it has
overcome so much initial difficulty, is the prime success of the
historian. So with Carlyle. It is not astonishing that he should
have written the " Frederick," it is astonishing that he should have
written the " Revolution"; and our admiration for the effort and for
its result increases with every new thing we learn about Carlyle,
and with every new difficulty which we discover to have lain in
his way.

A particular instance of this will emphasise my contention. It
has been truly remarked of Carlyle as of Dickens, that there was
never a single gentleman in his books. The French Revolution
was crammed with gentlemen ; very few indeed of the actors in it
were of another social rank than that which is called in England
by the name of ' the gentry.' Consider, then, Carlyle's portrait
of Mirabeau; he certainly makes him something too much of an
actor, and something too little of an artist. The inherited dignity
of bearing, the firmness of gesture, and the regard for proportion
which mark his rank are not present in these pages.[1] But read
this passage, and ask yourself whether it has ever been excelled by
any writer but Michelet.

"Towards such work, in such manner, marches he, this singular
Riquetti Mirabeau. In fiery rough figure, with black Samson-
locks under the slouch-hat, he steps along there. A fiery fuliginous
mass, which could not be choked and smothered, but would fill
all France with smoke. And now it has got *air;* it will burn its
whole substance, its whole smoke-atmosphere too, and fill all
France with flame. Strange lot ! Forty years of that smouldering,
with foul fire-damp and vapour enough ;—and like a burning
mountain he blazes heaven-high ; and for twenty-three resplendent
months, pours out, in flame and molten fire-torrents, all that is in
him, the Pharos and Wonder-sign of an amazed Europe ;—and
then lies hollow, cold forever ! Pass on, thou questionable Gabriel
Honoré, the greatest of them all : in the whole National Deputies,
in the whole Nation, there is none like and none second to thee."

The words are theatrical. ' Whole national deputies ' is simply
bad English. The ' thou' and the ' thee' are grotesque—but the
touch is true.

[1] In the fourth chapter of the fourth book of Part I.

What I mean is this, that if you had known Mirabeau yourself and had read this passage long after his death, you would have said, 'Good lord! how vivid!' long before you had begun to criticise this or that slip in the appreciation. You would in that portrait of Mirabeau have had called up before you Mirabeau as you had known him. So powerful is the modelling that its failure to give the *refinement* of the original would have lain lightly upon your mind, as you were filled with a recollection of his *force*. Carlyle would seem to you to have put a living spirit again into the body of the man, and that living spirit would have been the spirit that you had known.

So is it almost universally where he has to draw the portrait of a man.

Whether the second of the Lameths knew English (I believe he did), or whether in his old age he ever read this book (he had ample time to do it, for he survived its publication by seventeen years), whether he was even acquainted with the name of Carlyle—I do not know; but I am certain that he, who had known Mirabeau, did, if ever he read this passage, stand startled at a resurrection from the dead.

There are exceptions. It is no just appreciation of Carlyle's work to ignore them; on the contrary, these exceptions help us even better than his successes to appreciate the quality of his genius. These exceptions are even numerous. They are to be discovered wherever a character of some complexity and, if I may so express myself, of 'varying grain,' is presented to Carlyle's deep and rapid carving, where the man he is dealing with is not of one stuff throughout.

Two very excellent examples of such failures are his pictures of the King and of Robespierre. In both, the delineation is a task of very considerable difficulty; both had characters highly complex and to some extent self-contradictory; both escape from the power of a pen which was creative, but incapable of analysis.

Louis XVI. was not a weak lump of a man. He never upon any single occasion—and he lived through greater dangers than any modern ruler has lived—showed a sign of fear. He fought for his principles to the very end; he conscientiously deliberated every act of importance which he undertook, and that is a rare and convincing sort of strength. Louis XVI. came of a stock nervous to the point of disease. He would have grown up (under most circumstances) shy, thin, perhaps consumptive, and even more terrified than was his grandfather of intercourse with statesmen and soldiers. He would probably have died young. The extreme care spent upon him by doctors, a careful and continually ordered diet, perpetual exercise in the open air, all these artifices bestowed upon him before he was twenty a sort of factitious health. He grew up robust, somnolent, of a large appetite, and with all his nervous weakness run to lethargy. Here was a man who could not be jotted down in a few deep strokes of the graver, nor to be seen clearly in high lights and shadows. Here was a man who could not by any manipulation be made into a dramatic figure; therefore, to put it bluntly, Carlyle dismisses him.

Robespierre was descended from a long line of squires, probably Irish. He was eloquent, pedantic, enthusiastic, cold, of excellent breeding, of a convinced faith, readily angered against persons, passionately loved, of a valueless judgment in dealing with masses of men, and often at fault with individuals. Here, again, is a character which cannot by any possibility serve the purposes of melodrama; he was not a monster or a coward, nor even a great ideal figure, as Hamel would regard him. You cannot deal with Robespierre unless you deal with the complexity of his position and of his mind. You must analyse the phenomenon closely, and you must put him in a separate place right aside from the furious and simple passions by which he was surrounded but from which he lived apart. Carlyle was either unable to do this or did not know that he had to do it; the result is that his Robespierre has no resemblance either to the original or to any possible man. He is of wax.[1]

But these, I repeat, are exceptions, and the very causes which make Louis and Robespierre escape him are proofs of the driving energy which lay behind his mind. The very fact that he cannot work in some material enhances the extraordinary power with which he moulded all other material that fell to his hand.

When it is objected that Carlyle could not deal justly with history on account of his preoccupation of exciting the emotions, we are on firmer ground. We are dealing here with his art rather than with his history, and we are dealing with the great vice to which art such as his is tempted.

In very early youth a man capable by his style of violently arousing the emotions of his readers, of striking time and again the spring which moves us like a phrase of music, may forget him-

[1] For instance, the famous epithet "Sea-green," is based on *one* phrase of Mme. de Staël's misread. What Madame de Staël said was that the prominent veins in Robespierre's forehead showed greenish-blue against his fair and somewhat pale skin. But his complexion was healthy, and his expression, if anything, winning.

self, and may merely over-indulge his power. He will fall into such an excess as it were unconsciously. But as his life proceeds, as his style is criticised and acquires public recognition, he cannot but become conscious of his art; he will tend to repeat certain tricks of it, and he cannot but depend too much upon those tricks to secure him a perpetuity of success and save him the fatigue of creation. He suffers the temptation which falls in another sphere to the orator (for both are rhetoricians), and he tends to yield to that temptation; to force the note. From this fault Carlyle's style after his thirtieth year undoubtedly suffers. As he grew older his straining for the vivid got worse and worse, like Swinburne's alliterations, Browning's obscurity, Wordsworth's "common phrases," or Gladstone's trick of a verbose confusion. Such temptations come only to the great, and it behoves us to be very careful how we charge them with their faults, for we must remember how hardly any great man has escaped them, and how, to lesser men, the temptation itself is impossible. Nevertheless, it is true that the temptation, as it was presented to Carlyle, was only too successful. His art is spoilt by a perpetual tautening of the bow.

I will here quote two passages which should support my contention: the first, as I think, spontaneous; the second false.

The first is near the opening of the seventh chapter of Book IV. in Part III., and begins the trial of the Queen: it is as follows:—

"There are few Printed things one meets with, of such tragic, almost ghastly, significance as those bald pages of the *Bulletin du Tribunal Révolutionnaire*, which bear Title *Trial of the Widow Capet*. Dim, dim, as if in disastrous eclipse; like the pale kingdoms of Dis! Plutonic Judges, Plutonic Tinville; encircled, nine times, with Styx and Lethe, with Fire-Phlegethon and Cocytus named of Lamentation! The very witnesses summoned are like Ghosts . . . they themselves are all hovering over death and doom. . . ."

Consider the qualities of these lines. They open with a simple phrase. The phrase, the consideration of his subject, excite him at once to dithyramb. The rhythm is natural and open. The very vowels of the syllables are consonant to horror, the cadence rises to the wail of the word 'Lamentation.' Its consonants possess the regular though not excessive alliteration of poetical English. It falls and ends like a gong sounding the word "Doom."

Turn now to the second, and see whether these same qualities are not here purposely and forcibly struck upon the metal of his writing rather than appearing as something inherent to the quality of that writing itself.

"One other thing, or rather other things, we will mention ; and no more : The Blond Perukes ; the Tannery at Meudon. Great talk is of these *Perruques Blondes :* O Reader, they are made from the heads of guillotined Women ! The locks of a Duchess, etc., etc." . . ., and so forth to the end of the chapter, twenty lines more : "Alas ! then, is man's civilisation only a wrapping through which the savage of him . . ." and so on.

This is bad. It is all forced. The perpetual 'we' of his emphatic manner is introduced to no great purpose. He is writing rapidly. He intended to 'mention' one thing—he thinks of a second (both are false) and is too hasty to remould the sentence. He adds 'no more,' to hide his error and make it pompous. Each phrase is affected. Why 'Great talk is'? Why 'O reader'? Why the excessive commonplace and well-worn tags of the last sentence picked out in an unusual order? It was because he felt his own interest flagging and his pen at fault that he had deliberate recourse to tinsel of this kind.

So much then for the chief fault which can justly be discovered in this great and enduring work. It is easier to take up again the task of defence. I will allude in particular to the charge of inaccuracy, and say at once that Carlyle is without question one of the most accurate historians that ever put pen to paper.

He writes in that method which of all others most compels a man to errors in matters of detail. Fugue : a very vivid presentment : the making of one's subject move before one ; the giving of its characters a life of their own such as we give to the characters of fiction—all these high efforts in an historian are direct causes of minute inaccuracy. The extent to which Carlyle escaped that inaccuracy is positively astounding. It has latterly been my business to comment upon one of the latest editions of his work which has been produced with voluminous footnotes at Oxford. Here there was no excuse at all for inaccuracy. The book was dull, pedantic, and badly put together. It was a purely mechanical piece of work, and all the Editor had to do was to verify every reference he made and to see that the spelling and the dates were correct.

Yet I have found in this edition at least five errors to one of Carlyle's.

Here is a curious and instructive instance. In speaking of Napoleon's rank before Toulon, Carlyle calls him a major at a moment when he *may* have held that rank or *may* have been colonel: it is a point not yet decided, and perhaps never to be decided. The records are imperfect: the time was a hurried and muddled one. Napoleon was certainly in a higher than a battery command, but not yet a general officer. The Oxford edition elaborately corrects Carlyle and makes Napoleon a captain!

It cannot be too often repeated by those who have the honour of English historical science at heart that we have in Carlyle not only in his "Frederick"—where every one concedes it—but here in the Revolution an admirable instance of care and of correction. Michelet is perhaps a greater man, and certainly a greater historian, but in accuracy Carlyle is his superior. Mignet's little book alone perhaps of the early authorities falls into less errors, while in the midst of modern research Aulard is perhaps the only worker who would have a right to contrast his painstaking with that of the English writer. Taine is nowhere; but then Taine was not even trying to tell the truth, and that makes a vast difference where accuracy is concerned.

It is again true of Carlyle that he had but an imperfect acquaintance with the French language, and hardly any acquaintance with the French character. It remains true that by some sort of miracle he accomplished successfully the task he had set himself. It is somewhat as though Victor Hugo had managed to write not a great play (which he did write), but a thorough history of Oliver Cromwell.

Thus Carlyle comprehended one chief factor of the Revolution: the mob. Alone of all European peoples, the French are able to organise themselves from below in large masses, and Paris, which wrought the Revolution, can do it better than the rest of France. A French mob can march in column without a leader, and a Parisian mob can not only march in column, but in a rough fashion deploy when the column debouches upon some open space. It is almost incredible, but it is true.

Now of all the writers of his time Carlyle was, one would have thought, the least able to understand this. He could see nothing in acephalous mankind. It was the whole of his philosophy that men cannot so organize themselves, that they need leaders and strong men, and all the rest of it. Yet so thoroughly has he got inside his subject, so vitally has he raised it up and made it move of its own life that in his book you see the French mob doing precisely what he would have told you, had you asked him, no

mob could do. When he describes them you see them doing
what as a fact they did, and moving in a fashion which, as a fact,
was their own. When he stops to comment upon them, as he
does from time to time, he is often wrong, but when the description begins he becomes right again by a pure instinct for visual-
ising, and for making men act in harmony and in consort in his
book.

His inacquaintance with the French character does certainly
make him misunderstand the battles. Where he is at his best in
his other works, there he is at his worst in the Revolution. His
fighting is all wrong. Everybody knows for instance that Bona-
parte lost one of his guns in Vendémiaire, there was no " whiff of
grape shot," and what is worse he does not present the great
battles of '93 and '94 in their true perspective. He does not show
the victories " Pursuing the Terror like furies," and throughout
the work 'the armies which are the meaning and the guidance
of the Revolution come in as it were by accident and give no
clue.

But there is another point where his ignorance of the French
people and his peculiar ignorance of their religion might have led
him far more astray, and where he is triumphantly successful ;
and that is in his portraiture of French violence, and of French
ferocity. He had not in his life seen anything violent or
ferocious. It was sheer creative power which enabled him to
project upon his screen the actualities of which he had read, and
there is perhaps no other English writer who has done it ; so alien
is violence to our national character and so utterly removed is it
from our national experience.

The energy of the Revolution, one might conclude, found in the
depths of this man who had never been near the sound of arms or
the vision of an insurgent populace, something congenial : some
ancient strength in the Scotch inherited from mediæval freedom
arose in him and answered the French appeal. It did for him
what the story of Napoleon did for Victor Hugo : it 'blew the
creative gale'—'le souffle createur.'

Here is the peculiar merit of this book, and here is what may
preserve it even when taste has so changed that its rhetoric shall
have become tedious and that a classical reaction shall have
rendered repulsive the anarchic outbursts of its prose. He was
inspired. The enormity of the action moved him as the
Marseillaise can still move the young conscripts upon the march
when they hear it from a distant place and go forward to the call

of it. The Revolution filled him as he proceeded, and was, in a sense, co-author with him of the shock, the flames and the roar, the innumerable feet, and the songs which together build up what we read achieved in these volumes.

H. BELLOC.

Life of Schiller (*Lond. Mag.*, 1823–4), 1825, 1845. (Supplement published in the People's Edition, 1873.) *Wilhelm Meister Apprenticeship*, 1824. *Elements of Geometry and Trigonometry* (from the French of Legendre), 1824. *German Romance*, 1827. *Sartor Resartus* (*Fraser's Mag.*, 1833–4), 1835 (Boston), 1838. *French Revolution*, 1837, 1839. *Critical and Miscellaneous Essays*, 1839, 1840, 1847, 1857. (In these were reprinted Articles from *Edinburgh Review, Foreign Review, Foreign Quarterly Review, Fraser's Magazine, Westminster Review, New Monthly Magazine, London and Westminster Review, Keepsake, Proceedings of the Society of Antiquaries of Scotland, Times.*) *Chartism*, 1840. *Heroes, Hero-worship, and the Heroic in History*, 1841. *Past and Present*, 1843. *Oliver Cromwell's Letters and Speeches: with Elucidations*, 1845. *Thirty-five Unpublished Letters of Oliver Cromwell*, 1847 (Fraser). *Original Discourses on the Negro Question* (Fraser, 1849), 1853. *Latter-day Pamphlets*, 1850. *Life of John Sterling*, 1851. *History of Friedrich II. of Prussia*, 1858–65. *Inaugural Address at Edinburgh*, 1866. *Shooting Niagara: and After?* 1867 (from "Macmillan"). *The Early Kings of Norway; also an Essay on the Portraits of John Knox*, 1875.

There were also contributions to Brewster's *Edinburgh Encyclopædia*, vols. xiv., xv., and xvi.; to *New Edinburgh Review*, 1821, 1822; *Fraser's Magazine*, 1830, 1831; *The Times*, 19 June, 1844 ("Mazzini"); 28 November, 1876; 5 May, 1877; *Examiner*, 1848; *Spectator*, 1848.

First Collected Edition of Works, 1857–58 (16 vols.).

Reminiscences (ed. J. A. Froude), 1881. *Reminiscences of my Irish Journey in 1849*, 1882. *Last Words of Thomas Carlyle*, 1882 (ed. by J. C. A.). *Last Words of Thomas Carlyle*, 1892. *Rescued Essays* (ed. P. Newberry), 1892. *Historical Sketches of Notable Persons and Events in the Reigns of James I. and Charles I.* (ed. A. Carlyle), 1898.

Introduction

We have arrived at a phase in English
literary criticism when it is possible to
regard steadily and to appreciate justly a
talent such as was that of James Russell
Lowell.

In the generation just past, it was not so
much the fashion as the genuine appetite
of fine literary sense to despise and even
to neglect wholly gifts of this kind. The
prose or verse emanating from a brain of
Lowell's texture—and there were many in
the same category—was observed to delight
a great number of people among that small
minority of English men or women who
read English prose or verse at all; but it
was taken for granted among the critics of
pure literature that this admiration was
directed entirely to the matter and not at
all to the manner of the thing admired.
The crowd of admirers were essentially
middle class and suburban, and in general
your close surveyor of a generation ago

iii

would simply deem Lowell contemptible, nay, what was worse in his eyes, Colonial —and would pass him by. This attitude was essentially erroneous, and, I repeat, the time has come when it can be totally reversed. James Russell Lowell possessed abilities in the field of literature of a sort which make for partial and occasional but permanent effect, and it behoves all those who have a regard for English letters to recognize these qualities in however unheroic a form they may appear, or to whatever cause, from the fantastic to the commonplace, they may be devoted.

Now before speaking (as it will be necessary to speak) of what it was that caused Lowell to be unjustly neglected, let us note what these qualities of excellence and permanence were.

In the first place he was capable of composing what I may call for the purposes of this essay a "final" line, by which I mean a line satisfying the intelligence and the ear so completely as to achieve a character of perfection which will save it from the effects of time: not of perfection in the sense of a thing being sublime and absolute, defying challenge in its own sphere, but of perfection in the original sense of the word: finished, completed, not to be added

iv

INTRODUCTION

to, satisfying and fulfilling the mould upon
which the artistic creation was conceived.
Lines of this sort become the permanent
quotations of a language, and it is worth
remembering that they do not proceed from
the greater writers alone, but also from the
lesser; so true is this that in more than
one case the author of such lines has been
completely forgotten, and in many cases
remains wholly unknown to the culture of
his race . . .

> " John P.
> Robinson he
> Says they didn't know everything down
> in Judee "

is a quotation certainly permanent.

> " The silent headsman waits for ever "

applied as a metaphor to the self-punish-
ment of crime has the same character.
It is used foolishly in the poem *Villa
Franca* of a subject which a man in
Lowell's position could not understand,
but the excellence of the line does not
depend upon the knowledge or ignorance
of the poet, though it *does* depend (and this
brings me to my next point), it does depend
to no small extent upon the virtue of the
writer.

v

INTRODUCTION

This last assertion—that artistic excellence depends to no small extent upon the virtue of the writer—is a doctrine that needs some defence even at the present day. A few years ago it might (in England) have seemed mere paradox; yet it is a sound doctrine, and one which has behind it the common sense and experience of mankind. It has been most nobly expressed perhaps in the immortal couplet of Ronsard.[1] It has been put forward as a philosophic truth by Aristotle himself, and it is a matter capable of continual test in contemporary literature: not that mere virtue is a seed of good verse or prose, but that virtue or virtuous emotion of a certain intensity is potentially full of high expression, and, conversely, without any doubt an imagination tarnished by an opposition to virtue is to that extent warped in artistic expression. There is no permanently satisfying poem or essay in defence of or tainted with cowardice, cruelty, avarice, or hypocrisy. The moment such motives appear in a composition an irritant appears along with them which destroys its flavour. Nor is it possible to achieve

[1] " . . . Ceux dont la Fantaisie
Sera religieuse et devote envers Dieu
Tousjours acheveront quelque grant Poesie ".

excellence in such a direction save under the safeguard of irony, and the necessity of that irony is proof that direct expression of such emotions is not matter for art.

Now James Russell Lowell, though intent upon matters very remote from us, was not only frequently filled, and to an intense degree, with just emotions, but was evidently possessed of a passion to have those emotions satisfied. This is that driving force which Our Lord (according to the tradition of the Church) blessed under the title " a hunger and thirst after justice ", or some such words—at least this is the form which Episcopal councils have sanctioned.

Many reading this may be inclined to quarrel with so high a praise. They will point out that Lowell was almost invariably upon what is to us in Europe the wrong side. That he had with regard to our affairs in France and Italy and Ireland and the rest a monstrous newspaper-manufactured opinion. His Irishman, for instance, is the comic Irishman of *Snapshots*. His French revolution resembles that of Mr. Arnold Forster. His Englishman is a Yankee. I can imagine a critic exclaiming: " But good heavens! the man thought that Napoleon III was in league with the Jesuits!" or again: " But good

vii

heavens! the man was taken in by our governing classes' sudden conversion and their hugging of the North when the South was hopelessly beaten!" Perfectly true. But a virtuous emotion is quite independent of information upon the subject of its affection, and that "hunger and thirst after justice" can but act upon symbols in the mind. If a man *thinks* the things are thus and thus, and thinking so takes the right line, it matters nothing to his soul nor anything consequently to his literary production whether they *are* thus and thus or no. His conscience has acted upon the facts presented to his intelligence, and it could do no more.

Attached to this erroneous form of cavil against Lowell and men like Lowell is a much truer exception which is sometimes taken to such men and their work. How, it may be asked, can good verse proceed from one who, though possessing the emotions just described, and to an intense degree, is also affected with mental vices utterly inimical to poetic effort? It is evident that Lowell suffered from two vices (among others) which are as disastrous to poetic inspiration as they are to the allied enthusiasm of military valour. These are, *first*, the vice so wittily hit off by Butler

viii

118   Lowell / *Poems*

INTRODUCTION

as compounding for sins one is inclined
to by damning those one has no mind to;
secondly, the hatred of that which one has
defeated and the respect of that which has
defeated oneself. Both emotions are rooted
in the same religion and philosophy, both
are despicable and both servile. Those
who can savour striking verse will not despise the antepenultimate stanza of the
tenth Biglow paper.

" My eyes cloud up for rain; my mouth
    Will take to twitchin' roun' the corners;
I pity mothers, tu, down South,
    For all they sot among the scorners:
I 'd sooner take my chance and stan'
    At Jedgment where your meanest slave is,
Then at God's bar hol' up a han'
    Ez drippin' red ez yourn, Jeff Davis!"

It is striking verse, but we in Europe
feel how revolting is that last allusion to
the defeated cause and to the heroic tenacity of its chiefs.

The poem is a fine poem from beginning
to end. It is so fine that any reader unacquainted with the main facts of history
might pass by the line in question without
comment and imagine Mr. Davis to have
been some traitor upon the Northern side
whose treason had prolonged the war.

INTRODUCTION

Why it may be asked should that be praised
as good verse which contains this very un-
poetical emotion of hatred for the weak?
The answer is simple enough; there is
no kind of humanity—poet, soldier, pawn-
broker, priest, or thief—but has a vice or
vices, and the presence of such an admix-
ture will not overbalance a strong and
right emotion until it be present in a very
high proportion indeed. These two servile vices, respect for the strong and zeal
against the weak (though both were present), never produced the main emotion of
Lowell's verse. The first series of Biglow
papers (which made his fame) were written
from the standpoint of a Minority, not of a
very small or persecuted minority, but still,
of a minority. They were written against
the stream, and though Lowell certainly
had not in him the stuff of which martyrs
are made, yet he had in him a sufficient
energy of conviction to do more than drift
with the stream—at least in early manhood. Moreover, though we are dealing
in Lowell with a type which was capable
of occasional poetic achievement we are
not dealing with a type which could comprehend military affairs. The great military poems of our race, the *Battle of
Brunanburgh*, the *Chanson de Roland*, the

INTRODUCTION

Iliad, to quote great things; the words of the *Marseillaise*, the *Wacht am Rhein*, and the fine songs of Campbell, to quote small things, rely upon emotions which Lowell had no opportunity of feeling, and which, even had he survived to hear of the treatment of the prisoners in the Philippines, would hardly have come within his psychical experience. It was but an accident that his time compelled him to write of matters connected with war: by nature he was a rhymer for small merchants.

One final objection must be met before we leave the causes that have unduly belittled his reputation. It may be asked how that man can be praised as a poet who wrote with such ease and at such length so very many hundred lines which no one could pretend to be poetry. I have deliberately included what is perhaps the most striking example of this defect by putting within this collection a short twenty-two lines of his entitled *Mahmood the Image-Breaker*, in order that the reader may justly appreciate how deep Lowell could sink into bathos. The first couplet has much the same effect upon the critical reader expectant of poesy as would have upon a gourmand a lump of half-cold mutton fat popped into the mouth by mistake for a new potato.

Here it is—

" Old events have modern meanings; only that
    survives
Of past history which finds kindred in all
    hearts and lives."

Scansion, sentiment, choice of words, order, everything, are things to groan at! Here is another:

" Then the revulsion came that always comes
After these dizzy elations of the mind ".

It is from that long poem on the Cathedral of Chartres, which from respect for him and for the reader I have omitted from this collection.

He was always at it. But my answer to those who might choose to quote the innumerable occasions upon which Lowell was thus guilty is to quote another stanza, and to beg their close attention upon it. It is from the famous *Ode to France*.

" As, flake by flake, the beetling avalanches
Build up their imminent crags of noiseless
    snow,
Till some chance thrill the loosened ruin
    launches,
In unwarned havoc on the roofs below,

INTRODUCTION

So grew and gathered through the silent
   years
The madness of a people."

Here again the history is deplorable—
but much of the verse is excellent. That
very poem of *The Cathedral* from which
I have quoted that amazing couplet, has
embedded in its monstrous bulk eleven
austere words that do not miss their mark.

" A shape of vapour, mother of vain dreams
   And mutinous traditions. . . ."

Lowell, indeed, was possessed (though
not to a high degree nor upon frequent
occasions) of that gift which his fellow
countryman, Longfellow, remarkably enjoyed : the gift of detecting, while a poem
is still in formation within the mind, short
groups of rhythm and of verbal arrangement which will satisfy the genius of the
language. It was this that led him, as it
led Wordsworth, to lift unconsciously a
whole line out of another poem. But at
least Lowell did put in one new word. " I
have loved thee Freedom : as a boy . . ." is
not absolutely identical with Byron, whereas the chunk of Milton in Wordsworth's
Excursion (I think) is literally exact. It is
a debatable point whether it is well or ill

to be slightly original in efforts of this
kind.

Lastly, how much of Lowell will survive?   To this no answer can be given.
There are poets so long dead, and with
reputations so mature, that, big or little,
they must necessarily endure with the language in which they wrote.   There are
others so universally praised during so
sufficient a time that one may be certain of
their endurance also, as Keats and André
Chénier.   There are others again who,
though they be but recently dead (or even
still living), are by the bulk and solidity
of their contemporary fame secure.   Thus
Byron, Victor Hugo, Dryden, Corneille
could justly be thought immortal before
they died.   There are others, a very few,
who gradually grow to fame long after
death.   Their quality always secures them
a band of enthusiasts from the beginning.
Lowell, of course, belongs to none of these,
but the chances for and against his survival
may be summed up, though no issue may
be arrived at.   They are as follows :—

Against him : that he wrote such masses
below the level even of mere verse; that
much of his best stuff was written in dia-
lect; and worst of all that the illusions,
a sympathy with which made so many

xiv

INTRODUCTION

readers sympathetic with his verse good or
bad, are already moribund. The fond picture nourished for a whole generation in
Cambridge, Massachusetts, in Balham, and
in no small section of the university of Oxford has faded. The future is not to the
middle classes of the puritan states of New
England, nor to "the residential suburbs"
of our industrial hells. The future is to the
victor in a struggle of proportions quite
beyond any scale with which men like
Lowell could measure—a struggle in which
the opponents of the Catholic Church, for
instance, will not worry about "enlighten-
ment" nor waste much time in speechify-
ing before Garibaldi, a struggle in which
the opponents of private property in land
and machinery will not waste much ink
over the Prince of Peace. Lowell is handicapped by his being immersed in interests
that were always petty, and seem to-day
ridiculous. He was further handicapped
by that fundamental ignorance of history
which is to a politician the most fatal
lacuna in knowledge, because history is
the science of mankind.

On the other hand he has provided quotations fairly fixed in the language, and
his is the principal, popular commentary
upon the destruction of the old English

civilization of the Southern States of America; a catastrophe which, whatever be the fate of the cosmopolitan North in the future, will always possess historical interest as one of the three or four great National Tragedies of the nineteenth century.

H. BELLOC.

Introduction

SO long as man does not bother about what he is or whence he came or whither he is going, the whole thing seems as simple as the verb " to be "; and you may say that the moment he does begin thinking about what he is (which is more than thinking that he is) and whence he came and whither he is going, he gets on to a lot of roads that lead nowhere, and that spread like the fingers of a hand or the sticks of a fan; so that if he pursues two or more of them he soon gets beyond his straddle, and if he pursues only one he gets farther and farther from the rest of all knowledge as he proceeds. You may say that and it will be true. But there is one kind of knowledge a man does get when he thinks about what he is, whence he came and whither he is going, which is this: that it is the only important question he can ask himself.

Now the moment a man begins asking himself those questions (and all men begin at some

A   I

time or another if you give them rope enough)
man finds himself a very puzzling fellow.
There was a school—it can hardly be called a
school of philosophy—and it is now as dead as
mutton, but anyhow there *was* a school which
explained the business in the very simple
method known to the learned as tautology—
that is, saying the same thing over and over
again.   For just as the woman in Molière was
dumb because she was affected with the quality
of dumbness, so man, according to this school,
did all the extraordinary things he does do
because he had developed in that way.   They
took in a lot of people while they were alive
(I believe a few of the very old ones still survive), they took in nobody more than themselves; but they have not taken in any of
the younger generation.   We who come after
these scientists continue to ask ourselves the
old question, and if there is no finding of an
answer to it, so much the worse; for asking it,
every instinct of our nature tells us, is the
proper curiosity of man.

Of the great many things which man does
which he should not do or need not do, if he
were wholly explained by the verb "to be,"
you may count walking.   Of course if you
build up a long series of guesses as to the steps
by which he learnt to walk, and call *that* an
explanation, there is no more to be said.   It is

as though I were to ask you why Mr Smith
went to Liverpool, and you were to answer by
giving me a list of all the stations between
Euston and Lime Street, in their exact order.
At least that is what it would be like if your
guesses were accurate, not only in their statement, but also in their proportion, and also in
their order. It is millions to one that your
guesses are nothing of the kind. But even
granted by a miracle that you have got them
all quite right (which is more than the wildest
fanatic would grant to the dearest of his geo-
logians) it tells me nothing.

What on earth persuaded the animal to go
on like that? Or was it nothing on earth but
something in heaven?

Just watch a man walking, if he is a proper
man, and see the business of it: how he expresses his pride, or his determination, or his
tenacity, or his curiosity, or perhaps his very
purpose in his stride! Well, all that business
of walking that you are looking at is a piece
of extraordinarily skilful trick - acting, such
that were the animal not known to do it
you would swear he could never be trained
to it by any process, however lengthy, or
however minute, or however strict. This is
what happens when a man walks: first of
all he is in stable equilibrium, though the
arc of stability is minute. If he stands with

his feet well apart, his centre of gravity (which is about half way up him or a little more) may oscillate within an arc of about five degrees on either side of stability and tend to return to rest. But if it oscillates beyond that five degrees or so, the stability of his equilibrium is lost, and down he comes. Men have been known to sleep standing up without a support, especially on military service, which is the most fatiguing thing in the world; but it is extremely rare, and you may say of a man so standing, even with his feet well spread, that he is already doing a fine athletic feat.

But wait a moment: he desires to go, to proceed, to reach a distant point, and instead of going on all fours, where equilibrium would indeed be stable, what does he do? He deliberately lifts one of his supports off the ground, and sends his equilibrium to the devil; at the same time he leans a little forward so as to make himself fall towards the object he desires to attain. You do not know that he does this, but that is because you are a man and your ignorance of it is like the ignorance in which so many really healthy people stand to religion, or the ignorance of a child who thinks his family established for ever in comfort, wealth and security. What you really do, man, when you want to get to that distant place (and let this be a parable of all adventure and of all desire) is to take an enormous risk, the risk of coming down bang and breaking something: you lift one foot off the ground, and, as though that were not enough, you deliberately throw your centre of gravity forward so that you begin to fall.

That is the first act of the comedy.

The second act is that you check your fall by bringing the foot which you had swung into the air down upon the ground again.

That you would say was enough of a bout. Slide the other foot up, take a rest, get your breath again and glory in your feat. But not a bit of it! The moment you have got that loose foot of yours firm on the earth, you use the impetus of your first tumble to begin another one. You get your centre of gravity by the momentum of your going well forward of the foot that has found the ground, you lift the other foot without a care, you let it swing in the fashion of a pendulum, and you check your second fall in the same manner as you checked your first; and even after that second clever little success you do not bring your feet both firmly to the ground to recover yourself before the next venture: you go on with the business, get your centre of gravity forward of the foot that is now on the ground, swinging the other beyond it like a pendulum, stopping your third catastrophe, and so on; and you

have come to do all this so that you think
it the most natural thing in the world!

Not only do you manage to do it but you
can do it in a thousand ways, as a really
clever acrobat will astonish his audience not
only by walking on the tight-rope but by
eating his dinner on it. You can walk quickly
or slowly, or look over your shoulder as you
walk, or shoot fairly accurately as you walk;
you can saunter, you can force your pace, you
can turn which way you will. You certainly
did not teach yourself to accomplish this
marvel, nor did your nurse. There was a
spirit within you that taught you and that
brought you out; and as it is with walking,
so it is with speech, and so at last with
humour and with irony, and with affection,
and with the sense of colour and of form,
and even with honour, and at last with
prayer.

By all this you may see that man is very
remarkable, and this should make you humble,
not proud; for you have been designed in
spite of yourself for some astonishing fate, of
which these mortal extravagances so accurately
seized and so well moulded to your being are
but the symbols.

Walking, like talking (which rhymes with it,
I am glad to say), being so natural a thing to
man, so varied and so unthought about, is

necessarily not only among his chief occupations but among his most entertaining subjects of commonplace and of exercise.

Thus to walk without an object is an intense burden, as it is to talk without an object. To walk because it is good for you warps the soul, just as it warps the soul for a man to talk for hire or because he thinks it his duty. On the other hand, walking with an object brings out all that there is in a man, just as talking with an object does. And those who understand the human body, when they confine themselves to what they know and are therefore legitimately interesting, tell us this very interesting thing which experience proves to be true: that walking of every form of exercise is the most general and the most complete, and that while a man may be endangered by riding a horse or by running or swimming, or while a man may easily exaggerate any violent movement, walking will always be to his benefit—that is, of course, so long as he does not warp his soul by the detestable habit of walking for no object but exercise. For it has been so arranged that the moment we begin any minor and terrestrial thing as an object in itself, or with merely the furtherance of some other material thing, we hurt the inward part of us that governs all. But walk for glory or for adventure, or to see new

sights, or to pay a bill or to escape the same,
and you will very soon find how consonant
is walking with your whole being. The chief
proof of this (and how many men have tried it,
and in how many books does not that truth
shine out!) is the way in which a man walking
becomes the cousin or the brother of everything round.

If you will look back upon your life and
consider what landscapes remain fixed in your
memory, some perhaps you will discover to
have struck you at the end of long rides or
after you have been driven for hours, dragged
by an animal or a machine. But much the
most of these visions have come to you when
you were performing that little miracle with a
description of which I began this: and what is
more, the visions that you get when you are
walking, merge pleasantly into each other.
Some are greater, some lesser, and they make
a continuous whole. The great moments are
led up to and are fittingly framed.

There is no time or weather, in England at
least, in which a man walking does not feel
this cousinship with everything round. There
are weathers that are intolerable if you are
doing anything else but walking: if you are
crouching still against a storm or if you are
driving against it; or if you are riding in extreme cold; or if you are running too quickly

in extreme heat; but it is not so with
walking. You may walk by night or by day,
in summer or in winter, in fair weather or
in foul, in calm or in a gale, and in every case
you are doing something native to yourself and
going the best way you could go. All men
have felt this.

Walking, also from this same natural quality
which it has, introduces particular sights to
you in their right proportion. A man gets
into his motor car, or more likely into somebody else's, and covers a great many miles
in a very few hours. And what remains to
him at the end of it, when he looks closely
into the pictures of his mind, is a curious
and unsatisfactory thing: there are patches of
blurred nothingness like an uneasy sleep, one
or two intense pieces of impression, dis-
connected, violently vivid and mad, a red
cloak, a shining streak of water, and more
particularly a point of danger. In all that
ribbon of sights, each either much too lightly
or much too heavily impressed, he is lucky if
there is one great view which for one moment
he seized and retained from a height as he
whirled along. The whole record is like a
bit of dry point that has been done by a hand
not sure of itself upon a plate that trembled,
now jagged chiselling bit into the metal; now
blurred or hardly impressed it at all: only in

some rare moment of self-possession or of comparative repose did the hand do what it willed and transfer its power.

You may say that riding upon a horse one has a better chance. That is true, but after all one is busy riding. Look back upon the very many times that you have ridden, and though you will remember many things you will not remember them in that calm and perfect order in which they presented themselves to you when you were afoot. As for a man running, if it be for any distance the effort is so unnatural as to concentrate upon himself all a man's powers, and he is almost blind to exterior things. Men at the end of such efforts are actually and physically blind; they fall helpless.

Then there is the way of looking at the world which rich men imagine they can purchase with money when they build a great house looking over some view—but it is not in the same street with walking! You see the sight nine times out of ten when you are ill attuned to it, when your blood is slow and unmoved, and when the machine is not going. When you are walking the machine is always going, and every sense in you is doing what it should with the right emphasis and in due discipline to make a perfect record of all that is about.

Consider how a man walking approaches a little town; he sees it a long way off upon a hill; he sees its unity, he has time to think about it a great deal. Next it is hidden from him by a wood, or it is screened by a roll of land. He tops this and sees the little town again, now much nearer, and he thinks more particularly of its houses, of the way in which they stand, and of what has passed in them. The sky, especially if it has large white clouds in it and is for the rest sunlit and blue, makes something against which he can see the little town, and gives it life. Then he is at the outskirts, and he does not suddenly occupy it with a clamour or a rush, nor does he merely contemplate it, like a man from a window, unmoving. He enters in. He passes, healthily wearied, human doors and signs; he can note all the names of the people and the trade at which they work; he has time to see their faces. The square broadens before him, or the market-place, and so very naturally and rightly he comes to his inn, and he has fulfilled one of the great ends of man.

Lord, how tempted one is here to make a list of those monsters who are the enemies of inns!

There is your monster who thinks of it as a place to which a man does not walk but into which he slinks to drink; and there is your monster who thinks of it as a place to be reached in a railway train and there to put on fine clothes for dinner and to be waited upon by Germans. There is your more amiable monster, who says: "I hear there is a good inn at Little Studley or Bampton Major. Let us go there." He waits until he has begun to be hungry, and he shoots there in an enormous automobile. There is your still more amiable monster, who in a hippo-mobile hippogriffically tools into a town and throws the ribbons to the person in gaiters with a straw in his mouth, and feels (oh, men, my brothers) that he is doing something like someone in a book. All these men, whether they frankly hate or whether they pretend to love, are the enemies of inns, and the enemies of inns are accursed before their Creator and their kind.

There are some things which are a consolation for Eden and which clearly prove to the heavily-burdened race of Adam that it has retained a memory of diviner things. We have all of us done evil. We have permitted the modern cities to grow up, and we have told such lies that now we are accursed with newspapers. And we have so loved wealth that we are all in debt, and that the poor are a burden to us and the rich are an offence. But we ought to keep up our hearts and not to despair, because we can still all of us pray when there is an absolute necessity to do so, and we have wormed out the way of building up that splendid thing which all over Christendom men know under many names and which is called in England an INN.

I have sometimes wondered when I sat in one of these places, remaking my soul, whether the inn would perish out of Europe. I am convinced the terror was but the terror which we always feel for whatever is exceedingly beloved.

There is an inn in the town of Piacenza into which I once walked while I was still full of immortality, and there I found such good companions and so much marble, rooms so large and empty and so old, and cooking so excellent, that I made certain it would survive even that immortality which, I say, was all around. But no! I came there eight years later, having by that time heard the noise of the Subterranean River and being well conscious of mortality. I came to it as to a friend, and the beastly thing had changed! In place of the grand stone doors there was a sort of twirlygig like the things that let you in to the Zoo, where you pay a shilling, and inside there were decorations made up of meaningless curves like those with which the demons have punished the city of Berlin; the salt at the table was artificial and largely made of chalk, and the faces of the host and hostess were no longer kind.

I very well remember another inn which was native to the Chiltern Hills. This place had bow windows, which were divided into medium-sized panes, each of the panes a little rounded; and these window-panes were made of that sort of glass which I will adore until I die, and which has the property of distorting exterior objects: of such glass the windows of schoolrooms and of nurseries used to be made. I came to that place after many years by accident, and I found that Orcus, which has devoured all lovely things, had devoured this too. The inn was called "an Hotel," its front was rebuilt, the windows had only two panes, each quite enormous and flat, one above and one below, and the glass was that sort of thick, transparent glass through which it is no use to look, for you might as well be looking through air. All the faces were strange except that of one old servant in the stable-yard. I asked him if he regretted the old front, and he said "Lord, no!" Then he told me in great detail how kind the brewers had been to his master and how willingly they had rebuilt the whole place. These things reconcile one with the grave.

Well then, if walking, which has led me into this digression, prepares one for the inns where they are worthy, it has another character as great and as symbolic and as worthy of man. For remember that of the many ways of walking there is one way which is the greatest of all, and that is to walk away.

Put your hand before your eyes and remember, you that have walked, the places from which you have walked away, and the wilderness into which you manfully turned the steps of your abandonment.

There is a place above the Roman Wall beyond the River Tyne where one can do this thing. Behind one lies the hospitality and the human noise which have inhabited the town of the river valley for certainly two thousand years. Before one is the dead line of the road, and that complete emptiness of the moors as they rise up toward Cheviot on the one hand and Carter Fell upon the other. The earth is here altogether deserted and alone: you go out into it because it is your business to go: you are walking away. As for your memories, they are of no good to you except to lend you that dignity which can always support a memoried man; you are bound to forget, and it is your business to leave all that you have known altogether behind you, and no man has eyes at the back of his head — go forward. Upon my

soul I think that the greatest way of walking, now I consider the matter, or now
that I have stumbled upon it, is walking
away.

H. BELLOC.

PREFACE

IF men would, or could, detach themselves from their own time and place, Lourdes would be the most interesting business in the world.

'Lourdes' means, of course, the complex of emotion, marvel, site and religious theory, for which that word stands.

Now it is very difficult for men of our time to detach themselves. We are not living in a moment when sheer intellectual force has a social value. Intrigue has the high value it has always had and gains the rewards it has always gained, of shame, accumulated wealth and the contempt of one's fellow-men. Intuitive creative genius still has social value, though it is of less importance in the community than ever before. But intellectual power and the results of an intellectual process have nowadays, for the moment at least, and particularly in this country, no 'market.' I do not mean no market in money, though that is important; I mean no reward attached to them in fame or respect such that a man will be content to exercise them.

On this account there is always an impediment

v

opposed to those who would discuss with their fellows in modern England those problems which chiefly exercise the intelligence. One feels it to be beating the air. And to propound matters that demand an intellectual process and the strong grasp of the mind always feels in modern England something like speaking to the deaf in a foreign language—not only to the deaf but to the bored. And speaking to the bored, even if they can make something of what you say, is a very disheartening process.

Nevertheless, such is the driving power of mere truth and the strong appetite of mere curiosity, that men once engaged in an intellectual adventure can hardly refrain from communicating their interest to their fellows. And those who discover what Lourdes means, not to the pilgrim, but to the mere observer who has muscle enough in his mind to detach himself from any modern bias—those, I say, can with difficulty refrain from challenging the attention of their contemporaries to the amazing thing Lourdes is.

Let us present first the popular or newspaper view of Lourdes. Let us next recapitulate in series the known facts about Lourdes. The contrast is almost comic. Lastly, let us judge as soberly as we can what we may say for and against the religious theory about Lourdes based upon these facts.

Well then, the newspaper (which is also the financial) world, the world of the English press in particular, and of such sheets as the *Matin* or the *Tribuna*, and other anti-Christian financial sheets abroad, will have Lourdes to be something after this fashion :—A number of people belonging to a certain sect called Catholics (in England the insular term is ' Roman ' Catholics) frequent a town under the Pyrenees where, under the influence of very strong emotion, there are produced certain effects upon them such as strong emotion will produce : the nervous are less nervous, the stammerer and the twitched recover control, and in general men and women under the influence of a violent emotion discover aptitudes abnormal to their daily powers just as they will discover such abnormal aptitudes under any other great strain or shock.   This superstition is commoner with peasants than with townsfolk, and commoner, of course, with the poor than with the rich, and with the ignorant than with the cultivated. Meanwhile it is fostered by those who can profit by it even at the expense of reason and dignity.   The priests of the sect naturally foster the illusion and accentuate the abnormal mental conditions of those who come to be ' cured.'   They claim as ' miraculous ' cures what are often temporary phenomena, and always phenomena of suggestion.

That is not an unfair summary of the way in which the kind of people who control our press, and whose· chief concern is the Stock Exchange, desire the mass of Europeans about them to consider Lourdes.   That is the way they talk about Lourdes, and that is quite possibly the way they really think about it : for the men who control our press to-day are as ignorant as they are brutalised by intrigue and avarice, and blinded by these and other appetites to reality and to proportion.

A 3

Now, as against this newspaper legend, let us put a few facts. I shall be careful not to put them in any fashion postulating the Catholic Faith. I shall put down only what posterity will clearly see, whether that posterity remain Christian and civilised or no. I shall set down only what academic people call ' objective ' truth : things as they are. In other words, what ordinary people call ' the truth.'

The truth about Lourdes is simply this. A long lifetime ago the young daughter of certain poor parents in the Pyrenean town of Lourdes said that she had seen in a grotto overlooking the river of that place a figure. She alone saw this figure, her companions who were with her did not. The figure was that of a young and beautiful woman. The figure spoke, proclaiming itself to be Mary, the Mother of that Personality Whose worship is embodied in a certain organism known as the Catholic Church; that organism being in its turn the spiritual aspect and the Form of European civilisation. In other words, the child claimed to have had a vision of one of those figures associated with what is, when they have religion, the determinant religion of European men. The words spoken by this vision inculcated repentance, the frequentation (with the object of a cult) of this grotto, the drinking of the water which flowed from it and bathing in the same. Further, the figure said ' I am the Immaculate Conception.'

There was a great deal more, but I am giving only the essentials of the story, as a detached but rationalist historian would present it.

What next followed is exactly what might have been expected. Since this child alone perceived this figure and heard those words it was taken for granted that she was either lying or the victim of an hallucination. But, what is more remarkable, so obvious did this conclusion appear (and it is that which we should all at once have come to upon hearing any similar tale) that even those who could most have profited by making something of the tale were the first to ridicule it. The child's parents, and in particular the priests of religion, the local religious official, and the Bishop of the Diocese himself, thought it unworthy of any other solution.

So far so good : not only history but most private experience is full of things of that kind. But what follows is of a different sort. Certain individuals, willing to test the story or chancing for themselves some cure which they had despaired of, begin to bathe in and to drink those waters. Of those individuals many are cured of their ailments. Time passes. The cures continue and increase in number. These cures have, roughly speaking, only one common feature. They are physical cures, cures of physical ailments. They have NOT in common the feature that the cures so effected are cures of nervous trouble which a strong affection of the mind might reasonably be supposed to promote, at least for a time. Certain of the cures, many of the cures are of this nature. For instance, dumb persons recover their speech, just as dumb persons have often recovered their speech elsewhere under the influence of violent emotion. But then certain other cures, and those exceedingly numerous, are concerned with ailments of a totally different nature—for instance, ulcers. With every passing year the multitude, and what is more remarkable, the *external quality*, of the cures develop. With every year the accumulation of cures admittedly insusceptible to suggestion increases.

We must note this last item in our series of mere facts as a true and plain fact ; a fact like any other, to be admitted by Catholic and non-Catholic alike and a simple piece of contemporary history ; it is evidence no court can refuse, and it is the key to the whole case. With every year the original hypothesis of hallucination, or suggestion, becomes less tenable to the average mind. The average sane visitor to Lourdes who admits miracles in his philosophy, but comes to Lourdes doubtful of phenomena which have been utterly misrepresented in the press, is generally convinced that what he sees at Lourdes is something altogether different from what he had hitherto thought possible or had expected. The average visitor who comes to Lourdes not accepting the miraculous in his system of philosophy has exactly the same experience. Both kinds of men go away either converted or puzzled. Of those who have really and carefully watched the affair in what is sometimes called a ' scientific spirit ' only a very small number remain simply contemptuous and simply postulating a material or even ' psychical ' solution of what they see.

This last fact is exceedingly important. It differentiates Lourdes from all historical parallels to Lourdes.

You can, if you will, deny the great miraculous Christian shrines of the past—Canterbury for instance—because the witnesses to them are dead.   The evidence is overwhelming indeed in its amount and detail; but its credibility ultimately depends upon the character of the witnesses—and these are no longer available.   The close network of contemporary experience upon which all our judgment of character is built has faded or been obliterated altogether, and you can call the witnesses fools or liars: for they are dead.   But you cannot do that about Lourdes.   All up and down Europe you will find men still living and submissible to your own judgment, men of the first intelligence and of the widest culture who have visited Lourdes and watched the thing, and who will tell you, if they are at one end of the line that they have seen Heaven open and the power thereof, if they are at the other end of the line that they have been wonderfully puzzled.   But you will only find a very few men, and those not usually of the best judgment or of the highest culture, who will tell you that the matter was easily explicable or negligible.

Now when we consider this series of facts let us see what we are to conclude.   I do not mean what we are to conclude in the matter of religion, nor even in the transcendental matter, hardly subject to positive proof, of *why* these things arose and What is that which brings them about.   I mean only, What is the nature of these things in their relation to us—are they from us or from outside ?

I conceive that by a mere dry process of reasoning

we must determine that there is proceeding at Lourdes an influence affecting mankind independently of mankind and not proceeding from mankind.

For myself I have come to a much nobler and to a much happier conclusion, and, from the year 1904, about Easter time, I have had no doubt that here the best influence there is for men (I mean that of our Blessed Lady) is active.   But I am not here concerned to present a rhetorical or an emotional argument : only a rational one.

If what happens at Lourdes is the result of self-suggestion, why cannot men, though exceptionally, yet in similar great numbers, suggest themselves into health in Pimlico or the Isle of Man ?   It is no answer to say that here and there such marvels are to be found. The point is that men go to Lourdes in every frame of mind, and are in an astonishing number cured.

Again, it is to be noted that when a definition is asked, ' Where will you draw the line ? What physical ailment will you say is capable of a cure by auto-suggestion and what is not ? ' those whom you interrogate are as chary to-day of giving a reply as they were ready to give it some twenty or thirty years ago.   They had but to formulate a test for that test immediately to fail them in the next cure examined. They had but to say, strong emotion can induce from within the cure of alpha but not the cure of beta, for a case of beta and a cure thereof immediately to appear.

I remember a wealthy and foolish woman saying some years ago at dinner that she would believe in miraculous powers if a man who had lost a finger or a hand by amputation could have it joined again at Lourdes. To which a priest present at the table replied, with great judgment, that if or when this kind of miracle were worked those who still believed the phenomena of Lourdes to proceed from the cured themselves would invent a bastard word, half-Greek, half-Latin, ending in ism and signifying in plain English the growing together of severed flesh and bone. In the same way men who now admit that saints in ecstasy have been raised into the air call that exercise ' levitation.'

But all this is mere reasoning on paper, and that is not by any means the most convincing process. It is my advice especially to those who have no devotion or faith, but whose minds are none the less free and who have the means and the leisure, to go to Lourdes and see what they shall see. It is much the greatest experience in travel they are likely to have in the modern world.

H. BELLOC.

PREFACE

By Hilaire Belloc

Mr Chesterton's book is an attempt to accomplish a very difficult task. It is a task which, perhaps, I think more difficult than he does, and it is a task comparable in nature to more than one that he has lately undertaken in public affairs.

To put it in the most general terms, it is the task of making what was an aristocracy and is now a plutocracy act like a democracy.

But in the present case—the matter of the war and its peace—the need is so urgent, and the punishment threatening ignorance, corruption, or a bad political machinery, so evident and so tremendous, that he has a better chance of accomplishing his object than heretofore.

Let me give an example that will show both the difficulty and the nature of such a task.

Mr Chesterton and I worked side by

9

side for months in making public the nature of Parliamentary decline.

After a general exposure in book and newspaper, we proceeded to a particular case in proof—the Marconi business.

It was only one out of dozens of such things which are native to the atmosphere of Westminster, but it was an excellent working model with which to move our contemporaries.

Mr Chesterton put it forth most clearly and fully. Of course all that could be concealed by the culprits was concealed—and still is; but the Marconi ramp was made an object lesson so reiterated and so insisted upon that nobody could ignore it. After several months of this prolonged action even the official "Conservative" Press was compelled to discuss the misdeeds of the "Liberals." In something like a year all the middle classes and great sections even of the populace had at last appreciated—though imperfectly—what the governing classes had known all along : that bribery was a commonplace in public life, and that the professional politicians gave themselves and their relatives

sums of money obtained, directly and in-
directly, by monopolies, special contracts,
etc., out of the public pocket. I say, so
far as plain statement and proof were concerned, all were at last convinced.

What was the result?

Under the old aristocratic conditions,
which had been the strength of Protestant
England since the fall of the monarchy in
the seventeenth century, the Marconi men
would have been done for. Not that aris-
tocracies are other than cynical, but that
their power depends upon a certain pres-
tige, and members of their oligarchy discovered and exposed in an undignified
moral position are thrust out of that oligarchy for the sake of its own preservation.

Under a democracy the culprits would
have been punished; for under a democracy public men are regarded not as
masters but as servants. Dishonesty
upon their part, though more frequently
attempted perhaps than under other forms
of Government, is checked before it grows
dangerous by the simple process of attaching unpleasant consequences to corrup-

tion.   At best the culprits are imprisoned
(like Garfunkel) or driven to suicide (like
Reinach) or they fly the country (like
Hertz).   At the least they suffer general
contempt.   Honest men refuse to associate with the tricksters.   They have to
hide and retire.

But under our present regime of plutocracy neither of these two salutary processes of excretion, the aristocratic or the
democratic, were at work.   The Marconi
men remained in public life, and not only
so remained, but were regarded by their
colleagues as peculiarly suitable to further
and graver responsibilities as a consolation for their recent sad experience.

Why was this?   It was due to effects
of plutocracy working quite openly and
patent to the observation of all : the first
an indifference to right and wrong—the
chief moral consequence of plutocracy;
the second the direct power of great wealth
in a plutocracy to govern to its own advantage—its chief material effect.

As to the first, men told you upon every
side that it was quixotic and fanatical to
set up an impossible standard of purity in

public life; that there was no great harm in such things; that a fellow caught in some rather dirty action was probably fairly cunning or he would not have engaged in it, and that cunning was the chief requisite in an administrator and his greatest claim to our reverence. Of wisdom in contrast with cunning, of the fact that cunning is the opposite and corrosive of wisdom, as sloth and luxury are the opposites and the corrosives of good breeding, opinion in general had become oblivious.

As to the second, it was simply a question of mechanism. There was no organ of expression that was not owned by the same plutocratic forces as had, in another aspect, worked the Marconi business. All the principal newspapers—almost in proportion to their circulation—first falsified and then hushed up the issue. A peerage was given to one newspaper vulgarian (the second Harmsworth); a few other honours and salaries to the lesser ones, and the thing was over.

How does all this apply to the present crisis?

In the following manner :

The country is at the present moment under the acute, imperative necessity of destroying Prussia. Its only impediment in the full accomplishment of this salutary execution is the power of a few rich men. If this country is persuaded to lag behind its Allies in the hard task of victory, if it does not (1) fully support all its Allies up to the complete defeat of the enemy, (2) use that defeat fully and help its Allies whole-heartedly to eliminate the criminal power, then the future of Britain—whatever be that of her Allies —is beyond doubt. She will remain for long a great, somewhat amorphous commercial power, bound together by the interests of her merchants and financiers, but increasingly lacking in co-ordination and losing wealth. As a spiritual and political force in the world she will decline very rapidly indeed.

Britain is clearly at once the chief objective against which a surviving Prussian State would direct itself, and, from her dependence upon the sea, Britain is also the most vulnerable objective offered to such a foe. Her dependence upon the sea makes her the most vulnerable objective because any one power commanding the sea excites the jealousy of all others, and because sea power depends in a great degree upon mechanical and limited things. A determined enemy with great material resources can far more easily and quickly build a great fleet than he can re-create a dominant army after defeat. Further, certain changes in marine attack and defence due to quite modern invention make security at sea much more gravely threatened by a much less expenditure of money than ever before.

Now the organism of a nation thus politically threatened is, perhaps, better defended by an aristocracy than by any other form of government. An aristocracy is vividly alive to the national interests, and is prompt, ruthless, and exhaustive in the pursuit of them.

The old aristocratic England (which perished in our own time and before our own eyes) would have fallen upon this problem with the rapidity and directness of lightning. Its governing members would not only have expended all their energy against the foe, but would have seized the first moments of the struggle for the development of the fullest possible policy of aggression. Finally, it would have had no sort of hesitation about the end in view. It would have gone straight for the total destruction of the adverse power menacing the State.

We may call such a spirit unscrupulous and even vicious if we disagree with it. But we cannot deny that it would have been the most efficient spiritual force for achieving the end—the salvation of the country.

A democracy would in another fashion have been equally determined and direct, though perhaps less prompt, and certainly less informed. It would have worked more by instinct. It would probably have made initial mistakes. But it would have attempted to correct them by its later energy, and above all it would have no doubt whatever of the prime necessity to-day. Everyone among the people is to-day agreed. The speech of all in the street and in the crowds is the same. Those who with the terrible necessities of the moment, who divert themselves with "Pacifist" theories or who continue, in the academic classes, the old rubbish of "Teutonism," are numerically quite insignificant and utterly out of tune with masses around them.

The danger lies in the fact that what really governs us is plutocratic, and that the aristocracy is gone and the populace impotent to act—not even conceiving their action possible, but ready to submit to anything the rich impose.

There are three separate ways in which this danger of a false policy proceeding from the new plutocracy has manifested itself.

First, it has been clearly seen that private interests in trade—the advantages of private fortunes—have been allowed to weigh, if not against the commonwealth, at any rate on a par with the interests of the commonwealth. We have seen it in the handling of freights; we have seen it in the exceptions to blockade; we have seen it in the field of contracts. But this evil is particularly apparent in the hesita-

B

tion shown by many when they discuss the commercial terms to be imposed upon the enemy, and their fear lest a complete victory should interfere with private gain in commerce.

From the point of view of the nation as a whole, a victorious people has no economic advantage whatsoever in leaving the vanquished wealthy. There is every advantage in leaving the vanquished laborious and *productive* of wealth; but the whole effort of the victor should be turned to the draining of that wealth, once produced, *away* from the vanquished and *towards* themselves.

Thus to exclude the goods of a conquered Germany from these islands is the act of an idiot. To permit a conquered Germany to build up new wealth wherewith to attack again is the act of a traitor. Yet these two policies alone are suggested by the stupid and the more intelligent sections of our plutocracy irrespectively.

There is but one obvious public policy —the maintenance of a continual drain of wealth from a Germany conquered and compelled to export to our advantage. It is a policy the richer can impose most simply by life-long indemnity, most drastically by the confiscation of mortgage and scrip with garrisons to maintain the treaty.

Private interests are at issue with such a public policy. The financier has interests bound up with German interests; the merchant fears the ruin of his client.

There is here a very interesting example of private fortune misunderstanding its own advantage from its very avarice.

The financial interests—which are by far the strongest things in this country —thoroughly understand the taking of tribute from the occupied and subject territory of those whom they think very weak.

The whole history of Ireland is nothing else than that. Ireland, until George Wyndham's Land Act (and to some extent even since that Act), was sending overseas masses of material, vast in proportion to her wealth, as interest upon loans, which loans had been advanced to the landlord class by cosmopolitan finance.

The whole history of modern Egypt is

nothing else. What the Egyptian peasant produces beyond his bare livelihood and the cost of administration is paid as interest to their same cosmopolitan financiers, who caught in their net long ago the foolish and irresponsible monarch of the country.

It is perfectly clear that the economic fate of any conquered country could be modelled upon the same lines. You can always so arrange matters that the vanquished have to *produce* wealth indeed, but, instead of *retaining* that wealth, shall regularly pass it over to the victors. If those members of our plutocracy who happen to have no personal interests in Germany or Austria could be got to see this almost self-evident economic proposition, the power of their great fortunes would no longer be an impediment to the complete destruction of the enemy.

But they cannot be got to see it. Even those wealthy men who have no interests in the enemy's country will almost certainly work to prevent the terms of peace from impoverishing the enemy.

Meanwhile those who *have* personal interests in the enemy territory (and these are very numerous) will be directly interested in preventing a complete victory; they are working actively against it at this moment. That is the first way in which the fact the new plutocracy imperils the final success of the national arms.

The second way in which the danger manifests itself is through the preference of private fortune to public good in the matter of direct military expense.

The great war has cost the belligerents in material goods per month far more than the material goods which they can themselves produce or economically command as interest or tribute from abroad; at least, it has cost them an expense of material goods at a far higher rate than the rate at which wealth can be produced or demanded over and above the current necessities of national sustenance.

Therefore the great belligerent nations have had to fall back upon their accumulated reserve of wealth to withdraw it from the production of further wealth : to consume it immediately and irrevocably upon the field of battle.

In part this accumulation has been directly expended in the prosecution of the war. In part it has been exchanged for material obtained from neutral countries. For instance, the getting rid of American shares held in Britain simply means that whereas a resident of Britain formerly owned, say a group of buildings in America, and received the rent thereof in England, he has now been compelled to forgo this rent for ever in exchange for a number of shells the Americans have made for him; which shells produce no further wealth in consumption, and therefore, when consumed, leave nothing in their place. The British revenue drawn from America has disappeared. It has disappeared in those little puffs of white against the grey of the Flanders sky.

Now the accumulation of capital during the long peace of the West was so enormous that the first two years of this great struggle could be " financed "—that is, in plain English, the coal, the chemicals, the cloth and the iron and wheat, etc., could be obtained—without any form of true confiscation. The possessors of these

accumulations were for two years willing
to give them up on condition that the State
promised them a certain yearly revenue
in their place—which revenue it could
probably raise. But this process after
about two years of war is reaching its
term. The great accumulation of material
still remaining available will hardly be
obtained in this voluntary fashion. The
State may try to obtain it by promising
greater future rewards than it is ever
likely to be able to pay—but such inability
will be patent to those who are approached
for a loan.

Therefore, if the war should proceed
beyond a certain period—I have suggested
some time in the third year as the probable
beginning of the new phase—owners of
great wealth would be faced, not merely
with severe taxation upon their current
revenue for short time, but with an actual
diminution of their permanent revenues
throughout all the future. They would
be faced with the beginning of a confiscation from private stock for the public weal.
To fight against this by quite obvious and
direct means, the masters of our plutoc-

racy might not dare. But to fight against
it by indirect means, they would; and the
most obvious indirect means would be to
spread the conception abroad that further
struggle had become "impossible" on account of some mysterious thing called
"financial exhaustion."

In plain economics it would only mean,
of course, that the price of victory was
the reduction of fortune. But plain
economics are always presented nowadays
as a mystery beyond the ken of ordinary
mortals. It would be easy to flood the
public with the technicalities of the money
market; to ascribe to this "financial exhaustion" a rise in the prices of food, or
any other evil of which the populace as a
whole was acutely conscious. And the
very men to do it are the men of the
Marconi ramp, the Indian balances and
the Rupee scandal—all of them actively
in power.

Such is the second form of the peril:
the second way in which the fact that we
are a plutocracy may interfere with the
achievement of victory.

But it may be asked by what instrument

the plutocracy could act thus rapidly to pervert opinions in a matter so vital and so clear?

This question leads me to the *third* way in which the peril of it appears; and that is through the plutocratic control of the Press.

The people of our great towns—that is, between four-fifths and nine-tenths of our population—have no information save through the Press. The things they care for and discuss are not real experiences, but phantasms presented to them by the Press.

Now the Press means to-day in England a very small number of very wealthy men, and on the patriotism and the public spirit of those very few wealthy men depends the true information of the people : upon their baseness, ignorance, folly, avarice, or cowardice—or all five combined—depends the mal-information of the populace. By mal-information we may suffer (we are already beginning to suffer) the weakening of the national will, and the failure to insist upon national success.

This handful of rich newspaper-owners

is, like all other categories of men, diverse in character; and we find some portion of the Press resolved on victory and refusing to spread panic, although the resolution bids fair to impoverish its owners. But you will find another portion, from whatever of the five motives I have enumerated (and usually from all five combined), playing the traitor.

It will probably be the very newspapers which were most vulgarly violent against weak opponents in the past, which have shown the most offensive lack of chivalry in military matters, which have shrieked the loudest while opinion was still violent and tenacious in the earlier phases of the present great war, that will try to create towards the end of it a current of opinion leading towards an inconclusive peace.

That is the third way in which a plutocratic form of Government can manifest itself, and it is far the most effective of the several ways in which that form may ruin England, and of those individuals most dangerous, through a lack of education combined with avarice and fear, I should name Alfred Harmsworth as the most obvious type.

Such then are the dangers besetting the full achievement of victory as I see them in the Society to which we belong. Against them we must set the fact that the marvellous effort the country as a whole has made, and made spontaneously, is a guarantee of something very different in the commonwealth, a resurrection of forces at which the plutocracy under which we had begun to live hardly guessed.

It is possible—it is to be prayed for most earnestly—that these new popular forces will, handicapped though they are by the profound popular ignorance of public men and public affairs, prove too strong for any anti-national conspiracy. It is to these popular forces that such a book as this principally appeals. Not so long ago the appeal to aristocracy might have had its force—but to-day that factor is quite dead. The aristocrats are dining with the Samuels and sneering at their hosts.

I may add in conclusion that Mr Chesterton's book is largely directed to argument against those in whose singular philosophy justice does not demand the punishment of any powerful criminal nor common sense the rendering of a wicked maniac impotent for further evil.

It seems to me personally (I give it only as a private opinion) that Mr Chesterton has here somewhat exaggerated the importance of a clique with which we are brought so directly into contact whenever we engage in political discussion that we may over-estimate its real strength. I mean the intellectuals.

The fool who says " all war is wrong " —(a perfectly meaningless phrase, as who should say, " all hammering is right whether on the head of my aunt or of a tenpenny nail "), and the more perverted fool who cannot reconcile justice with charity (for he has no creed), has indeed an influence in our society quite out of proportion to his numbers. That is because he is to be discovered almost exclusively in the wealthier classes. His subscriptions to secret political " pools " and to the private necessities of individual politicians give him considerable power; while, in the absence of a common religion, he has a field for action upon some portion of the public mind. He still has an influence. But I do think that this element can no longer be regarded as a chief factoɪ in the situation.

The suffering has been so great, the heroism so simple and so sublime, the sacrifice so spontaneous and so superb that these mere negative follies of the Garden Cities and the Universities—and a small minority even of these—can hardly deflect opinion or control policy.

No, the danger does not lie there. It lies in the presence at the head of affairs of the low-born men who for years defied opinion while they took bribes from shady company-promoters and their families, while they rifled the silver interests and the taxation-balances of India, while they robbed ignorant investors—as in the Howard Union attempt or in American Marconis—while they still more cynically affirmed—what was, alas! true—that their colleagues, the political lawyers in the Courts, so far from punishing *them* would condemn any public-spirited critic to fine or imprisonment.

It lies in the presence behind such scum in office (and now actually upon the bench) of newspaper-owners—men of similar origin, similar morals, similar immunity from the law, and yet masters of our public life.

Long before the war these things had become a common jest against us throughout Europe. We were bid neglect the foreign critics—our shame was only a moral, an intangible weakness. We were told to ignore such flimsy stuff as honour.

To-day the awful issue proves that Mr Chesterton and I were right, and that our shallow and timorous advisers of but four years ago were desperately, tragically wrong.

If the country fails at the end and patches a peace the crime will proceed from just such secret powers as gave us Marconi, and the weakness and the folly will lie at the door of just those professional politicians who permitted what followed and obeyed their private masters.

There is no logical connection between swindling and inefficiency, but there is an organic connection. God is not mocked.

INTRODUCTION

I HAVE been honoured with the request to write a few words of Preface to this Memoir of my very valued and very much lamented friend Mr. John Lewis Griffiths, formerly Consul-General for the United States in London.

There is so much that could be said in such a connection, and which I know myself only indifferently able to express, that I hesitate a little to undertake the task : poignant as is my memory of its subject and strongly as I feel it my duty to bear such testimony as I can in the company of so many others.

I shall, I think, render the best service if I restrict my attempt to one narrow field and speak of Mr. Griffiths only in connection with that : I mean the aid which such men as he gave, subconsciously, as it were, and yet at the critical moment, to the general business of the world, which is the right issue of the present war. For John Lewis Griffiths was one of those—I think I may say without exaggeration the most completely successful of those—who established personal relations between Englishmen and Americans ; and the establishment of those relations in sufficient strength to bear the strain of the present alliance is at this moment a definite and large part of the work necessary to the world.

ix

Others will express far better than I can the charm of his personal character : a charm which I think reposed even more upon integrity than it did upon the power of vivid expression, although this last and rare gift was most noticeable in him.

Others, of course, can speak as I cannot, of his career in his own country, of which I know nothing. Others can describe and have described his most exceptional gift of moving, lucid and arresting speech, which made him the best deliverer of an address—especially of such addresses as required reading and judgment combined—whom I have ever heard. But that other matter—his popularity and success in establishing what I have called personal relations between considerable groups of Englishmen and Americans before the war—must be my only object in so restricted an effort as this.

The two societies are more difficult to introduce the one to the other than either is prepared to recognize. The root cause of this difficulty is that you have here a community of language and a partial community of institutions. There are some who would call such a statement a paradox, and a paradox is out of place in any serious study. But for my part I do not think it a paradox at all. On the contrary it seems to me something so obvious that I am astonished men do not perpetually recognize it.

When you frankly regard a foreign nation as wholly foreign, when you are prepared for a shock at every turn ; when every word used by the foreigner is unfamiliar to you, and language, the form of thought, is the strangest part of all his strange apparatus ;

when his institutions arouse in you bewilderment or ridicule or mere blank incomprehension—*then* you may proceed to a deliberate study of his society, to a grasp of its character and at last perhaps to a full appreciation of it.

Thus Angellier, for instance, of the *École Normale* in France, one of the many Frenchmen who made themselves expert in British things, so soaked himself in the English language and in the Scottish dialects, with all the society and tone of thought which these connoted, that he was able to produce a great monograph on Burns; superior to any rival book.

Apart from these experts, the mass of opinion, the bulk of educated men when they know they are dealing with something completely foreign make allowances for what irritates or confuses them. But when you have a community of language between societies which are in spirit very different, a cause of friction at once arises. When there is not only community in language, but to a large extent in religious formation (for religion is the root of all action) and even in some institutions, the danger of friction grows greater yet. Familiar words mean to the one party what they do not mean to the other. Expressions of the mind which we are expecting in connection with our own speech we find lacking in the similar speech of the stranger. It is like looking into a distorted mirror, or like listening to a conversation passing between others and not meant for ourselves.

If this is true of language it is still more true of institutions. When certain fundamental institutions are similar between independent and different nations, but though similar are not identical—when the common factors of life are mixed in different proportions and the synthesis of the whole is correspondingly at variance, there is bewilderment or confusion or irritation. In religion, for instance, both nations are Protestant, but the proportionate numerical strength and influence of Catholicism in England is nothing to what it is in America. Again in both nations there is a considerable sceptical class : nowadays a very large one ; but in America there is no tradition left of aristocratic scepticism. In Britain that form of scepticism is the oldest and the most rooted.

The fundamental institution of the law, of legal forms and terms, and even of the legal spirit, is a very striking example of what I mean. There is so much in common between the two countries, that the precedents of the one can be quoted in the other. Every act in an English court, every form, is easily followed by the American visitor of the legal profession, and yet the social spirit which underlies the two systems of courts differs more widely than the social spirit between any two European nations of the West.

This is a hard saying. It will be denied by most of those who read this perhaps, and even violently denied, but it is true. The society of the United States, taken as a whole, is frankly and inevitably egalitarian, that of England is especially and will always be aristocratic—for aristocratic states will never adopt any other form ; they never have in history and, indeed, it is impossible to see how they could. Government by the populace or through the populace is inconceivable in an aristocratic state. No other form of government is conceivable beyond the Atlantic. The necessary strain between popular government and centralization is at once solved there by the intensive practice of local autonomy—the very core of American political ideas. Here the central control of small closely connected bodies, magisterial, financial, political, is complete and absolute.

It would be tedious to pursue this. The point is, I think, clear. The two societies, profoundly differing, are in a special danger of friction from the fact that their language is identical and that parts of their institutions are closely similar.

Now the reconciliation of such differences is a subtle and difficult thing. I have watched not a few attempts at it and many more imitations of it, which were the more failures because they boasted of success. The intermixture of a few rich people with a foreign society—they are but a handful—does nothing towards helping the comprehension of that society by those from whom such immigrants have come. On the contrary it only breeds a worse friction. The very considerable interchange of literature does something, but it does it badly. The Englishman does not really know what America is thinking through the American books he has thrust upon him or accepts. The American in America reading a much greater proportion of English work is certainly even more deceived about England. I have noticed, for instance, that novels describing English political life if they are accurate and vivid can obtain no sale in America whatsoever, but that the novels which give a conventional picture of the two English Houses of Parliament and their personnel—a conventional picture as wide of the mark as can be and simply neglected by people actually living in politics—do obtain a considerable sale upon the other side of the Atlantic. Occasionally efforts in philosophy do more to explain the one nation to the other. This was very noticeable in the case of Mr. James and his brother. But most of all is done by those rare men who establish a personal contact in which is mingled understanding, affection and humour. They are, in truth, the ambassadors between the two peoples.

It may sound ungracious, or even unpatriotic, but I fear it is true that work of this kind is far more rare as from us to the Americans than it is from the Americans to us. This is perhaps inevitable. Europe is for the American a subject of travel far more than is America a subject of travel for us. And the Americans see Europe more as a whole than do we see the United States as a whole. We think of the United States—at least we are too much led to think so through our newspapers and many of our books —as a product of British expansion : something originally colonial which afterwards grew up to have an independent life.

The American often sees Great Britain as the nearest and most comprehensible to him of many European states, but still only one of many such states. It is the American who establishes the interpretative relation much more often than it is the Englishman, and of the Americans who established such relations Mr. Griffiths—in my experience at least—was by far the most successful and the one whose influence will most certainly endure.

This was in no small measure due—apart from that extraordinary talent for expression which I have already mentioned—to the immediate affection by which he drew both private acquaintances and great audiences towards himself. The vague and quite insufficient word " popularity " I have heard used of him only too often. It was much more than popularity. It was the recognition of fundamental goodness and sympathy. Everybody felt it. I am happy to count myself one of those who have had opportunities of feeling it most strongly. When such a temperament, with its advantages, is united to the talent or even genius for comprehension and exposition which was present in him, the effect is not only immediately considerable but above all lasting.

This talent for exposition, of which public speaking is only a part, means, when it is generally stated, something diffuse and vague. But in the case of Mr. Griffiths it had a rare, peculiar, and personal quality which caused me to listen to him in something of the same mood as that in which one watches a skilful performance upon a difficult instrument. A man in his position is called upon to address audiences of very different sorts, at short notice—often with no notice at all ; upon subjects now agreed, now novel, now controversial, now perilous, now enthusiastic. I have many times, as I listened to him, contrasted his method before the audience he was immediately addressing with that which he had used, and which I had also heard (perhaps but a week before) when he had to meet other minds and deal with other matters. The skill with which he grasped at once the air in which he spoke and the line that would lead his immediate hearers to conviction or to interest, was something so individual, that I have not found it in any other man.

In all this I am speaking only of talent ; high and admirable, but still talent only. I am saying nothing of virtue, which is incomparably more. The true source from which all this effect sprang was that virtue in the mind of which the French use the phrase " *rayonnant de bonté.*"

I feel as I conclude these very few lines, how inadequately I have dealt with something which is very near my heart and which I could have wished to have put in better terms. A personal emotion is at work— an emotion of reverence, of great regret and of established admiration which if I gave it rein would make me write very differently and perhaps with too individual a note. I have concerned myself only with the public effect of this man's work and virtues coming just before so critical a moment in the history of the world, and coming, as I believe, with a real benediction about it, and a purpose greater than in all his neighbours.

It is the characteristic of those who have done well that when they die their influence does not fade or diminish, but in some way we do not understand bears increasing fruit. It is the test of what those now dead have done. It is their title in the history of the world. And I have no doubt that this friendship with which I was myself honoured and which was extended indeed to all who met and knew its object, will be of increasing value.

HILAIRE BELLOC

PREFACE

Homo faber. Man is born to make. His business is to construct : to plan : to carry out the plan : to fit together, and to produce a finished thing.

That human art in which it is most difficult to achieve this end (and in which it is far easier to neglect it than in any other) is the art of writing. Yet this much is certain, that unconstructed writing is at once worthless and ephemeral : and nearly the whole of our modern English writing is unconstructed.

The matter of survival is perhaps not the most important, though it is a test of a kind, and it is a test which every serious writer feels most intimately. The essential is the matter of excellence : that a piece of work should achieve its end. But in either character, the character of survival or the character of intrinsic excellence, construction deliberate and successful is the fundamental condition.

It may be objected that the mass of writing must in any age neglect construction. We write to establish a record for a few days : or to send a thousand unimportant messages : or to express for others or for ourselves something very vague and perhaps very weak in the way of emotion, which does not demand construction and at any rate cannot command it. No writer can be judged by the entirety of his writings, for these would include every note he ever sent round the corner ; every memorandum he ever made upon

A   I

PREFACE

his shirt cuff. But when a man sets out to write as a serious business, proclaiming by the nature of his publication and presentment that he is doing something he thinks worthy of the time and place in which he lives and of the people to whom he belongs, then if he does not construct he is negligible.

Yet, I say, the great mass of men to-day do not attempt it in the English tongue, and the proof is that you can discover in their slipshod pages nothing of a seal or stamp. You do not, opening a book at random, say at once: " This is the voice of such and such an one." It is no one's manner or voice. It is part of a common babel.

Therefore in such a time as that of our decline, to come across work which is planned, executed and achieved has something of the effect produced by the finding of a wrought human thing in a wild. It is like finding, as I once found, deep hidden in the tangled rank grass of autumn in Burgundy, on the edge of a wood not far from Dijon, a neglected statue of the eighteenth century. It is like coming round the corner of some wholly desolate upper valley in the mountains and seeing before one a well-cultivated close and a strong house in the midst.

It is now many years—I forget how many; it may be twenty or more, or it may be a little less—since *The Wallet of Kai Lung* was sent me by a friend. The effect produced upon my mind at the first opening of its pages was in the same category as the effect produced by the discovery of that hidden statue in Burgundy, or the coming upon an unexpected house in the turn of a high Pyrenean gorge. Here was something worth doing and done. It was not a plan

2

PREFACE

attempted and only part achieved (though even that would be rare enough to-day, and a memorable exception) it was a thing intended, wrought out, completed and established. Therefore it was destined to endure and, what is more important, it was a success.

The time in which we live affords very few of such moments of relief : here and there a good piece of verse, in *The New Age* or in the now defunct *Westminster* : here and there a lapidary phrase such as a score or more of Blatchford's which remain fixed in my memory. Here and there a letter written to the newspapers in a moment of indignation when the writer, not trained to the craft, strikes out the metal justly at white heat. But, I say, the thing is extremely rare, and in the shape of a complete book rarest of all.

The Wallet of Kai Lung was a thing made deliberately, in hard material and completely successful. It was meant to produce a particular effect of humour by the use of a foreign convention, the Chinese convention, in the English tongue. It was meant to produce a certain effect of philosophy and at the same time it was meant to produce a certain completed interest of fiction, of relation, of a short epic. It did all these things.

It is one of the tests of excellent work that such work is economic, that is, that there is nothing redundant in order or in vocabulary, and at the same time nothing elliptic—in the full sense of that word : that is, no sentence in which so much is omitted that the reader is left puzzled. That is the quality you get in really good statuary—in Houdon, for instance, or in that triumph the archaic *Archer* in the Louvre. *The Wallet of Kai Lung* satisfied all these conditions.

3

PREFACE

I do not know how often I have read it since I first possessed it. I know how many copies there are in my house—just over a dozen. I know with what care I have bound it constantly for presentation to friends. I have been asked for an introduction to this its successor, *Kai Lung's Golden Hours*. It is worthy of its forerunner. There is the same plan, exactitude, working-out and achievement; and therefore the same complete satisfaction in the reading, or to be more accurate, in the incorporation of the work with oneself.

All this is not extravagant praise, nor even praise at all in the conversational sense of that term. It is merely a judgment: a putting into as carefully exact words as I can find the appreciation I make of this style and its triumph.

The reviewer in his art must quote passages. It is hardly the part of a Preface writer to do that. But to show what I mean I can at least quote the following :

" Your insight is clear and unbiased," said the gracious Sovereign. " But however entrancing it is to wander unchecked through a garden of bright images, are we not enticing your mind from another subject of almost equal importance ? "

Or again :

" It has been said," he began at length, withdrawing his eyes reluctantly from an unusually large insect upon the ceiling and addressing himself to the maiden, " that there are few situations in life that cannot be honourably settled, and without loss of time, either by suicide, a bag of gold, or by thrusting a despised antagonist over the edge of a precipice on a dark night."

4

Or again :

" After secretly observing the unstudied grace of her movements, the most celebrated picture-maker of the province burned the implements of his craft, and began life anew as a trainer of performing elephants."

You cannot read those sentences, I think, without agreeing with what has been said above. If you doubt it, take the old test and try to write that kind of thing yourself.

In connection with such achievements it is customary to-day to deplore the lack of public appreciation. Either to blame the hurried millions of chance readers because they have only bought a few thousands of a masterpiece ; or, what is worse still, to pretend that good work is for the few and that the mass will never appreciate it—in reply to which it is sufficient to say that the critic himself is one of the mass and could not be distinguished from others of the mass by his very own self were he a looker-on.

In the best of times (the most stable, the least hurried) the date at which general appreciation comes is a matter of chance, and to-day the presentation of any achieved work is like the reading of Keats to a football crowd. It is of no significance whatsoever to English Letters whether one of its glories be appreciated at the moment it issues from the press or ten years later, or twenty, or fifty. Further, after a very small margin is passed, a margin of a few hundreds at the most, it matters little whether strong permanent work finds a thousand or fifty thousand or a million of readers. Rock stands and mud washes away.

What is indeed to be deplored is the lack of

5

PREFACE

communication between those who desire to find good stuff and those who can produce it : it is in the attempt to build a bridge between the one and the other that men who have the privilege of hearing a good thing betimes write such words as I am writing here.

HILAIRE BELLOC.

6

PREFACE.

———

NEARLY all the historical work worth doing at the present moment in the English language is the work of shovelling off heaps of rubbish inherited from the immediate past.

The history of Europe and of the world suffered, so far as English letters were concerned, from two vital defects rising at the end of the eighteenth century and lasting to the end of the nineteenth : when the wholesome reaction began.

In the first place it was not thorough.

In the second place it blindly followed the continental anti-Catholic tradition and particularly the German anti-Catholic tradition.

Now that the historian should not be thorough, that he should scamp his work, is an obvious defect. We have suffered from it in England, especially our two old Universities of Oxford and Cambridge, which do not set out to be seats of learning so much as social and aristocratic institutions.

But the second defect was worse still. History may be scrappy and superficial and yet, on the whole, right ; but if its whole orientation is warped by a wrong appreciation of the past, then, however detailed and full of research, it is worse than worthless ; it is harmful and it had better not have been written at all.

These preliminary remarks apply to the history of Europe as a whole and especially to the history of Europe between the coarsening of the foundational Roman administrative system in the fifth century and the rise of modern culture in the seventeenth.

They do not apply to late local history. Late (post 1600) local history *was* thoroughly well done. The history of England itself, when it deals only with the England which sprang out of the completed Reformation century (still more the local history of the United States) was detailed and exact. What is more important than exactitude in detail, it was consonant with the spirit of the thing described. The writers on either side of the Atlantic, but especially upon the American side, understood the material with which they were dealing. Here in England (where I write this Preface) the work on *later* history was also national and well done, though it suffered from no small defect in that the original Catholic England (which was like a foreign country to the writers in question) lingered on as a dwindling minority till at least 1715 and somewhat disturbed the picture; so that our modern English historians are never really at home until they get to the Hanoverian dynasty. Before that they have to deal with a remaining remnant of the vigorous Catholic spirit, and they are perplexed and bewildered by it, so that it vitiates their conclusions. That is why they cannot write of the later Stuarts, and especially of James II, with any proper sense of proportion. They cannot conceive how strong nor even how widespread was the support of the national dynasty, because that support was mixed up with the (to them and in our time) utterly alien Catholic idea.

I say that the main task of an historian writing in the English language is the shovelling away of rubbish; and this is particularly true of the rubbish which has accumulated over the record of the Dark and early Middle Ages (A.D. 500 to 1000; A.D. 1000 to 1500).

From the very beginning of the affair popular history was warped by the spirit of ridicule (Voltaire's creation propagated in the English language by Voltaire's pupil Gibbon). against the formation of Christendom and that tremendous story of definition upon definition, council upon council, from which emerged at last the full Christian creed. The decisive conflicts of Nicea, of Chalcedon, were made a silly jest, and generations of boys and young men were taught to think of the most profound questions ever settled by the human mind as verbal quips and incomprehensible puerilities.

Next the gradual transformation of our Catholic civilization from the majestic order of our pagan origin to the splendid spring of the twelfth century was represented with incredible insufficiency as the conquest of the

Occident by barbarian Germans, who, though barbarians, possessed I know not what fund of strength and virtue. Institutions which we now know to be of Roman origin were piously referred to these starved heaths of the Baltic and to the central European wilds.   Their inhabitants were endowed with every good quality.   Whatever we were proud of in our inheritance was referred to the blank savagery of outer lands at no matter what expense of tortured hypothesis or bold invention.   This warping of truth was indulged in because the northern part of Europe stood (in the nineteenth century when this false "Teutonic" school had its greatest vogue) for a successful opposition to the rest of Christendom, and for a schism within the body of civilized men.

But the worst fault of all, worse even than the superficial folly of Gibbon's tradition in our treatment of the great Christian foundation and worse than the Teutonic nonsense, was the misunderstanding of those four great centuries in which our race attained the summit of its happiness and stable culture—the twelfth, the thirteenth, the fourteenth and the fifteenth.   And of these, the greatest, the thirteenth, was in particular ignored.

Men did indeed (partly because it enabled them to "turn" the position of true history by concession to, partly from the unavoidable effect of, increasing historical knowledge) pay lip service in England, during the later part of the nineteenth century, to the greatness of the true Middle Ages.   In his early period, Ruskin is a conspicuous example of a writer who, without in the least understanding what the Middle Ages were like, hating yet ignorant of the faith that was their very soul, could not remain blind to the vivid outward effect of their expression.   Even Carlyle, far more ignorant than Ruskin and far more of a player to the gallery, could not altogether avoid the strong blast of reality which blew from those times.

But these concessions, these partial admissions, did but deepen the blindness of such historians and their readers towards the formation and the climax of our race ; upon the Dark and the Middle Ages, history as written in the English language was warped beyond recognition.

Then came the reaction towards historical truth : it has

already far advanced and the book for which I have the honour here to write a Preface is a notable example of that progress.

" History" (said the great Michelet in a phrase which I am never tired of repeating) " should be a resurrection of the flesh." What you need for true history is by no means an agreement with the philosophy of the time which you describe (you may be wholly opposed to that philosophy) but at least a full comprehension of it and an understanding that those who worked its human affairs were men fundamentally the same as ourselves. Humanity has not essentially differed from the beginning of recorded, or, indeed, of geological time. Man as man (the only thing which concerns history, or, indeed, the morals and philosophy of mankind) has been the same since first he appears fully developed upon the earth. But in the case of Western Europe during the Middle Ages the thing is far more intimate. We are dealing with men who are not only of our genus but of our very stock ; wholly of our particular blood, our own fathers, our own family. What is more, in those ancestors we should take our greatest pride. For never did our race do better or more thoroughly, never was it more faithfully *itself*, than in the years between the First Crusade and the effects of the Black Death : 1100-1350. Those three long lifetimes were the very summit of the European story.

Now I say that to treat properly of this affair it is not indeed necessary to agree with the philosophy of those men—that is, with their religion. It is certainly not necessary to agree with the details of their action, as, for example, their lapses into cruelty on the one hand or their fierce sense of honour on the other. We may be baser, or more reasonable, or more gentle, or more lethargic than they, and yet remain true historians of them. But what one must have if one is to be an historian at all, and not a mere popular writer, repeating what the public of "the best sellers" wants to have told to it, is a knowledge of the spirit of our ancestors *from within*.

Now this can only be obtained in one fashion, to wit, by accurate, detailed, concrete record. Find out *what* happened and say it. Proportion is of course essential ;

but to an honest man proportion will come of itself from a sufficient reading, and only a dishonest man will after a sufficient reading warp proportion and make a brief by picking out special points.

The trouble is that this period has been dealt with in the past without minute research. There has been plenty of pretence at such research, but most of it was charlatan.

Let me take as a specific instance by way of example:

Freeman's huge volumes upon the Norman Conquest were long treated as a serious classic. He pretended to have read what he had not read. He pretended to have studied ground he had not studied. He wrote what he knew would sell because it was consonant with what was popular at the time. He attacked blindly the universal Catholic religion of the epoch he dealt with because he hated that religion. But scholarly he was not and did not attempt to be; yet scholarly he pretended to be, and upon supposed scholarship he based his false representation. I will give three examples.

He calls the Battle of Hastings "Senlac." He found the term not where he pretends, in Ordericus Vitalis, but in Lingard, who was the first man to commit the error. Lingard was the great quarry from which Freeman's generation of Dons dug out its history without ever acknowledging the source. "*Senlac*" could not possibly be a Saxon place-name, but Freeman understood so little about the time and was so ignorant of the genius of the language, that he took it for Anglo-Saxon. Perhaps he thought in some vague way he was restoring a "Teutonic" name; more "Teutonic" than Hastings itself!

To this religious motive of his there was undoubtedly added the motive of novelty and of showing off. What the ridge of Battle was originally called by the people of the place, before the Norman invasion, we cannot tell. It may have been "Sandleg" (which would be Sussex enough), or it may have been "Senhanger," also sound Sussex, or it may have been something ending in the Celtic and Latin "lake." But "Senlac" it most certainly could not have been; and that Freeman should have pretended to scholarship in a matter of that kind damns him.

The second point is far more striking and can be tested

by anyone who visits the localities mentioned in the five principal contemporary authorities. He desires to reduce the numbers involved in the battle; partly from a silly prejudice against anything written by a monk, partly from a desire to belittle the actions of the early Middle Ages and the whole of its civilization, partly (mainly, perhaps) from a desire to be novel. He make up the estimates out of his head, grossly reducing the forces actually engaged.

We have contemporary evidence which allows for more than 50,000 men upon Duke William's side and something of the same sort upon Harold's. The evidence not only of those who saw William's host mustered and who must actually have handled the lists on the Norman side, such as the Duke's secretary, William of Jumièges, but the evidence of topography also proves this. Pevensey, the harbour in which the great Norman fleet of 3,000 vessels moored, was a vast expanse of water comparable to Portsmouth to-day; you may still trace its limits accurately enough round the contour of the present marsh. The position held defensively at Hastings by Harold's command is only just under a mile long and is one of the most clearly defined positions in Europe, absolutely unmistakable. Freeman, with no appreciation of military history, conceives this line of a mile (held by men closely interlocked and in dense formation capable of withstanding hurricanes of cavalry charges for nine hours) to have been held by a handful of men! It is the wildest nonsense, and yet it passed for a generation as history.

Lastly, as an example of bias and charlatanry combined, you have the confident statement that Pope Sylvester had given a Bull to Duke William in support of the invasion. Here Freeman has at least the grace not to give a sham reference in a footnote, for the thing is completely false. If Freeman had taken the trouble or had had the science to look up the Bullarium, or even the letters and documents of Sylvester in Migne, he might have been spared the contempt of all competent critics. As it is he preferred a legendary piece of nonsense in a piece of popular verse to exact history.

The motive through which Freeman invented this Bull was the motive of his place, time, and generation: hatred

of the Catholic Church, that is, against the religion of the
people with whom he was dealing, and a desire to satisfy
the animus of his Victorian readers against the Papacy.

In contrast to nonsense of this kind, haphazard, ill-
evidenced and invented history, note the admirable
description you will read in the following pages of the
battle of Muret.

Here is a real knowledge of ground and, what is more
important, *a careful estimate of time and movement.* I
know nothing better in the reconstruction of a mediæval
battle than this first-rate piecing together of evidence
through common sense upon the flanking surprise movement executed by Simon de Montfort against Foix's
division of the enemy at Muret. It is an unbreakable
chain of calculation, and at the same time a full explanation of what happened. This piece of work, in the fifth
chapter of the volume here presented to the reader, is as
good as anything can be of its kind, and an excellent
representative of that new, modern, accurate work now
ridding us of the loose stuff which encumbered history
through the past two generations. That is the way to
reconstruct a mediæval battle in the absence of detailed
evidence, to see the movements as they actually took
place.

I have laid emphasis on this particular section of the
book by way of contrast to the insufficiency of so typical
a name as Freeman's. I ought rather, perhaps, to turn
to the book as a whole and then again to certain other
specific points of excellence which have struck me.

Mr. Nickerson's study is mainly concerned with explaining the nature of the early Inquisition ; incidentally he
gives us a very clear view of the Albigensian War, and
what is especially remarkable in the clarity of his view is
the arrangement of the episodes. I note that the author
has done what is of first importance in all military
chronicling, and that is, the division of episodes *not*
in equal measures of time but by their separate military
characteristics.

It is a principle too often forgotten even by professional
military historians. A war may take twenty years, or fifty,
or one. It may, by accident, divide itself naturally into
two or three episodes of fairly equal length in time or
it may by coincidence fall into episodes corresponding

more or less with a successive series of years (e.g.,)
Marlborough's Campaigns in Flanders in the early eighteenth century). But much the greater part of military
history is concerned with episodes which have no relation
to such more or less equal time-chapters. The general
rule is that three or four successive phases of a campaign
(or battle) occupy the most disparate lengths of time.
The proper way to treat *military* history is to give to the
capital episodes their relative *military* importance; not, as
in the case of a civilian chronicle, to weigh that importance
by the time involved.

For instance, no one can read a clear account, however short, of the great European War without seeing it
as a siege; it is therefore, like every siege (not raised, nor
degenerated into a blockade) essentially divided into three
episodes :—

(*a*) The preliminaries of containment, that is the war
of movement prior to the establishment of siege conditions.

(*b*) The siege itself.

(*c*) The storming of the siege line and the collapse of
the besieged.

Now if we were to take the Great War in *years*—1914,
1915, 1916, 1917, 1918 would appear. If we divide it
into chapters of more or less equal lengths of time we have
a confused, meaningless picture such as is given us by
nearly all the popular histories as yet published of that
great event. However much these accounts succeed in
pleasing each its national audience they fail as histories
because they think a month of war must be thirty times
more important than a day and need thirty times as much
telling. The moment we divide the Great War according
to its *military* values the scheme falls into place and becomes clear. You have three divisions, of which you can
make, if you like, three volumes or three chapters. The
first is absurdly short in comparison with the length of the
whole. It only seriously begins with the great shock of
August 20, 21, 1914, in Lorraine and in Flanders, and it
ends when the Germans went to earth less than a month
later—on the Aisne. From that moment onward the
war was a siege.

Next you get the second division, the completion of
the siege lines in the West to the sea (which is over before

the middle of November, two more months), and then the solid three and a half years of effort on the part of the besieged to break out in great sorties and on the part of the besiegers to break down the defence of the besieged.

In mere length of time this episode is prodigious and includes all the better known stories of the war. It lasts for over forty-four months and sees the collapse of Russia; the first sorties of the besieged Prussian alliance through Poland; the tremendous efforts made by the Allies to break the enemy's siege-lines in Champagne, on the Somme, and in Flanders, on the Asiago plateau and on the terrible Carso Plateau in front of Trieste. It sees the failure of the attack on the siege wall at the postern of the Dardanelles, and even in remote Mesopotamia, as well as in the Balkans. It sees further great sorties, especially the violent struggles of the besieged at the end to get out of their net: Caporetto, St. Quentin, the Chemin des Dames. That second division ends on July 15, 1918, when the last effort of the besieged to get out was made against Gouraud and broken by him in front of Rheims. On July 18, 1918, three days later, the third division begins and lasts exactly four months to the Armistice on November 11. It is nothing but the successive breakdown of the defence, the crumbling of the siege wall and the collapse of the besieged.

See the Great War on these lines, and you see it clearly, as it was. Try to write of it by successive years, and you get nothing but a fog.

Now Mr. Nickerson has done exactly that right thing for the Albigensian War. He clearly divides the struggle into its *military* episodes; the first great rush; the long struggle of de Montfort; the curious but inevitable fruit of the whole business after de Montfort's death in the lapse of the South to the crown of France, that is to the North.

In this connection one cannot praise too highly the simple and clear fashion in which the author has presented to the reader the real nature of mediæval warfare. There are two points to be established in which, I think, he has been permanently successful. First, in making the reader understand the narrow limits of time to which any effective work on a large scale by a powerful army was then confined.   Secondly, the contrast between the feudal forces which were, as it were, normal to the times, and those supplementary mercenary forces, which, though they were not regarded by the time as normal, were the real backbone of all continuous military effort in the West.   It is an idea which one might develop in many epochs of military history besides the Middle Ages. Over and over again a particular form of recruitment is regarded as normal and after use for some generations begins from causes inherent in itself to yield insufficient results ; whereupon a supplementary form of recruitment, which for long continues to be regarded as exceptional, becomes, as the close observer may discover, the essential of the new fighting force, e.g., the Auxiliaries and the Legions after, say 180, and especially after 312.

It was one of the advantages of the English, by the way, in the later Middle Ages that the difficulty of transporting large feudal forces over the sea led to an early development of their mercenary forces and produced the highly trained professional bowmen who are the mark of the Hundred Years War.

Mr. Nickerson is also right in saying how considerable was the degree of military organization in the early thirteenth century.

Too often in military history anything earlier than the seventeenth century or the middle of the sixteenth is treated unscientifically by the writer, who seems to imagine that if he gets far enough back he can treat armies as herds moving about at random.   The truth is of course that no great body of men ever so moved or could be moved without a high degree of organization, and that when you are dealing with the *rapid movement* of a very large body the organization must be nearly as detailed as it is to-day.   There is a certain minimum of organization below which you cannot fall without breaking down, when it is a case of great bodies moving quickly ; and that minimum is so high that it does not vary very much between the very first epochs of recorded history and the latest.

The next point I have to notice is Mr. Nickerson's presentation both of the Inquisition as an *idea* and of the contrast between its *methods* and those of modern times.   The task undertaken is the most difficult of any that lies before the historian; yet it is also the most essential. The wrong way of dealing with the remote past when it presents acts or states of mind quite unfamiliar, and even repulsive to us, is to express horror or ridicule and leave it at that. Thus we have Mr. Davis in his typical Oxford textbook upon the Angevin period sneering at the massacre at Beziers as "pious butchery"; thus we have another typical Oxford textbook, Mr. Oman's, dealing with an earlier period, sneering at the piety of Gildas; and thus we have yet another textbook—from Cambridge this time—in which the Regius Professor of History, Dr. Bury, sneers at a vision of St. Patrick's as the result of a "pork supper."

Now that way of writing history, which is, I am sorry to say, still the common way in our English Universities, is worthless. Your business in writing of the past is to make the past comprehensible. More: you ought, as I quoted at the beginning of this, to make it rise from the dead; and that you certainly cannot do if you are so little able to enter into its spirit that everything in it which differs from yourself appears small, repulsive, or absurd. Anyone, however ignorant, can discover what is repulsive and absurd in standards different from their own; and one's learning, no matter how detailed, is wasted if one gets no further than that. The whole art of history consists in eliminating that shock of non-comprehension and in making the reader feel as the men of the past felt.

We have a very good example of the same difficulty in the case of travel-books. We all know how intolerably boring is a book of travel in which the writer can get no further than decrying or laughing at the foreigner, and we all know how the charm of a book of travel consists in its explaining to us, putting before us as a living and comprehensible thing, some civilization which at first sight seemed to us incomprehensible.

It is just the same with history. In the case of the Inquisition it is particularly difficult to make the modern reader understand the affair because all the terms have been, so to speak, transliterated; but I think we can arrive at a fairly satisfactory result if we translate the terms involved into things which the modern man is familiar with. Instead of physical torture, for instance,

read cross-examination and public dishonour; instead of
the sacrifice of all civic guarantees to the preponderant
interest of united religion, read the similar sacrifice of all
such guarantees to the preponderant interest of a united
nation; instead of clerical officers using every means (or
nearly every means) for the preservation of religious
unity, read civil officers using *every* means for the
preservation of national unity in time of peril. If you
do that, I think the modern man can understand. Had
you presented to the early thirteenth century the spectacle
of the whole male population medically examined,
registered, and forcibly drafted into a life where a chance
error might be punished immediately by death or by
some other terrible punishment; had you shown him
men, doubtful in their loyalty to the nation, condemned
to years of perpetual silence, secluded from their fellow
beings after being made a spectacle of public dishonour
in the Courts; had you even sketched for him our
universal spy system whereby a strong modern central
Government holds down all its subjects as no Government of antiquity, however tyrannical, ever held them
down—could you have shown a man of the thirteenth
century all this, he would have felt the same repulsion and
horror which most modern men feel on reading of the
Inquisition, its objects and its methods.

A man who should so explain our modern life to a man
of the thirteenth century as to make it *comprehensible* to
him (a difficult task!) in spite of his repulsion and horror
at our cruelties, blasphemies, and tyrannies, would be a
good historian. The converse also is true.

There are many special points in the book on the
consideration of which I would delay did space allow.
Thus my own knowledge of the time and place enables
me to make certain suggestions. I see that the author
inclines to the Cerdagne route for the march of Pedro of
Aragon. I should do more than incline—I should be
morally certain of it—at least on the evidence to our
hand; and that in spite of Pedro's presence at Lascuarre
in August. If, which is very unlikely, further evidence
comes forward, we may have to accept the Somport
sallent or even the Val d'Aran, but the more I think of
it, the more the latter seems to me out of the question.
I know the steep and dangerous approaches upon

either side, especially upon the Aragonese side. I consider the great difficulty of reaching them from the point
of concentration at Lerida. The Cerdagne is the one
really open road. It was the only easy pass of value
then to large armies ; as for the second pass, the
Puymorens, into the valley of the Ariege, it is perfectly
easy, a mere lift of land. I have crossed it a dozen times
under all conditions of weather. Again I would find it
most interesting to contrast the procedure even of the
late Inquisition with contemporary civilian procedure,
e.g., Torquemada's procedure with Henry VII's Judges
in a treason trial. It is to the advantage of the former.
Better still, a trial under Philip III and Cecil's Judges in
his carefully nursed Gunpowder plot.

But such detailed discussion of a hundred matters of
history raised in this book would unduly prolong what
is already too lengthy an introduction of a work to
which the reader must be anxious to turn.

Kings Land, Shipley,   H. BELLOC.
Horsham.

PREFACE.

By HILAIRE BELLOC.

IT is sufficiently clear to those who survey Europe in the mass and follow the full outline of their time, that our civilization must return to the Faith or be destroyed.

It is a conclusion arrived at in a hundred ways by observation, by instinct, by history. There stands in support of it the evident formation, insistent throughout the West, of growing intellectual superiority upon the Catholic side : so that to-day no-one is worthy to stand as an equal against the Catholic controversialist save that rare being the pure sceptic. We have to-day against the full and convincing system which Catholicism permanently presents, opponents, who, for the most part, do not know what they are attacking, and, therefore, in their attack can do little more than abuse. The moral and the intellectual tide of the *moment* is clearly with the return of that philosophy which is more than a philosophy ; that fulness in which alone the human spirit is at rest and the mind of man finds its home : that living thing which is called the Catholic Church : that Sufficient

v

Community which at the same time enfranchises, decides, and nourishes.

But this does not mean that our future contains the victory of the Catholic Faith. It means only that when or if the worn filaments of authority still binding non-catholic society together are torn, that tottering bundle will collapse : for so great, so complex, an organism as Christendom can only be bound by organic, and by inter-connected habits and ideas ; not by a few reluctantly admitted mechanical rules of property and of law, but by a communion in innumerable sanctities and certitudes. No idea or institution provides such a communion, or offers any organic support to society save one: The Catholic Church.

That the moral and intellectual forces of our time are clearly with the Catholic Church and increasingly so, does not mean that the Catholic Church will triumph. Frequently enough in human history, it is the barbarian that has killed the cultured man ; the half-educated, self-assured fool that has obscured to oblivion the ideals and the perceptions of his superiors.

It may be, then, that the inferior forces, the lesser intelligence, what the French call " The Primary Minds," the people nourished on " Universal Histories " and on the mythology of most uncertain guess-work in physics and in pre-history, will triumph at the expense of their betters, and that Europe will cease to be. It would then fall into that barbarism with which it has been threatened four times at least during its recorded history.

There are present to-day the makings of such
a catastrophe, and we all see them before us.
We can read them in those writings which sell
most widely, in the crudities of our demagogues,
and in the incapacity of our greatest leaders to
take any sufficient hold upon the mass.

The avenues whereby salvation can come to
men ; whereby the essentials of civilization can
be re-introduced to the declining social mind
about us ; whereby the increasing substitution
of affirmation for reason and of hypothesis
for knowledge can be checked, are many. One
of them, to my mind the most powerful, is the
historical : and it is the historical method which
is put forward in this book.

It is put forward so clearly that it needs no
praise and no criticism of its thesis. I would
only suggest this : that our reversion is not to
paganism, which we associate with that great
antiquity from which we sprang, and upon which
the Catholic Church itself is founded, but rather
a return by a short cut to savagery.

For though the parallel between our time and
that of Theodosius is accurate enough, yet there
is all the difference between a rising and a falling tide.

The main argument against the claims of the
Catholic Church, an argument which had very
great force with our highly cultured ancestors
of the eighteenth century, and which still held
the ground during the nineteenth, is the argument that Catholicism attended the breakdown
of the old civilization in the dark ages, and was
native to the insufficient knowledge of the middle

ages ; only as Faith weakened (we are told) did the modern conquests in the sciences appear.

I have called this set of propositions " an argument." It would have been more just to have called them an *attitude*. That was the *attitude* of our fathers. Since all cultural ideas gradually sink slowly down through the social strata, that is the attitude to-day of your popular " best-seller " in what may be called " Railway Bookstall history." It is the normal attitude of the half-educated man, who is to-day the active, as he has always been the potential, poison of society.

The answer to that argument, or rather attitude, is simple enough : the argument or attitude is historically false. The Catholic Church did not cause, nor even assent to, the material decline of civilization after the second century. The whole vigour and spring of the Catholic Church was derived from the very highest moment of antiquity, and it was the preservation of that vigour during the decline of a *non*-Catholic society which saved the world. It was the *conversion to the Faith of a society in peril of death which warded off that death*. It is further true that the fruition of the Catholic spirit led to an achievement, to a multitude and a magnitude in colour, in form, in device, in speculation, in the attaining of intellectual and moral certitude, in law and in all social institutions, which we still precariously enjoy to-day.

Here is the truth which must be rubbed in if we are to change the attitude of our opponent. Especially does primary education suffer every-

where from the anti-Catholic legend. Even they
of the Faith, for the most part, take that legend
for granted ; especially in countries such as our
own where the Catholic culture is known only to
very few and where the Catholic tradition has
been broken. The Catholics themselves in such
circumstances boast of any special Catholic action
in any field of learning as though it were an
exception to be singled out. They accept the
hostile interpretation of the Catholic past which
is in the air around them. They measure contemporary national values by the false standards
set them, conceiving, for instance, that Prussia
is a success and Italy a failure.

The task of reversing that anti-Catholic system
is the hardest of all modern tasks. Yet must it
be undertaken ; for, although the most profound
and the most active agent of change must always
be spiritual action upon the individual, yet corporate action upon the mass is essential ; and
to-day *history* will act there as nothing else
can do. In *history* we must abandon the defensive. We must carry the war into Africa.
We must make our opponents understand not
only that they are wrong in their philosophy,
nor only ill-informed in their judgment of cause
and effect, but out of touch with the past :
which is ours.

PREFACE

MISS BUCKLEY has very kindly asked me to write a word or two of introduction to her thorough and scholarly thesis upon the public life of my grandfather Joseph Parkes, of Birmingham. I do so with the greatest pleasure, though with little ability and no desire to add anything to the details, nor even to the general impression, of her work. A family tradition, which preserves whatever was living about a man of energy and influence, may also distort; and I should fear, if I said anything intimate of my grandfather's memory, that I might seem to exaggerate his place in the formative time through which he lived and which he did so much to mould. The absence of publicity (which his survivors thought strange enough) is easily explained. Men are sharply divided into those attracted and those repelled by publicity. He hated it. His appetite was for achievement, and this he enjoyed beyond his own expectations. For he lived to see in the early half of a most active life the triumph of social theories which for him and his contemporaries were a burning creed, and to pass the later half in an England which had come into an apparently permanent state of security and wealth at home, supremacy abroad. His patriotism, which grew in concentration as his life advanced, was satisfied; his own deserved prosperity in his profession contributed to such a mood, and he died one of those who end in content. He did not live—he could not have survived—to see the great change in all this, but especially in the nature of those political institutions to whose health and continuance he had given his life. During my own membership and close examination of the House of Commons in its present state I remembered the contrast daily: and knew what he would have made of such a revolution. He was happier still in that he died when the international position to which his country had risen seemed eternal. Such men of such a stock, long centuries of free yeomanry moulding them, still move among us: healthy in frame and intelligence, direct, sure of their principles, with his own vivid yet contained strength of feature and his own integrity and humour. But they no longer affect the State, nor ever, I think, will now again affect it. They were once its prime factors. To-day their servants have some blind power. The gentry with which and under which they worked is dissolved, and a new Plutocracy, of which Joseph Parkes could not have dreamed, is master. But I still find it some consolation to remember that, not so long ago, there was here a society consonant to such men as he.

H. BELLOC

KING'S LAND
HORSHAM
March 1926

INTRODUCTION.

By HILAIRE BELLOC.

Mr. Albery has done a particularly useful work in thus compiling a Parliamentary History of Horsham.

There remains in departments of this kind a vast field still to be explored, and nothing can be of more service to English History as a whole than the faithful examination and publishing of local records, especially when the work is done, as in this case, with sound judgment in selection and presentation.

England is particularly rich in documents upon which such work can be based. They exist (much of the same type throughout Western Europe until the seventeenth century) in all the other countries of Christendom. But this country has been especially fortunate in the absence of disturbance by invasion on a large scale or by violent civil war. What are called the Civil Wars in our history are no more than small and fairly orderly operations conducted by well-to-do leaders without any element of destructive social unrest. The only losses on any serious scale we have to deplore are the great sacrifice of manuscripts in the dissolution of the monasteries and the struggle against the old learning in the Universities, together with the exceptional local but important case of the Great Fire of London under Charles II. The latter was, I believe, the only example in our later history of any loss of civil record on a large scale ; the former undoubtedly caused grievous loss of chronicles and of classical texts, but did not, presumably, greatly affect detailed local record of the civic kind.

iii

On this account it is possible for an Englishman devoted to the history of his own town to make, as a rule, a fuller compilation than a Foreigner can, and this characteristic of English historical work is of the highest service to men's understanding of their own country.

For instance, in this book of Mr. Albery's, how clearly we grasp the truth that a common name and title corresponds to utterly different institutions in varying times.

The term " House of Commons " meant at first—that is from the end of the thirteenth century onwards for about 300 years or a little less—a body of fairly well-to-do townsmen and local squires who were sent up, not at all as an honour nor to their liking, to the neighbourhood of the King's Court at irregular intervals, there to be detained in the irksome business of deciding how much the places from which they came could pay, not in the way of *normal* or regular taxation (that was allowed for by custom and needed no grant), but for exceptional and novel taxes. Their presence came gradually to be required also in confirmation of important laws. They were allowed to petition, but they had nothing to do with the main Government of the Country or with the framing of the new statutes ; still less with the general policy of the State on which they were heard only in grave crises or on petty details usually connected with the taxes arranged for.

Then comes the great and rapid change of the later sixteenth and earlier seventeenth centuries. The House of Commons becomes, almost suddenly—well within a lifetime— the organ of the newly-enriched wealthy classes which are determined to destroy the old power of the Crown. By the end of the seventeenth century it has taken on the full function of Government and is typical of that aristocratic State which England had then become. A seat in the House of Commons is henceforward a most valuable possession leading to great salaries in the legal profession and in public life, to all manner of opportunities for acquiring commercial and landed wealth, and for other direct forms of power.

It is not till quite modern times that the idea of exact

representation emerges—largely under the influence of the French Revolution. The old conception was that a locality must have some one to speak for it in the National Assembly, not that the nation as a whole was voting and declaring by a majority which way its feeling lay on any disputed question. Hence the bewildering diversity of town franchise, in which the men of the past saw no anomaly or injustice : although in one town the vote was with pretty well every household, and others with the corporation, in others with a compara-tively small number of people holding burgess right as here in Horsham, where for generations fifty-two was the fixed number, only slightly increased in later times.

You may read in Mr. Albery's pages how comparatively late was the idea of a contested election, and too, how even more modern is the idea of an election representing any par-ticular party or interest.

The truth is that all our way of thinking in the House of Commons to-day, what it stands for to us, and the part which it plays in our economy is a recent thing in the history of England.

It is most interesting to note that Horsham appears as a Borough sending two Burgesses to Parliament at the very origin of the English House of Commons in what has been called by recent historians "The Model Parliament of 1295." We have the names of the first two members, Walter Randolph and Walter Burgeys.

This body came late in the story of European parliaments, 200 years later than the first gathering of the kind in Aragon, and later than the corresponding bodies in the south of France from which Simon de Montfort derived his model. But it has had the fortune, unlike its fellows abroad, of maintaining an unbroken continuity till our own day.

There are many points in Mr. Albery's admirable and ex-haustive study which I should have liked to have touched on had space permitted me. Thus the reader will note the characteristic change which comes with the cessation of payment for Members' expenses and services when their presence had ceased to be a task and had become a privilege. He will also read with the highest interest the story of the struggle between the local aristocratic interests which began with the eighteenth century and continued long after the reform. He will be particularly struck, I think, with the contrast between election to-day and election as it was within the memory of all elderly people while Horsham still retained its separate representation. Though I have not space to go into this and the many other points that give this book its value, I hope I have said enough to recommend it heartily to what I am sure will be his large circle of readers.

H. BELLOC.

KINGSLAND, SHIPLEY,
NR. HORSHAM, 3rd August, 1926.

PREFACE

MANY years ago I was walking with a friend through Burgundy.

We came down off the high hills into a lovely valley, with pastures along the banks of a little river and with lines of spinneys bordering those meadows.

Upon the edge of one of these, where the shorn turf and the trees met, two old gate-posts of stone (with no gates left between them) flanked a somewhat neglected earthen road which led through the wood to a house once noble and still majestic, but now half ruined and bare and held as a farm.

As we were looking at this side of the old house—the woodland, the meadows and the high hills all around—we noticed with pleasure and astonishment a strange piece of stonework lurking in the tall weeds and brambles to the side of the way. It was a statue of I know not what date, but ancient, set upon its little pedestal, not mutilated though much worn by time: the effigy of some monk or other, singularly living, but powerfully restrained and not at all of our time.

While we were looking at it, the man who owned the place came up to us and we talked to him of our journey and our destination, of the beauty and fertility of his countryside. We asked him what this old statue might be. He was a strong-faced, weather-beaten old man, vastly interested in his

5

land : "And as to the statue," he said with indifference, " they call it St. Bernard ; it is very old."
Then he shrugged his shoulders and asked us into
the house where we drank *marc* with him and then
went our way.

. . . . . .

The classical spirit has not fallen into disrepute
among us : it has been forgotten. It has become
alien and strange, so that men coming across it
to-day, in our society, are like rustics coming across
some marble of the ancients. It does not repel
them, but it hardly attracts them at all—they can
make nothing of it.

That reaction against the classical spirit, which
began in England with the turn of the eighteenth
century and the opening of the nineteenth, the
romantic extravagance, the search for violent
sensation, the test of poetry by poignancy, the loss
of measure, provoked elsewhere a fairly strong
resistance and, before long, a reaction.

Here, neither resistance nor reaction came.
The romantic expansion in England ran its whole
course like a wave getting more violent as it spreads
into shallower water. Men ceased to attempt profound effect within a convention or to excel within a
set framework ; or, rather, such as did attempt the
great traditions of that mood failed lamentably.
Blank verse was written—Tennyson excelled in it
a score of times—but the rhythms were new and,
above all, the vision was strained. There was no
success in the rhymed heroic iambic pentameter
at all—not even by Swinburne. But, much more

6

important than the manner, the matter of classical creation had gone : the spirit of it. To be more accurate, one should say perhaps that that spirit was to be found occasionally reappearing in certain great lyrics, never upon a large scale and, even in these, only rarely. The poise, the fulness, the solemnity, the disdain of sharp effect, the glory in control, the magic of proportion—all these were no longer conceivable.

It is said that men who drink spirits lose their taste for wine and certainly men who use violent sauces lose their taste in cooking. Under the effect of the romantic extravagance, the general sense of the classic died. But the last extravagances of that extravagance were left for our time to suffer. It is within the lifetime of men now middle-aged that there arose such strange conceptions as that verse could not be profound if it were lucid and that a miracle in words must be sought either (as in the tradition of Wordsworth) by an affectation of the absolutely common, or—what is even worse—by an affectation of the unusual.

I have found in Miss Pitter's verse, which I here set out to praise, an exceptional reappearance of the classical spirit amongst us. It is as odd to come upon such an excellence to-day as it is to find sustained irony or the noble rhythms of sixteenth century prose. It seems to me even unique. I know of no other contemporary example.

To get your rhythmic effect without emphatic lilt ; to be subtle in your management of results without any apparent complexity ; to be an artist without

7

showing your art, is a thing pretty well unknown amongst us to-day—I except Mr. Housman.

Meanwhile, the writers who will be read at all costs, through their patriotism or any other popular and worthy sentiment, through deliberate absurdity and mountebank tricks, through the use of obscenity or of cruelty or of panic or of blasphemy or of mere inversion of morals increase enormously ; but, as they increase in number, they tend to a complete exhaustion.

For it is of the nature of Art that, when it forgets limit and measure, it piles excess upon excess, reaching out towards unattainable expressions of emotion, and becoming in that attempt first ridiculous, then null. It is as when a singer concerns himself not with the beauty of his song but with the attainment of some impossibly high note or some impossibly loud noise. There is soon an end to that. It is a spending of capital.

It may be objected against the classical spirit that its higher expression is continuously achieved only by very few and that all those who are inspired by it are in danger of dulness in patches ; to which it may be answered that the opposite of the classic positively forbids sustained success ; it depends on occasional sharp lines, and the rest of what its votaries see fit to publish is often dull, but always pitiful. The classical spirit may be compared to a building of squared stone in which there may be an excess of empty unornamented space, though all is satisfying and solid ; the romantic, to those buildings which are a conglomerate of shining ornament and rubble.

8

When I first read Miss Pitter's verse in the *New Age*, some little time before the Great War, I said to myself, " This is a resurrection of what people have forgotten. This bears the authentic mark and it will tell." I was too charitable to my generation ! The first volume appeared and fell dead. The later poems could not be published till now ; and I ask myself as I write these lines whether their beauty will be understood or no ? Abroad, with the very restricted audience which follows English work, her reputation is established. In her own country it is yet to come.

It is customary to say that good verse must of its nature survive and establish itself in men's minds. I have often repeated that judgment myself. At a time of life when men commonly begin to despair of ultimate justice, I am still of that opinion. Really good verse, contrasted with the general run of that in the midst of which it appears, seems to me to have a certain quality of *hardness ;* so that, in the long run, it will be discovered, as a gem is discovered in mud. I say that I still believe the ancient doctrine to be true and the forces of excellence and of the Muse to be, in the long test of years, invincible.

But we live in a time and place where the handicap is very severe. The numbers of those who know good verse when they see it is far smaller in England to-day than ever it has been in England of the past—and it is rapidly diminishing. It is laughable to pretend that those few millionaires who control our press have the least conception of it. Some few pre-servers of tradition remain among the diminishing

9

number of those who care for beauty ; but their influence also is sinking to nothingness.

However, for such as still love beauty, I beg humbly to present it here.   Here is beauty and right order, singularly apparent in the midst of such a moral welter as perhaps no society of men ever yet suffered.

I have no faith in the attempt to demonstrate beauty.   You can no more demonstrate it nor impose an appetite for it than you can impose a taste in physical things or demonstrate their excellence. So I will conclude in the old fashion, by a mere comparison.   I will take in contrast to Miss Pitter two writers of verse each typical of our day for very different reasons.   I will take one writer very widely read and choose what is a fair example of his popular style :   I will take another writer who is widely talked of and choose a fair example of her characteristics.   I will then set down a few lines from the pen for which I have written this introduction.

Here are the three extracts :

The first is from the poetic works of Miss Sitwell :

> " I bring Branches green with Dew
> And fruits that you may crown anew
> Your whirring waspish gilded hair
> Amid the Cornucopia."

The second is from those of Mr. Kipling :

> " My son, said the Norman Baron, I am dying and you will
> be heir
> To all the broad acres in England that William gave me
> for my share
> When we conquered the Saxon at Hastings, and a nice
> little handful it is ;
> But before you go over to rule it, I want you to under-
> stand this."

10

The third from the book to which I write this preface :

" With his red beak and marble plume
Uttering his wild, his pulsant cry,
The Swan into the wild did fly.
Into the fiery dawn rode he,
And many burning cherubim
That know the face of the Most High
In godlike flight did go with him."

Now that all standards have gone and that society is but a dust, every reader must judge for himself. For my part, I prefer the third.

H. BELLOC.

11

PREFACE

I DO not know why I should have undertaken to write a Preface for Mr. Wyndham Lewis' *Villon*. It was a presumption, and one which perhaps I ought not to have made. I am putting these few words introductory to a work of great scholarship and research wherein the author has discovered all that Villon was, within and without. I myself can pretend to no such scholarship. I have no more position in the matter than that of the man of general education who from early youth has felt an unchanging admiration for that distinctive and typical voice of the later Middle Ages and of its France. All I could do was to put, as best I may, the effect produced by Villon upon myself; and what I believe to be the essentials of his greatness: though in this I know that I have no standing, and that Mr. Wyndham Lewis' work is there to tell the reader a hundred times more than I can.

Villon, as it seems to me, attained at once the very high place he took, has increased in the scale of European letters, stands higher now even than he did in the height of the Romantic movement, and will in the future (if we retain our culture—which is a big "If") appear as one of the very few unquestioned permanent summits in Western letters, through the quality of *hardness*.

Mr. Wyndham Lewis says it in this book (p. 297) in three words: *"clarity: relief: vigour:"*—and these are the marks of hardness: of the hard-edged stuff: the surviving.

They say that when men find diamonds in primitive fashion, they scrouch and grope in thick greasy clay till they come upon something *hard,* quite different in material from its surroundings; *that* is the stone. In the monuments of Europe, when they fall into

ix

ruin, there survive here and there what seem almoſt imperishable things; it is marble, it is granite which survives.

Now in letters the simile applies. I heard it well said by a great critic weighing one of the beſt of our modern versifiers (and "the beſt" is not saying much), that he liked the ſtuff well enough, but that it had no chance of survival because it was "carved in butter": an appreciation profound and juſt. It is with the production of verse as with the chiselling of a material. You handle a little figure of the fourteenth century in boxwood; it is smooth, ſtrong and perfeĉt. So is the cut oak of the medieval ſtalls. But the pine has perished.

Now this quality of hardness in any poet or writer of prose is difficult or impossible to define—more easy to feel.

It is to be discovered by certain marks which are not the causes of it, but are its accompaniments. Of these the chief is what the generation before our own used to call "inevitableness": the word coming in answer (as it were) to the appeal of the ear: the conviĉtion, when you have read the thing, that the leaſt change deſtroys it; the corresponding conviĉtion of unity through perfeĉtion.

Villon has that. There are times when he seems to have arrived at it by heavy ſtrain of search, "working the verse," as the French say. More often it seems to have come to him with what our fathers called "inspiration"—and after all, that is the beſt word. But everywhere in Villon, sought by him or discovered by him, you find it.

There goes with this, and is inseparable from it, a run, a sequence, which is not smoothness, but which is a sort of linking or leading on without the leaſt threat of dislocation; that also is a mark of hardness. Further, carving in hard matter is alive with the power of economy, which most certainly is not an economy of excision, but the economy of direĉt speech. And that again you find in Villon everywhere. He puts into a phrase all that could be said to ſtrike home:

Paradis paint, ou sont harpes et lus.

Or:

Sire, et clarté perpetuelle.

x

And again:

Emperiere des infernaux palus.

And again:

Helas! et le bon roy d'Espaigne
Duquel je ne sçay pas le nom?

Take the most famous, the Ballad of the Dead Ladies. Look how exact and immediate are the subsidiary phrases, the sharp arrowpoint of

Qui beaulté ot trop plus qu'humaine?

or the rise and swell of

Berte au grant pié, Bietris, Alis,
Haremburgis qui tint le Maine.

It will be said that this intensity of style—for that is "hardness" —does not alone make up a poet. The criticism is just. It is but the manner of the poet; were he not a poet no manner could save him. But still it is the manner which preserves his achievement.

As for the matter, Villon has, being French, that supremely national acquaintance with the grandeur and bitterness of reality, and therefore the power of jesting with it; bitter sometimes, sometimes sombre, and sometimes almost genial. And he has what goes with the bold appreciation of reality, the refuge in beauty, and the natural (not weak) refuge in affection. But of these last he is a little afraid—wherein again he is national.

If you desire one word to use as an antithesis to the word sentimental, use the word Villon.

Now apart from all this, Villon is also the ending of the Middle Ages. The verse is the living voice of a man speaking right out of fifteenth-century Paris, as though you heard him at your elbow. But were I to follow up the fascination of the historical, of the picture from the past, I should make this Preface much too long— with kennels and gables, spires, black icy water, Paris under a snowy winter of Louis XI. Since I must not make this Preface too long, nor keep you from your author, I will end.

HILAIRE BELLOC.

INTRODUCTION

W<small>HY</small> do men climb mountains? You may put the question more particularly: why did Englishmen begin to climb mountains in the nineteenth century and turn the effort into a national pastime; to be taken up wholesale and soon copied–but in far smaller numbers–by other Europeans, notably by Italians?

There is no answer except that a certain emotional wave passed over the English mind in those two generations, a wave the force of which is not yet spent. It was a mood under which those who felt it sought adventure under particular conditions.

Men have loved adventure in all places and times: that is, they have loved a combination of novelty and risk because these two quicken them, and commonly they have added a third element, the pursuit of gain or glory.

But the particular conditions of adventure to the Englishman in the nineteenth century were new. Security and wealth had led it into the form of a game; a game may be defined as conflict without anger or mutual killing or wounding between the combatants, and this the Englishman of the nineteenth century passionately developed.

Mountaineering was among the finest of these games. It had all the elements. It had danger, exhilaration, novelty, discovery, competition, and a peculiarly definite object. A hill has some highest point. If it seems impossible to reach that one point there is a clear challenge, and the spirit of which I speak at once responds.

To all this in mountaineering there is added landscape–the sense of which is peculiarly strong in the mood of adventure. The sense of landscape developed in modern England to a degree it had never reached in our ancestors. It was at its height–especially in English lyric poetry–during the same years as saw the maturity of English mountain climbing.

There were two things attendant on this modern English spirit of " the game," one good, one evil. The good one was glamour. That intense imagination which is a mark of the insular character in these Atlantic lands got hold of the game, and shed its coloured light powerfully over the sport of climbing. Climbs became epic and heroic in their narration; the recital of them was like the recital of Ballads. They became classical in the memory. How many of our generation can remember the delight of their boyhood in Whymper's *Scrambles*, with its pictures of the great hills?

The evil thing was mechanical complexity. The game took on a technique, acquired a long vocabulary, developed a mass of special instruments, and was always in peril of death through such relations: for a game grown professional and out of reach ceases to be a game.

This evil thing is at its worst in the sport of sailing. But at its least in climbing. Why climbing should be freer from it than, say, boxing or golf, I don't know—perhaps because its conditions are at once simpler than others, infinitely varied, and success more dependent on character than on skill acquired by mere repetition. Perhaps also because of its nature it cannot absorb a man's whole activities. It is a seasonal and spasmodic thing: not a continuous occupation.

Anyhow, there it is, and this record of a gallant attempt upon Mount Kenya is a shining example of it and answers for you, not by a definition but in experience, the question " Why do men climb mountains? " and especially " Why do Englishmen do so? "

In the narrative two points—among very many—particularly impressed me as I read them. One was the description of the point at which the effort was turned back; the other was the passage on the native sense of mystery and evil magic in these African wilds.

For the first, it reads better than a success. It makes one understand the heaviness of the task and the peculiar courage of the author in undertaking it. The description of the Diamond Glacier, which was not reached but seen and judged, is as though one had seen it with one's own eyes; as is that of the chasm which foiled the expedition and its " Gendarme " rock.

That word "gendarme," by the way, reminds the reader of another point in the story of English mountaineering: its new vocabulary is French, because the pioneers entered on their first tasks through France into French-speaking Switzerland. The Crevasse, the Glacier, the Pénitente, the Couloir, the Chimney, the Arête, all spring from that origin. Their survival would bear witness to the way the thing grew, even if all record of it was lost. And there is a parallel in the vocabulary of Geology in which

xii

the English were also Pioneers: " Devonian," " Silurian," mark the springs of that Science and its place of national origin.

The second matter, peculiarly impressive to me as I read, was that of the native appreciation of spiritual influence in material things. We have always heard of it, of course. Africans are specially profound in this sense—usually in its connection with horror.

All evidence of such things is of the deepest interest, and here there is evidence of an especially sharp and arresting sort. I mean the passage in the eleventh chapter on Omens and the evil Wood.

These things I have always taken to be real. I do not mean that a particular statement on Enchantment or a Shrine or a maleficent influence is necessarily true—on the contrary much the greater part of them are man-made illusions, just as most gods are false. But I mean that the general statement is true. There are influences beneficent and malicious, attaching to material things, and who is likely to recognize them better than those who dwell among them? We can lose our sense of such primary things by dissipation of value in town life and reading print and perpetual disturbance. So we can lose our sense of smell by too much smoking or our taste for wine by too much whisky. But it doesn't follow that the first sense did not emerge to a reality—and for my part I have never doubted either the good or evil influences underlying trees, rocks, and wells. There are gods also below the earth.

H. BELLOC.

King's Land,
  Shipley, Horsham.

FOREWORD

Reform Club,
Pall Mall, London, S. W.

My dear Father O'Connell:

Newman's Apologia has had an effect upon the world both greater than might have been expected and also of a different sort from what he himself would have expected. The book bears the character which you so often find in work that makes for the strengthening of the Catholic Faith, that it is an instrument in the hand of some other than its author.

In what then lies the peculiar effect of this book? In what its value?

Here any man may interrupt me and say, "In the style. Newman wrote a marvellous English. That accounts for the effect."

Now I admire to the very limits of admiration the prose style of the great Cardinal, and I think I may say without impertinence why I admire it, and that I have a right to admire it; for prose I would always distinguish from rhetoric. Lucidity—that is (a) knowing what you have got to say (b) saying it (c) so writing that what you intended is exactly reflected in the mind of the reader—lucidity is the test of prose. Now I turn over and over again to that book of Newman's written in his early vigor, "The Arians of the Fourth Century," and am lost in astonishment at the admirable quality of the prose. Here is a man writing upon a subject which only a few scholars consider; which has nothing in itself of general interest; which involves a quantity of tedious detail, yet the diction is such that it carries you on like a river, without effort: an amazing achievement.

If this be true of that book, how much more true must it be of the Apologia, written on what was a burning question of the time and round about what will be a matter of strong interest for ever—the approach of one mind towards the Catholic Church.

Yes, the Apologia of Newman conquers by its style, yet its style is far from being the main cause of its profound effect, its present (and increasing) position in European letters and in the story of our civilization. Its style alone, nay, its mat-

vii

ter alone, would not have achieved these things. What has achieved them?

The place of the Apologia is due to the fact that it puts conclusively, convincingly, and down to the very roots of the matter, the method by which a high intelligence, not only Anglican but of Oxford, and from the heart of Oxford, accepted the Faith.

It is one of the myriad converging proofs of Catholic Truth that its appeal is multiform. From its beginnings men appreciated that. It is all bound up in the story of Whitsuntide (in the octave of which this is written). One man and woman thus, another man, another woman in a wholly different way, from attitudes most adverse, from positions each, in the eyes of an opponent, impossibly hostile, repeats the famous words, "My Lord and my God."

Of all angles from which a man could approach that central reality of this world, which is called the Faith, of all points of departure from which the midmost of the sphere could be reached, Newman's was the most astonishing. Hence I think the effect, hence the excitement roused by his act, hence the stunning effect of his famous explanation. Not only did he come out of Anglicanism, but out of that very quintessence of all that Anglicanism meant—Oxford; and out of the quintessence of that quintessence; out of the pulpit of St. Mary's, the University Church.

Today, mainly on account of Newman himself, we are accustomed to the conception of a struggling, attempted compromise between things so helplessly antagonistic as Anglicanism and the Faith.

In Newman's time it was not so. The contrast was prodigious, the effort at unity, as it were, unnatural. True, there had been strong stirring because the high intellect of England had never completely acquiesced in the political arrangements of the sixteenth century. Long before Pusey and the rest began their reinterpretation of Protestantism in pseudo-Catholic terms, there had come from men still unknown appreciations of the truth. I have in my own library a very remarkable book (written at Oxford also) dating from long before the Tractarians; it is called "Sacramental Absolution at Oxford." It is a book racy, humorous, full of energy, delightful to read and, I am afraid, quite forgotten. It ought to be reprinted.

But, though things were thus stirring, not only was the overt act on Newman's submission to the church enormous; it was also revolutionary. You may potter about as much as you like with "isms" and half-truths and compromises, and all will be well; but make the great declaration of the Faith and you are in for martyrdom. Moreover, you strike a note quite different from anything the compromisers have ever heard before.

But all this requires an explanation. For to the great mass of the English-speaking world (a false category by the way— a common language is not a principle of unity, as is a common philosophy) the nature of Anglicanism is unknown, and Oxford is but a name. Let me try to explain both these terms. I have lived among them all my life and know something of them.

When the new millionaires of the sixteenth century, who had built their sudden enormous fortunes upon the loot of religion (with the Cecils at their head) puzzled how they might make those fortunes secure, they had to deal with the fact that the England of Elizabeth was a Catholic England. The anti-Catholic minority was less than it is today in numbers, in power far less, than it is in Italy or even in Ireland. But the quarrel between Reformers and Traditionalists (many among the latter being slack supporters of corruption) had not yet crystallized into two opposing religious camps. Thus many bishops of the French church were asking for the Mass in the vernacular, a delegate from the French monarchy had suggested the marriage of the clergy. All was still in flux.

The new millionaires under the guidance of the Cecils (Elizabeth had no real power) determined on two things; *first,* to make the change as vague as possible and as elastic as possible, (subject always to their determination that the Mass and the full Catholic spirit should not return, lest they lose their plunder); *secondly,* to use as a weapon against the Universal Church the particular and local spirit of patriotism. Hence what is called in England the National Establishment, that is, the Church of England.

It is not a body of doctrine (it has never professed any body of doctrine with definition); it is a National Institution, exclusive of the Catholic Church and particularly of the central rite of the Mass because these are universal and not local.

National feeling and the National Church were inextricably combined. The Catholic of the sixteenth century was the man who had asked help of the foreigner against his fellow citizen; the Catholic today is made to feel that he is an alien. This was the ardent emotion out of which Newman came. Let no one imagine that the English Established Church is a mere "Episcopalian sect." Its numbers even on the widest definition include but a small minority of the people, but every Englishman thinks of it as a national thing, and his. Every Englishman not a Catholic strongly affirms his right (as we have seen during the recent discussion on the Prayer Book) to have his say upon this English thing: part of his possessions.

Men must worship something, and this religion of patriotism was the religion out of which all Newman's training came. What an awful decision to break ties like these!

If it be true that Anglicanism is the expression of English patriotism in religion, Oxford is, as I have called it, the very quintessence of Anglicanism: not of doctrines, for there are no doctrines, save repudiation of the Catholic Church. A man may deny the Resurrection, the Incarnation or what he will, so that he remain national and deny the Universal Church. Oxford means the very heart of this national thing, the Church of England.

Now Newman was not only of Oxford, nor only in Oxford; he was, if one may use the metaphor, Oxford itself. He trembled with delight in his membership of this essentially anti-Catholic body; and when I say "essentially anti-Catholic" I mean the very word I use—"essentially." Not adventitiously, not as one out of many attributes, but as the very idea that makes Oxford what it is, you will there find opposition to the Catholic Church; to Ireland, to Poland, to Catholic culture as a whole, to Catholic history, to Catholic morals.

Out of all that came Newman. To have been an undergraduate at Oxford College was his happiest memory. To be elected a Fellow of an Oxford College his proudest moment. He lived within an extremely narrow Oxford circle, responding vividly to its every function. He was Oxford as Jane Austen was of the drawing room or Dickens of London. Even those parallels are not nearly strong enough. He was Oxford as Foch is of the French Army or as an intensely loving husband and father is of his own family.

Hence, not consciously at all, the "Branch Theory" of the English Church arose to save, if it might be, the Catholic spirit, in what of its nature exists for the destruction of Catholicism.

And out of that Newman came! And in what suffering!

Truly it may be said that they who bear witness are martyrs always.

The Apologia was written against a man, Kingsley, who had made an accusation which would not have galled in any other surrounding as it did in those surroundings. He had accused Newman of falsehood and insincerity. A Catholic from almost anywhere else in Europe than from Oxford would have laughed aloud at accusations of insincerity from the peculiar atmosphere of the English Church. Not so Newman. Newman well understood the penetrative power of that accusation in England. He knew to the quick the impact against which he must defend himself. We know what the re-action was. It produced the great, the strongly founded book, standing stronger after so many years, which the reader has here before him.

Almost for the first time Newman compelled his generation to the use of exact reason. Almost for the first time in the long controversies whereof his audience had heard but confused affirmations, he threw the enemy upon the defensive; and since the time when he so acted the effect of his counter attack has spread over wider and wider circles.

And here it is that I must conclude with the universal effect of the book. Of the Anglican Church Europe knows little and cares less, and will know still less and care still less as its dissolution proceeds. Of Oxford, European civilization as a whole takes no account, regarding it today for what in the main it is, a playground for rich young men, and certainly not the same kind of thing, nor even the tolerated equal of Paris or Leipsig or any other of the great universities of our time.

Yet over all Europe the effect of the Apologia continues increasing even beyond that of the noble "Grammar of Assent."

Such is the power of three things combined, interest in reality, an ardor to defend reality, use of the reason for the defense of reality. The appetite, the task, the weapon, the three between them are most worthy of a man.

Yours,

May 20, 1928

FOREWORD BY HILAIRE BELLOC

I first knew Margaret Douglas in connection with the agitation against the Insurance Bill in the year 1911. Until the introduction of this Bill (which had been ordered of the politicians by the great Capitalist monopolies, and especially by those Insurance companies which deal with the poorer classes) all Englishmen were equal in the sight of the law. But under this Bill a new political principal was introduced which created two classes of Englishmen: one class of poorer men who were to be subjected to a whole complicated machinery of registration and supervision: another much smaller class, the well-to-do people, who escaped. It was the first piece of servile legislation England had known, though much more of the same sort has been built upon that foundation. There was a universal and violent protest made against the Bill, and Margaret Douglas threw herself with characteristic energy and intelligence into the struggle against it. From that time we often worked together. She concentrated particularly upon the interference with the freedom of domestic service and the exceedingly unpopular and novel thrusting-in of officials between the various members of one household. In her courageous pursuit of this line she had rightly discovered the weakest point in the armour of our opponents. For while the ordinary industrial worker had no one to act for him, those in domestic service were supported by their employers who detested this latest manifestation of bureaucracy.

There was a moment when it looked as though Mar-

39

garet Douglas might possibly succeed in her effort. She organised great meetings, one in particular of exceptional attendance in the Albert Hall, which was packed to overflowing, and where I had the honour of speaking. She also organised provincial meetings all over the place. I spoke with her at Dover and sundry places in my own county of Sussex, in the suburbs of London, and, I think at Reading. But my work unfortunately prevented me from attending more than a fraction of the meetings which her untiring devotion to the popular cause had summoned.

The last one we spoke at together was at Portsmouth. By that time we had both of us come to the conclusion that the opposing forces were too strong to be defeated and the organised force of Capitalism would win. It was a melancholy conclusion, but inevitable in a society where there was no tradition of popular resistance to the rule of the rich. I remember our last talk about it in my house in Sussex, where she had come to stay, and the rather sad interest with which my wife and she and I discussed what ultimate good might result from an attempt which had failed.

Those who devote themselves wholeheartedly to the public good in spite of the appalling and increasing corruption of the times in which we live were rare in those pre-War days, and are to-day even rarer. But among the few whom it has been my great pleasure to know and admire in this field there is none whose memory is more sacred to me than this valiant lover of Justice.

40

PREFACE BY HILAIRE BELLOC

WHEN history began to be scientific the contemporary document took on a new importance. The word " scientific " when it is used accurately should mean, " knowledge according to a method which permits of exact measurement ". For instance, you can have a scientific statement as to the comparative volumes of the Cathedral of Seville and Broadcasting House in London. But you cannot have a scientific statement upon the relative beauty of these two buildings.

The contemporary document as a witness to history has the single advantage that the process of time will probably have warped it less with the growth of a myth than a later document. When it is not only contemporary but the writing of an eye-witness it has of course an added value in this regard ; and when the eye-witness has presumably written it down day by day as the events occurred, that value is further increased.

I need not waste the reader's time with a criticism of this kind of evidence in history. It must be enough to say that it is subject to the usual perils of deliberate falsification or inaccurate observation, the omission of the important and the resulting lack of proportion, etc. It is also true that tradition long established and mature conclusions, coming as they do through a multitude of men, will usually have more body, and as it were more " central truth " about them than a contemporary historical document. In other words, the spirit of our time has exaggerated the value of the contemporary historical document, as the spirit of any time will exaggerate the value of some particular kind of evidence suitable to itself. Nevertheless the contemporary historical document on the whole stands first in the list of particular witnesses, although of course it can never have the value of a broad and universal tradition.

Now the journal of Baron Gourgaud written at St. Helena stands very high in the list of original contemporary documents upon an important subject, and its value is felt to be the greater because on that particular subject such a vast amount of research had been done. There is, with the possible exception of critical examination of the New Testament, no historical subject upon which so much energy and ingenuity has been spent as the life of Napoleon. Pretty well everything that could be examined seemed to have been examined, and it almost seemed as though there was nothing further to come when, rather more than thirty years ago, at the very end of the last century, this diary of Baron Gourgaud was allowed to see the light. The effect of such a novel intrusion upon the mass of Napoleonic matter may be imagined. The man's name and attitude and to some extent his character were widely known. He had written considerably upon the events which he had witnessed during the Napoleonic wars, though, as what he had written was plainly inspired by violent personal feelings of irritation against others, his writings did not attain as much consideration as perhaps they deserved. But the diary was kept back, perhaps from a scruple which still has force among people of old-fashioned breeding, that matter of this kind should not appear while those who are attacked or exposed in it are alive, or even their immediate descendants.

The diary had the more effect because it came in support of a certain reaction against what may be called, according to one's philosophy, "The Napoleonic Legend" or "The Napoleonic Vision". For an active lifetime, some fifty to sixty years after the chief victories and the superhuman activities of the great man, the great bulk of our civilization exalted his memory in a religious fashion. It was exalted no less by his detractors than by his worshippers, for both combined to regard him as something almost more than human. The comparatively few who sneered at this enthusiasm and belittled the main European tradition in the matter were properly treated as negligible—as being incapable of understanding greatness. But a reaction took place following upon the fall of the Second Empire, upon the persistent propaganda of the clique of politicians who seized upon French public life after 1876 and upon the rise to a climax of Prussian power in Europe.

viii

Meanwhile the general decay of religion affected judgment in this as in all other matters. The classical spirit with which the name of Napoleon is naturally associated, the succeeding romantic spirit in the eyes of which his glory was transformed but enhanced was succeeded by the spirit first apparent in the Naturalists, now still further developed, which has a distaste for the worship of anything, and for that of beauty, glory and all the rest of it. Inevitably there went with this change an attack upon the vision of Napoleon, as there had come many years before with rationalism an attack upon the vision of the Saints. His glory, like all other glories, was extinguished, and whatever could emphasize the petty, the inconsequent or the offensive in his connection was put forward—whatever could correct the exaggeration of such things was left out.

By a remarkable but not unique piece of irony a hero-worshipper if ever there was one thoroughly served this spirit. Gourgaud's attitude towards the Emperor was more than admiration and adoration, it was exalted personal love filled with the highest measure of admiration. On this very account he exaggerated all slights and even all moments of indifference ; on this very account he noted too much what to others would have been but chance pieces of irritation, and therefore in the third step of this series the hero-worshipper becomes unconsciously the detractor.

There are two schools among those who would belittle Napoleon. There are those who would talk of him with admiration and even enthusiasm for this, that or the other side of his genius, but who let one feel all the time that they have taken him down from his pedestal, that he is not for them the chief or among the greatest of our Western race and that at any rate his primary purpose, which was more than half-conscious in him during his prime and was clearly perceived by him before his end—I mean the unifying of our civilization : peace through order and one restored Europe—is either indifferent or negligible. Of this sort I think at heart was the late Lord Rosebery, though he was a man of the highest talent and of excellent judgment who, if he had only avoided politics, would have been a much greater figure in English history than he is likely to become. For he had eloquence, style, and thought

ix

—three things incompatible with any long exercise of public life in its present condition.

There is another form of detractor who will make as little as he can even of Napoleon's talents, emphasizing his errors even in his own most conspicuous department of excellence, the military; but, more commonly, content to emphasize weak or evil moments in his conduct. To both of these, but especially to the latter, the sudden publication of Gourgaud's Journal so long after all seemed to be known was a godsend; it was hailed as a new revelation upon at least the end of Napoleon's life, and for the matter of that, upon his character as a whole.

To all however, whether they were detractors or worshippers, the thing was of capital import and will I think always so remain even when it has shaken down into its proper place. Lord Rosebery, as we know, not only made full use of it but may almost be said to have written his book on account of having read Gourgaud. What is, I think, more conclusive as a proof of Gourgaud's importance is the attitude taken by M. Bainville. M. Bainville is perhaps the best of modern historians—illuminating, conclusive, terse, observing exact proportion and happily releasing all that he does from the wretched pedantry of reference which has half-killed history in our time. His study of Napoleon should be read as a model, not indeed of judgment —upon which the reader is free to differ—but of how historical judgment when it has been arrived at should be set down. And M. Bainville in his recent great book on Napoleon—for it is not an exaggeration to call it great—particularly emphasizes the value of Gourgaud's evidence. He remarks that we have here something living, immediate, right from the heart of reality, and of a different quality from the other evidence upon Napoleon's last years—all of which suffered from advocacy, all of which was written for a purpose.

So much being said of the importance of the document— and it is of very great importance—let us examine as best we can its value to history. Before analysing this it is first to be remarked that the contrast between the national temperament not only of the writer but of those for whom he writes, his fellow Frenchmen, and the average English reader is so great that it may lead to confusion. The two nations have

x

followed divergent lines during the last 400 years or more, and especially widely divergent lines during the last century and a half ; the corporate tradition of each has become less and less appreciable by the other until at last what seems dignity to the one seems to the other an absurdity. And even in the conception of justice they differ so much that it is difficult for the readers in the one to follow judicial proceedings stated in terms of the other. The very conception of truth is not the same in the two minds. In so small a thing as the framework of a sentence this difference appears : the French use of rhetoric and the historical present jars upon the English mind as something insincere ; repeated and open expression in which a man often contradicts himself will strike the English mind as something contemptible where the Frenchman will rather regard the effort at repression, silence, and expressing emotions the opposite of what are really felt as something clownish and farcical. To put it in a phrase, " The Frenchman is still a comic figure in England and the Englishman a comic figure in France."

Allowing for all that, let us attempt to estimate the value of Gourgaud as a witness—not as a man, but as a witness.

First, let us calculate the points in favour of his evidence. There is the obvious and primary point that it " rings true ". All through the book which the reader will now have before his eyes you get that character. Look at the passage on p. 260 for example—it is only one of fifty—in which he jots down on the 30th of August, 1817, a chance phrase of the Emperor's upon religion. It is exactly what a man like Napoleon would have said at that moment when his mind was beginning to turn in the direction in which he finally reposed. It is the parrying of a thrust. Or again look at the little passage on p. 289, November the 5th of the same year, upon the use of grape-shot and ball. It is not a thought-out disquisition ; as it stands it would not mean anything ; obviously you could not use grape-shot at long range. Much must have gone before those last two remarks. If the diarist had been making things up he would have rationalized this passage : instead of that he just jots down hastily but vividly the end of a discussion. Or again, on the 21st of March the same year, " He continues to ignore my presence, and sings, and expresses to Montholon his satisfaction

xi

with the haricot beans." From an ironical pen that might be as false as you like, made up from the first word to the last, but from a simple soul it is vivid relation of what remained remembered when the dinner was over. The whole book is a series of passages of that kind. The second point in his favour is that the diary was almost certainly written self-regarding—that is, for the writer and for no one else. One can never be certain of this in any diary, however spontaneous it may seem; there is an ineradicable appetite in men to commune with their fellows, and when a man takes the trouble to write down for his own eye alone his most private and concealed miseries, he still has at the back of his mind some vague conception of a confidant. But I do think that in the case of Gourgaud you have as intimate a relation as can be found. The diary was not meant to be given to others, whatever afterthoughts the writer had in the matter. It was meant for his own consolation. I have known one case in my own life of one important diary the writer of which both kept it from day to day and deliberately falsified it upon mature consideration for the purpose of annoying the human race, or such of it as had come in contact with him. But then that diary was published as quickly as might be. Gourgaud wrote for himself, as adolescents write and as certainly no one would write who had ever written for fame, let alone for a living.

He is the more trustworthy because he was vain, and therefore was not proud. Proud people are always quite untrustworthy, they are liars to the core by the necessities of their vice; but vain people blurt things out and are sincere. They lack proportion, but what they do say is true so far as it goes. They are touchy as a rule, the two qualities can hardly help going together; they will make a prodigious case (as Gourgaud does) out of things which only concern themselves, and take an impatient cry—when their victim is bored beyond bearing—for a studied insult, but yet they do record the cry as it was given. They do not invent it.

But I think the best one can say for Gourgaud as a sincere and valuable witness lies in this: that though in his sense of proportion he is ridiculous, though he tells one fifty times too much of what Napoleon said or did which seemed to slight him and not one-hundredth of what he might have told us

xii

on the profundities of the Emperor's gesture, carriage and regard—yet on the large lines he was right. You get a living man before you ; his circumstance, his reactions to the characters around.

All this is in favour of Gourgaud as a witness. He must be read for what he is, a simple—too simple—straightforward emotional young man ; young even for his young years, the early thirties. There is virtue in him which we miss in the more accomplished cynics who illuminate but do not reveal. As against this, Gourgaud has two quite obvious disadvantages as a witness. In the first place he is a disturbed man. Evidence may be compared to the reflection of a real but concealed object in a sheet of water. We cannot see the mountain which is on the other side of the lake because it is above our windows, but we can see the reflection of the mountain in the lake. The surface of the lake is the mind of the witness. A calm unruffled surface will give a picture of an exact outline ; a ruffled surface will give but a blurred image and to that extent a misleading one. The simile is of course most imperfect, for the lake (not being human) will not set out to lie deliberately ; but it will serve my purpose and my reader will know what I mean. There is a quality of accuracy which accompanies the relation of those rare witnesses who are calm as well as honest (for your calm witness is commonly untrustworthy) which you do not get from an honest witness who is far from calm. Now Gourgaud is not only far from calm, but he is a man without intervals of calmness. He is in a perpetual irritation. Everybody offends him, every one is preferred to him, he is always being insulted and neglected and the rest of it. These defects go with virtue, but neither with social charm nor value in evidence. For instance, Napoleon comes into a room where there are several people and says, nodding to him, "Ah, Gourgaud——" and then goes on and says something else to some one else. Napoleon had been master of the world and still felt himself to be what he was—the greatest among men—and those about him felt it to be so, and no one more than Gourgaud. The Emperor was in a good temper that day, and probably thought when he said, " Ah, Gourgaud——" that he was being if anything specially warm in his regard. But the recipient of the remark

xiii

took it as a blow. Again, we know quite enough about the character of Montholon, and this perpetual bickering against Montholon is ridiculous. Napoleon said a mass of wise things applying to the human race as a whole, as well as a mass of things which he never intended to apply to anybody for more than a second, but he never said anything wiser than when he said to Gourgaud, " What you need is a little wife ! " And when he added that Gourgaud must consent to regard Montholon as more important he said something obviously true and sensible, which Gourgaud again takes as an insult.

In the reading of Gourgaud, as of any other intimate witness to the conversation and manner of the Emperor, it is important to emphasize once more the contrast between the national temperament of the reader and that of the writer, as also the contrast between the temperament of the reader and that of the subject of the book. Perhaps the most important rule to follow in this matter is to remember that Napoleon said many things which expressed his mind fully and permanently, but very many more which were not even intended to express his mind fully and permanently. To quote chance sayings of the Emperor's as permanent judgments is a proof of ignorance—ignorance of a foreign temper and ignorance of the human mind in general. Watch your contemporaries, and you will notice that a man who talks a great deal talks a great deal of nonsense, and that a man who talks very little hardly ever talks sense. When Napoleon said, " One bad General is better than two good ones," he was striking forth an immortal truth which ought to be written in gold wherever politicians or even kings are concerned with war. The moment a nation goes to war its first business is unity of command. If there be alliance, unity of command is still more imperatively necessary. If you had asked Napoleon his opinion upon that point a hundred times he would have given you a hundred times the same answer ; but when in exasperation he cries out against this or against that, and then a little later contradicts himself, it means nothing ; and indeed, to those who know that such exclamations mean nothing it is a marvel that anyone can take them seriously, or make of exact verbal consistency a necessity for their own self-respect. When you read in Gourgaud, as in any one of the contemporary records, of Napoleon's sayings—chance, irritable, merry, determined—distinguish between the categories : for he was a man who talked and talked and talked all the time, having—to put it without exaggeration—a creative brain.

Let me conclude by saying that I think there is in connection with Gourgaud's diary one very lamentable lack not due to the man himself ; and that is the absence in it of the last scenes. Far the deepest moment in the life of any man is the approach to death, so long as he is still conscious. Napoleon in that moment, as we know, fully returned to that from whence he had sprung. The very inward of the man was revealed. Had Gourgaud, with his sincerity, his simplicity, his hero-worship, been present in those last spring days of 1821 his relation would have been invaluable : there would have been no occasion for peevishness, he would have risen, I think, somewhat at last to the occasion. But he was not there. It is a great loss to history.

September 2nd, 1932.   HILAIRE BELLOC

PREFACE

THE connection between the Irish people and the French Revolution is part of the general connection between Ireland and France which forms a most important factor in the history of Western Europe.

Some will believe that there is an affinity between the two peoples based upon race; and, a generation ago, it was customary to use the word " Celtic " in such a connection. There is something in this idea of racial affinity, just as there is something in the idea of an affinity between the bulk of Englishmen and the bulk of Germans—or at least north Germans, and Flemings and Scandinavians. There are manifestly things in common to the two to-day, and probably one can discover, though somewhat vaguely, similar links in the past. The words " Celtic " and " Teutonic " which were for ever on the lips of our fathers, have been rightly discounted, but there is a basis, however vague, for making two categories of two kinds of people very roughly corresponding to such groups.

Of much more weight in the connection between two organised societies is a community of philosophy or religion, and even a community of language (though that factor has been vastly exaggerated) has its weight.

But the strongest and most real connection between the French and the Irish was a product of the great debate or conflict which fell upon Western Europe in the 16th and 17th centuries. The religious wars, lasting from the first years of the 16th century onwards, and not finally (though mainly) settled much more than a century

vii

later, had indirect effects which closely connected France and Ireland. They accentuated even if they did not create the Irish consciousness of permanent antagonism to England, they certainly accentuated and mainly did create the intense later antagonism of England to Ireland. Now as there had been, quite apart from the fate of religion, a continuous quarrel between the two Crowns of Paris and of Westminster, inherited from the old quarrel of the Plantagenets and their claims to the French throne, and heavily accentuated by the growth of nationalism, it was inevitable that, as the conflict betwen England and Ireland increased, France should appear as spiritually the ally, and often physically the ally, of the Irish.

This tie was strengthened by the ultimate victory of the Catholic culture in France in the 17th century, and by the very great place which France took in the general civilisation of Europe after the quarrel had been settled, as between the rebellious Huguenot nobles and the Bourbon Kings. The tie was further strengthened by the mass of emigration from Ireland to France (among other Continental countries) and by the memories of the aid which Louis XIV had given the efforts of the Irish at recovering their land and emancipating their religion. That aid was very far from being unselfish; it was strictly limited; and even at the height of its activity, when the King of France was attempting to restore the legitimate King of England, he was thinking more of his own complicated international policy than of Irish advantage. But the work had been done and the close intercourse between the real Ireland, which so astonishingly survived, and the great polity overseas foisoned and grew. All through the 18th century it increased. Perhaps the strongest impression which will be received by a reader of this book is the almost startling contrast in this respect between those days and these. It may be said that never since the 11th century had Ireland had a better knowledge of France and France of Ireland, had the two been more closely interconnected and sympathetic, than at the end of the 18th. It may certainly be said that never have they been further apart than now. The connection might have been permanent; it may perhaps be restored; but for the moment it is slighter than it has ever been before, and the cause of this revulsion is religion.

The cause was not the French Revolution—far from it. The Revolution was not unacceptable in its original principles to the Irish temperament. The enthusiasms appealed, the ideas underlying those enthusiasms were drawn from the Catholic culture of Europe, and the mere fact that there was a rising against what was felt by both rebels to be oppression at once established a common understanding; although the type of oppression resisted in France, in so far as it was oppression, was utterly different from the type of oppression which existed in Ireland. The enthusiasm for equality had a powerful effect upon men whose inferiority of legal status in their own country was an anomaly of the grossest sort.

There should be added to this the military turn which the Revolution took and which could not but at once appeal to the Irish character. When that military turn early in its career included aristocratic England as one of the main enemies of the new Republic, a seal was set and should apparently have set lastingly upon the spiritual contract between the two communities.

What ruined it was the fate of religion among the French: the fate, that is, of the Catholic Church in that country, its traditions, organisation and teaching.

Whether the great and flaming quarrel between the Revolution and the Church was inherent in the very nature of the new movement or was an accident which warped it, will be debated everlastingly. For my part I conclude that no such conflict was inevitable. As it

ix

seems to me, the Civil Constitution of the clergy upon the one side and the social sympathies of the then hierarchy in France upon the other lit the fire which began to blaze so fiercely in the second year of the movement, and the heat of which has affected all French affairs from that day to this.

Although it is true that the Masonic organisation played a large part in the fostering of the Revolution, although it is true that the original agents of the Revolution were at least indifferent to religion, and many of them hostile, and although there ran through the Revolution the Pelagian heresy which is as mortal to Catholic Faith as the Faith is mortal to it, yet the mass of the French nation was still so Catholic that I do not believe the new political constitution and the new social conception that went with it would have eradicated, even from a considerable part of Frenchmen, the immemorial traditions of Catholicism. The Church had made French culture, and from that culture are derived all those ideas which the Revolution set out to establish. Napoleon, had he completely succeeded (but complete success has never been in this world) would have reconciled the Revolution and the religion of the nation; just as the Third Republic has more and more divorced them.

But the religious quarrel rose, rose early and rose fiercely, and it had upon the French connection with Ireland two effects—the one spiritual and the other mechanical and both strongly adverse to the communion of the two peoples. In the spiritual sphere the actions of the Revolution against religion violently shocked the Irish conscience, and as with the march of the Revolutionary armies throughout Europe churches were pillaged, all Catholic institutions treated as enemies, religious communities broken up and looted, the Papacy challenged, Ireland was in disgust. A most powerful support of this spiritual effect was the passion of patriotism. Nationalism in Ireland had been associated

x

by the oppressed Catholics of that country both with their passionate claim for equality and freedom and with their national spirit. In France it was the other way. Until the Napoleonic settlement, national feeling was marshalled against the hierarchy in particular, and against the general constitution of the Church, the authorities of which were in alliance with the invaders of the country.

These spiritual forces were of course by far the most important, but the mechanical factor added to it. Ireland was largely cut off from the Continent and therefore from France during the period of the Revolutionary Wars. After the 1st of June, 1794, the English fleet became on its own element invincible and so remained for just over a hundred and twenty years, until the 4th of August, 1914. It formed a barrier, a new barrier soon to be made impermeable, and one through which facile communication was impossible. Further, for the first time since the great English families had destroyed the English monarchy more than a century before, it had necessarily become the policy of the British Government —the descendants of those families—to foster in some degree Catholicism in Europe and even in Ireland as a weakening of France. Hitherto the Irish priesthood had largely been trained abroad and the effect of this education had been profound. Henceforward as a direct result of English policy it was to be trained mainly at home. The chain hitherto binding Ireland and France was broken. The difficulty of renewing the tie has increased with every decade since those days.

In some degree even the last Great War helped to accentuate the change; for in the last Great War the French, fighting for life, were fighting in alliance with England who was also fighting for her life. But as the English Government had with incredible ineptitude maintained their quarrel with Ireland, the Irish people could not but be turned in sympathy against the

xi

PREFACE

Allies. It was the last and perhaps the most conspicuous example of the way in which the decline of aristocracy in England had been accompanied by a decline of political instinct; and we all know the price that has been paid for that last piece of folly.

Whether that ancient attachment between Ireland and France will revive, the future only can show; it will depend in part upon the settlement of the French religious quarrel, in part upon the new orientation of international forces, more perhaps upon new factors in the culture of the West which we are only now beginning dimly to perceive. It is an inquiry which can be made to no purpose, for never was the future in all matters more inscrutable than it is to-day.

H. BELLOC

King's Land
Shipley
Horsham.
1932.

PREFACE

A GREAT interest attaches to this book. It is the history of that opening part of the English Reformation which can only be called with strict accuracy "The Schism," for its characteristic was not an effort at doctrinal heresy but rather an effort to set up a National Church identical—or virtually identical—in morals and doctrine with the universal Church and yet separated from the unity of the latter. That was the distinctive note of what happened in the latter part of the reign of King Henry VIII. It was not a Protestant movement such as was taking place everywhere throughout the rest of Europe. It was not a popular movement, such as was to take place a little later in Scotland. It was not an aristocratic movement such as took place in France; it was purely political, dynastic, and wholly due to the initiative of the king, and, urging the king, Anne Boleyn.

Such a book as that which is now before the reader has especial interest in the fact that it is written by a man who is wholly French, wholly Catholic, and writing as such. We have, I think, no other example of a similar study under similar conditions.

The difficulties attaching to a judgment of what has been called "the Henrician Church" are very great. They are difficulties necessarily attaching to the subject itself, and present to anyone who attempts to write upon it; but there is also a special difficulty presented to such an author as Professor Constant, or indeed to any author, Catholic and not English, who approaches the period and the theme.

How great the difficulties are for any writer upon the matter may not always be appreciated. There are at least four major difficulties in the forming of an accurate judgment.

First, although the period, 1533–47, cannot but appear to us to-day as the beginning of the English Reformation, yet it was not, while it was in progress, attached to the Reformation

vii

as we understand that term. I repeat: it was not an heretical movement in the common use of the term heretical, that is, it did not combat any of the main doctrines such as were being combated so violently upon the continent of Europe. It did, indeed, deny the authority of the Pope, but it not only did not deny but fiercely affirmed Transubstantiation, the Mass, the whole of the sacramental system. We may put it simply by saying that to the ordinary man in his daily life and weekly religious duties things seemed to go on exactly as they had before. The destruction of the monasteries had nothing to do with doctrine. Vows of celibacy were insisted upon as much as ever they had been, and indeed under much worse penalties than the past had known, and though there was plenty of Protestant talk amid a small enthusiastic minority it was a minority which was persecuted as vigorously as, or more vigorously than, its colleagues were in any other part of Christendom.

Everywhere else the reformers had set out to destroy the Catholic system. The priest was their especial enemy, the Mass was in their eyes an idolatry to be overthrown. Everywhere else, wherever they had begun to form appreciable *nuclei* of revolt so early as 1533, they hated and sought to destroy the Catholic mind. In the Germanies especially, from Zurich to the Baltic, the religious life of the populace was revolutionised wherever the reformers had their way. It was an upheaval as startling and much more universal than the Communist movement in our time. But in England there was nothing of this. The denial of papal jurisdiction was made by an ultra-orthodox king and by the only king in Europe who professed himself to be a theologian. Henry had been intended for the priesthood and never forgot his theological lessons.

Now, an experiment of that sort is quite alien to our time. We have difficulty in grasping it. We conceive of a revolt against unity under the Papacy as a function of Protestant or other non-Catholic and anti-Catholic doctrine. The combination of a strictly conservative Catholic scheme with separation from Rome is something for which we can find no parallel and of which we have no experience.

In the second place, we are necessarily warped in our

judgment by our knowledge of what followed. To the men of the time, from whom their future was veiled, as our future is veiled from us, there was no apparent advance towards Protestantism. On the contrary, Henry's reign would have seemed, if anything, to the few but intense Protestants of his day (and, as we know from what they have left, did seem to them), to be a reaction from the movement of the Reformation. Their hopes that the quarrel with the Papacy would lead to a quarrel with the Mass and sacerdotal and sacramental system were violently disappointed. Had Mary lived, or had there been no such directing genius as William Cecil to found a new state of affairs in the second half of the century, the last fourteen years of Henry's life would have seemed a violent, irregular episode in the general history of Catholic England, filled with loot and followed by the very brief welter of a revolution that failed. But it would not have seemed more than that. Religious foundations would have reappeared—some no doubt would actually have been restored, and many created as the years passed. The Mass and all Catholic custom would have been continuous in men's experience save for three or four years of a grossly anti-national tyranny met by rebellion. But on account of what followed Mary's death, her father's last years are coloured for us with a Protestant tinge and we read into them an approach towards that later Protestant England which the men of the time would not have thought possible. Even as it was, England was not of a Protestant temper till a full lifetime after Henry's death, and a large minority of Catholic sympathies prevailed for nearly a century more.

Thirdly, the whole of the period was, politically, a reign of terror. England lay under not only the most absolute government in Europe, but the most centralised and the one which supported its power with the most cruel punishments. On this again it is difficult to discover facts, or even to catch the spirit of the time properly.

So true is it that this character of a "Reign of Terror" overhangs the whole period that we are misled even upon Henry's own pretty obvious private character. It is clear that he was despised by those who came most closely into contact with him in these latter years, and especially by the women who had the best opportunities for judging him as he was. But the tyranny and the cruelty of the punishments accompanying it were such that this weak character is made to appear strong.

But the last main difficulty preventing a right judgment of the period is much the most important. It is that, on account of the complete obliteration of Catholicism by the beginning of the eighteenth century, the great mass of our English historical writing is ignorant of what the Catholic Church may be. On this account the debates during Henry's reign are represented as a sort of see-saw, as though English people were being held half way between Catholicism and Protestantism. A vivid example of this is the way in which our writers talk of the Ten Articles. To read them one would imagine that the Ten Articles were an advance towards Protestantism, and that the Six Articles were a reaction towards Catholicism. Nothing could be further from the truth. In textbook after textbook we are told that the tenth Article modified the Catholic doctrine on Purgatory and on Masses for the dead. We are told it by men who do not understand what the Catholic doctrine on these matters is. The tenth Article is as orthodox as all the rest save on the point of papal power and therefore of papal indulgences, and the Ten Articles, apart from that sentence, might have been accepted by the Pope himself without hesitation.

I have said that there is a special difficulty present to a foreigner writing of the period. This special difficulty is the difficulty of appreciating that with us here in England to-day everything is official and nothing is more strictly or narrowly official than our history, the history taught in our public and elementary schools, the history required for our universal examination system which holds the doors of all professions, from the universities to the lowest branches of the Civil Service. This same official history appears in nearly all our historical fiction. It colours all our views of prominent individuals (Elizabeth, the Cecils, James II are examples).

It thoroughly falsifies our view of social history, making out the period 1560-90—which was one of declining wealth and great misery—to have been prosperous and materially advancing. It strongly falsifies our view of foreign policies, making out the Spanish power, which supported Elizabeth's advent, as her enemy from the beginning, not recognising the determining effect of the French religious wars, drawing an absurd picture of a Calvinist Holland nobly resisting an alien Spanish power.

It cannot be denied that the possession of a universal official history of this kind has been until lately of political advantage to England. It was a function of that complete political unity which England has achieved and which is, or at least was in the immediate past, the chief element of her strength. Yet the Continent is unaware of this official note in our textbooks. For a continental writer the word "official" means something very different and almost opposite to that which it means in this country. There is indeed an official history in France, but the very word "official" means in that country something *not* universally taught and held, rather something actually opposed to the best opinion. It signifies something dead and mechanical against which living criticism is exercised not only in direct opposition, but from almost every angle.

All *our* history has been standardised since the moral unity of England was achieved in the eighteenth century; a unity the like of which is not to be found anywhere else in Europe. Abroad, such standardised history is unknown.

One example will suffice to show what I mean. Drake was a great seaman and a man of exceptional courage; he was also a base character, very vain, a liar, an outrageous robber and guilty of murder wholesale. What is more, he worked for others who could at any moment have executed him for a pirate and who allowed him the modest commission of two and a half per cent on the proceeds of his buccaneering. Yet Drake gradually became a national hero and has been established in that position for now a hundred years. His contemporaries protested against him violently. His character was openly debated for another two generations, but the modern myth is now so firmly established, so deeply rooted, that you find no contradiction of it anywhere. The truth about him arouses a sort of scandalised astonishment.

Now compare this with a corresponding figure in French,

Italian or German history. In any continental nation you will find that the figure set up by one party, and especially by the official party, as a national hero is, with great bodies of critics, something very different, and to many something odious. That is because no European nation has established the sort of unity which the English have established and because the conception of such universal official history is not tenable by them.

Now, the foreign writer can with difficulty appreciate how strong this official history has become with us, still less is he likely to understand how universal is the feeling against the Catholic Church which this standardised official history represents.

Any foreign writer of the period, however much he may consult original documents, must be affected by the official history of our own time, as for instance, by the writing of such great scholars as Professor Pollard, our chief expert upon the fourteen years in question.

Professor Constant has, in the main, triumphed over this difficulty.

Thus he follows our official history in emphasising Warham's "*Ira principis mors est.*" But, both in a footnote on page 32 of this edition[1] and in his third chapter he remarks on Warham's courageous and most definite protest at the end of his life against what were as yet but threats of schism. The truth is that men did not grasp the full meaning of the Schism till it had come about. Still less did they see how the Schism would lead to heresy and at last to a general hatred of the Catholic name, and of all that spirit to which Henry himself was devoted. Gardiner of the "*non flevi*" was that same Gardiner who had.

Again, he fully appreciates the heretical character of Cranmer's Bible, which Henry was hoodwinked into accepting by the use of a false name, and he emphasises the opposition which it aroused, an opposition he further illustrates in a long note on the passage.

The Chapter on the Suppression of the Monasteries is a specially good example of the Author's detachment. He was here supported by the hesitation of most modern English

[1] Chap. 1, p. 32, n. 133.

authorities to continue, in this matter, the official history of the last generation, and our Author has an excellent passage in which he points out that some part at least of the reaction towards historical truth in this matter has come from clerical writers of the Church of England. But perhaps the most telling blow delivered against the monstrous old legend of which (characteristically) Burnet was the chief confirmer and final founder, was delivered by the late Cardinal Gasquet when he drew attention to the reports of the County Committees, which refute the accusations of evil living in the most striking manner. It is evidence which has not yet "pierced." It is not yet, as it will in time, become matter of common knowledge. But it is conclusive.

I should offer the criticism that in the first pages in the Divorce, our Author follows Pollard too closely. The evidence of a first attempt at divorce in 1514 is quite insufficient and the contention that, later, the Princess Mary was not regarded as a possible successor, is equally insufficient, or rather partial. One can give citations of opinion against a female successor, but there is no doubt that opinion accepted the princess and even accepted her enthusiastically. Henry desired a male heir, of course, but that desire was not the mainspring of the divorce. It is essential to history that we should grasp its true motive force: the will and tenacity of Anne.

Let it be said in conclusion that this fine book is typically French in the multitude and accuracy of its evidence. The Author has read everything, used everything and checked every date and name with the most industrious accuracy. It is in the best tradition of the "oeuvre documentée" which is the chief point, in historical study, of the University of France.

HILAIRE BELLOC.

PREFACE

ALL those who are sane and can see clearly
know that our civilization after the poisonous
effects of industrialization must come to one of
three conclusions; it may crash; it may
re-establish servitude; or it may re-establish
property. The observer of the moment, especially
if he knows nothing of Europe and the past,
concludes for one of the first two. All our
constructive legislation, that is all our present
efforts to escape a crash are directed towards
the permanent Servile State; those who think
that Socialism or Communism could be permanent may be neglected for they have no
knowledge of Man.

But the third solution, the restoration of
property, is envisaged even in this country
by a small but growing body. It is small
because the idea of property (save as the name
for a privilege of the few against the many), has
been eradicated out of the modern English
mind as thoroughly as the old National religion
was eradicated out of the eighteenth century
mind. Only a small number of pioneers can
ever be found to start a machine from cold.

But their number is growing simply because
their ideal is instinctive to humanity. No man
left a complete freedom of choice will be a
slave. He may come to think slavery inevitable.

v

He may from habit think of himself as a slave in a slave-society and regard its power to regulate his life as no more than the mitigation of his lot. Thus the shop assistant welcomes servile laws made by his masters, which in their interests as well as his own forbid him to work more than a certain number of hours. But give him complete freedom (a term which means, in England to-day, the possession of a large lump of capital) and he certainly would not welcome a law forbidding him to do any work he chose at any hour he chose to do it. Your rich young man who goes in zealously for painting would not be pleased to find himself punished if he went on painting after six o'clock of a summer evening.

There is no freedom without property and therefore, as freedom is natural to the desire of man—a desire for the restoration of property when it has been lost is natural.

The movement therefore though still in its small beginnings is destined to grow. To what extent it may reach we cannot tell, but we know that the air we breathe is hostile to its growth.

Now a necessary accompaniment of a system of re-established property and in practice the foundation of it, is a re-established property in land, in all land, but particularly in agricultural land. It is the perception of this truth that has created the Catholic Land Associations. Truth confirms truth and the general truths of the Faith promote this particular truth that the complete citizen is a free man working upon the land. It is for this reason that the Catholic culture of Europe has instinctively preserved the peasant. But if we are to recreate a peasantry in a Society poisoned to the very roots with industrial capitalism we need two things, a general and a particular thing. The general thing is the state of mind in which the possession of property by the poor man, and especially the property in land and more especially the property in land which he shall cultivate for a livelihood, is normal and widely accepted. The particular thing is a state of law favouring small properties. The first of these necessities, the general one, I will not discuss in detail, it requires a department to itself, for it is largely coincident with a change in religion.

What has made industrial capitalism is not the machine but the mind of man perverted by a false philosophy. In our civilization the French Heresiarch, Jean Cauvin, better known in the latinized form of "Calvin" stands at the origin of this perversion. The force that has destroyed property among us is greed. For if men regard wealth as the supreme good each will struggle to obtain the most of it, for himself. Under such competition, a smaller and smaller number obtain the desired thing and each new conglomeration swallows what is less than itself. In this the eternal paradox appears which was best expressed by Our Lord when He said that if you wonld save your life you would lose it.

Millions all snatching from each other, each in order that he may clutch a maximum in his claws, end by a general spoliation wherein the vast majority are left with nothing. It can only be after the purging out of this main product of the Reformation that right living can return.

But side by side with the effecting of so vast a spiritual change must go the protection of the few who are engaged in it. You cannot sow the seeds of private property save in ground properly prepared. They will not germinate save under favourable conditions.

To-day the state of law under which we live in England is poisonous to small property, especially in land. It is still more poisonous to the maintenance thereof. A heavy tribute must be paid to the lawyers' guild. A tribute which increases in inverse proportion with the amount of land to be acquired. Title is rendered, for the purpose of furnishing money to the lawyers, as complicated as possible and there is no public map on which title can be established.

The economic advantage in purchase which the large man has over the small (because he can wait, because he has better information, because he can pay for all manner of aid) is uncorrected by laws especially advancing the efforts of the small man to acquire and hampering the efforts of the rich man. In the absence of such laws the establishment of small property in land is impossible.

Once established it can only be maintained by another series of protecting laws, for unrestricted competition would kill it. There must be some marketing of produce. Unless the laws curb the power of monopoly the market will be controlled by a capitalist trust, as is the glaring case in milk to-day in England. There must be some transport for produce. Unless the laws favour the small man capitalist transport and its monopoly will ruin him, and when I say the laws I extend the term to mean every regulation however small imposed by Public Authority. For instance if a man desires to grind his own wheat to-day in England he is heavily handicapped by regulations which favour big capitalist milling and impose a serious fine upon himself.

Now the organ of legislation in this Country is Parliament. Of course we all know the real power is in the hands of the big Trusts, beginning with the banking monopoly of which the Politicians are either members or servants. Still, overtly and at the end of the chain of action comes Parliament.

But Parliament to-day means Plutocracy. It used to mean Aristocracy, which, whether liked or not, is a stable form of government and works in the open. Plutocracy is neither stable nor open, and is compelled to work through falsehoods.

The beastly condition of Parliament is a byword. The atmosphere of bribery and blackmail

—it is rather a stench than an atmosphere—
is the very air of what is called "Politics".

Until you have got rid of that you can do
nothing.

Those who insist upon the necessity of reform
in the moribund and degraded machine at
Westminster and better still its replacement by
popular and monarchic powers are often thought
futile precisely because that which they are
attacking has become so heartily and deservedly
despised. Yet the direction of their attack is
right. It is the key point. So long as the
legislative machine is controlled by and composed
of the monopolists, all effort at restoring healthy
economic life will fail.

My conclusion, then, is, that along with all
other items of a programme for restoring a
peasantry to England, there must go a programme for transforming the diseased centre
of political power.

H. BELLOC.

PREFACE

W. S. Gilbert, in one of the best poems in the English language, wrote, with regard to the apparition of a Red Indian at the gate of a Turkish house:—

To say that Ahmed ope'd his eyes
Would faintly paint his great surprise.
To say it nearly made him die
Would be to paint it much too high.

That is what Gilbert wrote, as well as I can remember after nearly fifty years, and if I have got it wrong by a word or two, that doesn't much matter; for I have noticed that when people change a text through quoting from memory they usually change it for the better.

Anyhow, this immortal quatrain is suitable to what I have here to say. When I first heard that Mr. Baring's Trilogy was at last to be bound up in one volume I cried out of my own accord, "The desire of the everlasting hills has come." The words are not my own but the emotion I think is. I now see that the emotion in cold print looks exaggerated. Either Talleyrand or somebody else said that whatever is exaggerated is worthless, and in saying so said something quite untrue. Still, exaggeration does take away from the value of a statement.

ix

On the other hand were I to say of the appearance of this book that it gave me peculiar satisfaction it would be to paint my feelings much too low.

Its appearance marks a day in my life. For years I have been praying in secret, canvassing in private and crying aloud in public that it was a duty to English letters to print these three masterpieces between two covers and to issue them as one book. There is thus an exact blend of savours for there is a subtle difference between the letters and the diaries, between the diaries and the letters and the dramas. Nor does it matter very much in what order you read them for they form not a sequence but a ring. Until they appeared as one book men knew some one or some other but not the whole. Now they will be known together and will achieve a permanence which they do not so much deserve as obtain of right.

There are now three books which stand out separate from the rest of the English prose work done in my lifetime. These three books are The Diary of a Nobody, The Wallet of Kai-Lung and this collection here before you. In each the character is that of a genus: a separate category. For it is true of these books as of angels. (Each angel we are told by those scholars who have studied the affair has a separate nature from every other angel. The angels are not in a lump but individual, differing one from another as much as an elephant does from a flea.) So it is with The Diary of a Nobody, so it is with The Wallet of Kai-Lung, and so it is with the present work. *Opus magnum et perdurabile.*

The Diary of a Nobody is the essence of the nation. The Wallet of Kai-Lung the essence of ironic wisdom, but this Trilogy of Mr. Baring's is something of yet another kind. It is the essence of what is civilised. It is the only thing in modern English letters which is wholly European and classic.

Here again I shall be told I have fallen over the edge into exaggeration. I don't think so myself but what a man thinks of his own opinion, of his own rooted opinion at least, is of no moment to his readers. What is of moment to his readers is what they think of his opinion. So if my readers think that the word "only" is an exaggeration, I will bow to them and leave it out. I will confine myself to saying that this book is, unlike the other two triumphs, European and classic; and that they may, my readers that is, go out to search for something else which shall be European and classic in modern English Letters. They will not find it.

The first mark, the chief test, of such a character in anything—a statue, an epigram, a life, a story—is economy: that is, the use of your material to its best effect: the making of it pull every ounce of its weight.

Look at a Greek marble head, or better still at the best Egyptian granite. Look at that great forearm and fist which are the glory of the British Museum and see with what excision of superfluity the thing is done. It is not a suggestion of beauty in the one case or of strength in the other: it is not an impression, or a hint, or an outline: it is the thing itself. By economy you get the soul of the thing. After seeing a work of art dependent for its triumph upon economy then the real thing of which it is an imitation, seems, by contrast, to be marred by too much detail. It seems to have less unity, to be less itself.

Read carefully the words used by Calypso to Mercury and then to Ulysses and you will see what I mean. Or again read Clytemnestra's letters in their order and observe the gradation. Then ask yourself how it is done. That is economy.

There is another way of putting it. If an enemy should desire to spoil Mr. Baring's book for posterity and render it worthless he would only have to go over it with the help of a commonplace mind and put in at every turn the redundant words which he himself would have written.

It is not only the exactitude of the terms the writer uses nor the order in which he puts them, it is also the numerical value of the total which counts; and this, in the case of words is the exact opposite of what it is in the case of money. The more sovereigns you give me, in the days when an angry people shall demand and obtain gold again, the better shall I be pleased. But the less words you give me, the better shall I be pleased also.

This is not to say that mere paucity of words is of value. There are fools who talk like that in universities. They are not all dead yet. But it is to say that, effect for effect, a similar effect with less words is stronger than one with more words, and, one with the least number of words necessary for the full statement bears the greatest weight.

It is not to say either that rhetoric or exuberance demand this restriction. With them it is the other way about. The repetitions of the Psalter, the cascades of Rabelais, depend for their value on verbal largesse. Yet even here there is economy in execution. For writing of that sort is only possible either because the writer has such a store that he will never overlap nor make two words do the work of one, or because his repetitions are calculated.

But though economy is the first mark of the writing

to which these lines form a paltry introduction there is a great deal more.

There is wit, acting as wit should, by simplicity and implication without trick or aid of any kind.

It is wit and not humour. Humour is founded upon folly but wit is founded upon reason; and where the reason works upon exact and multiple observation, upon the knowledge of men and things, there you get wit boiled down to its greatest strength, like a double consommé.

Wit is at its highest in Mr. Baring's work where he gives us the conversation or correspondence of the leisured woman. But it is present everywhere. It is present when he is laughing at his subject or when his subject is laughing at you. It is present in the remark of Lucullus about the dish of larks' tongues and it is present in the amiable simplicity of the Greek traveller reporting current talk about the Emperor. It is present perhaps at its best in the letter of King Lear's daughter.

But I do not very much believe in grading unsurpassed work and giving higher marks to this than to that in such a collection as the one now before me. Mere serial arrangement of that kind ignores quality. It tends to propose comparison between things which cannot be compared. But if one goes by what has most moved oneself I do feel the letter about King Lear's visit more even than I feel the banquet, the public banquet, at Puteoli.

Well there it is. I will not go on writing, for criticism is not my trade; nor writing either, for that matter. I have been compelled to take to writing from early youth as a drowning dog with a brick round its neck is compelled to treading water; but I was never born for it. Give me rather enjoyment, satisfaction, happiness;

which is the true end of man. And this Trilogy will always make me happy and after I am dead it will make happy I know not how many yet unborn.

As for those who do not understand what I mean, let them perish for what they are: deaf, dumb and blind.

H. BELLOC.

King's Land.
January, 1935.

FOREWORD

By HILAIRE BELLOC

THE English castle is one of the most illuminating objects
of study in history. It illustrates the whole of the English
Middle Ages and their military transformation under the
effect of artillery. The English castle is to-day one of three
things: a ruin, a restoration, or a fragment on to which has
been grafted a later dwellinghouse unsuited to war. In its
early development it followed the rule of all English things in
that it came tardily and developed tardily, because the arts,
military and civil, came from overseas and had been developed
elsewhere before they were established here. A further reason
for the tardy development of the English castle was the fact
that the English manorial lords took little part in the Crusades
of the twelfth century which were the mainspring of castle
building in Western Europe. Another reason was that save
for a brief breakdown under Stephen, before castle building
in stone had taken full root, English central government
remained stronger in England than on the Continent for over
three centuries. The greater feudal lords, whether on their
own account or as officers under the King, held the great
stone castles which in their new whiteness marked the English
landscape from the middle of the twelfth to the end of the
fourteenth centuries; but the smaller feudal lords and the
"one manor men," lords of single villages, had no occasion
to copy their superiors, having no chance of standing up
to them individually, a thing that the smaller feudal lords could
only do where central power was weak and social order confused. Therefore it is that the typical squire's house, which is
called in France to this day a "castle," rarely bears that name in
England, and when it does bear that name hardly ever derives
from the home of a petty local family but almost always from
one of the great barons or from the Crown.

Towards the end of the Middle Ages all this changed.
English architecture became in castle building as in everything else more particular and national. Even the language at
last became national in the fourteenth century and French,
which had been as common in England to the wealthier and

v

middle classes as English is common in Wales to-day, died out, and the new amalgam of dialects which we now speak and call English took its place. The Wars of the Roses offered opportunity for a certain amount of new castle building on a smaller scale, but they were not continuous. The end of the Middle Ages in England was more and more mercantile and less and less feudal. Castle building ceased, partly under the effect of that social change but also, towards the end, under the effect of artillery which gradually compelled the defensive to substitute earthwork for stone walls. It was this same artillery which destroyed the castles wholesale in the seventeenth century, here as abroad, but for very different reasons. Here they were destroyed during that rising of the landed class (including the more prosperous yeomen) against the Crown in the seventeenth century, known as "The Civil Wars." They were destroyed because they were "strong points" on which the national monarchy in process of defeat could fall back. Abroad and especially in France it was just the other way. Castles were destroyed because the Crown feared the defensive power they put in the hands of subjects. In each case it was the party with the most guns, the revolutionary oligarchy in the case of England and the monarchy in the case of France, which battered the old castles. In both countries the castle decayed or was transformed and ceased to be a fortress, and most castles, having no religious or social reason for survival, were abandoned to crumble or be used as quarries. At last in the late eighteenth and early nineteenth centuries what was left of their ruins appealed to the new Romantics and later to the new historical sense, whereby, in the main, they have been safeguarded, for good, let us hope, as national possessions.

H. Belloc

King's Land, *April* 1936.

vi

PREFACE

A COUNTRY is kept going by continual reform. Society is not aware of that truth because the process is not only continual but continuous; it gives an impression of something static and stable, though it is really in ceaseless movement. To keep things level and as they are is a perpetual effort; the process might be compared to treading water. And when this process of detailed and continual reform gets slack society sinks; it loses its powers, it becomes less capable, open to defeat, to loss of wealth and to decay.

One reform which we vitally need to-day in England is a reform of the Press. The English Press is more and more ceasing to perform its function of information, and as it sinks lower and lower in its exercise of that function our power of judging our own international position and our domestic affairs sinks with it.

All reforms suffer this major difficulty, that they have to combat inertia. But each reform has its own peculiar difficulties, and the peculiar difficulty confronting a reform of the Press is that it is an attempt to instruct that which is itself the source of instruction. You have to convince people of things they don't know, though you have blocked against you the only channel by which they get to know anything. Tell people of something of public importance which they have not seen in their daily paper, and they will have difficulty in believing you. In order to convince them that the Press misleads

ix

them you will have to use the Press itself. That is the
paradox of the situation. That is what makes it so
difficult to achieve the reform required.

There remains the use of th book, and it is by the use
of the book that the author of the present volume is
attempting the very necessary task of waking people up
to their danger. A book has of course nothing like the
effect of even one newspaper, let alone the general
Press; at its best the effect is delayed—it necessarily
begins, at least, in a comparatively narrow circle and it
is not reiterated—which is to-day a major weakness, for
the public has become so used to the ceaseless din of
reiteration that lacking in reiteration the truth will
hardly pierce.

Moreover, however vital the truth which a book
conveys, it may by accidental or deliberate neglect on
the part of the Press drop out: we have a first-rate
example of this in Admiral Consett's book on trading
with the enemy during the war (*The Triumph of the
Unarmed Forces*). It was quite clear from that book that
the politicians of this country permitted the enemy to be
supplied with material for continuing hostilities, and it
was equally clear that much of this material was supplied
by individuals resident in this country. That truth was a
vital truth which it was essential for all Englishmen to
know; its publication was met by boycott and misrepre-
sentation in the Press; to-day it is forgotten and its
lesson—which is a lesson of life and death—might as well
never have been delivered.

Nevertheless if a book is the only method available
then to that method we must turn.

Anyone with some slight knowledge of modern
Europe appreciates the decline of our Press in the matter
of information. It needs no great acquaintance with the
Continental Press, let alone with the conversation of men
who conduct Continental affairs, to find oneself appalled
by the lack of information in which the English citizen
stands to-day. But how many people can acquire that
little knowledge? How many people can by personal
experience test the gulf between the elementary knowledge they should possess and the ignorance in which
they remain? No foreign language is now familiar as
French was to educated men and women of the last
generation, the old intercourse between members of the
educated classes throughout the West of Europe has
broken down, modern travel is worse than useless, it is
actually a bar to information upon foreign things—it has
become impersonal and standardized. A man goes from
one international hotel to another to play bridge and golf
and then to come home. I continually come across men
who have returned not only from common travel of
this kind but even from international conferences, as
innocent of any useful material for forming a good judgment on Europe as they were when they set out.

When you add to such conditions the modern factor of
inflamed national vanity which separates the various
parts of Europe one from another more than they were
ever separated before, you have a situation which may
well make one despair of remedy.

There is, however, one avenue of approach whereby
something may be done. That is the use of examples. A
sufficient number of examples of the state into which our

Press has fallen presented to a sufficient number of readers may possibly start a demand for some national minimum of information. At any rate the attempt is here made.

HILAIRE BELLOC

INTRODUCTION

AMONG the many problems which English history presents, far the most important is this : ' What was the process of the Reformation in England ? ' The book for which I have the honour to write this introduction attacks that problem from an approach of the highest value : the numerical situation of the Catholics after they had become an opposition. It is only by grasping two points in this connection that we can appreciate with what difficulty and how slowly the unnatural severance between this country and the main body of Europe was accomplished. These two points are : first, the large number of acknowledged and open Catholics remaining *at each stage* in the affair ; second, the contemporary wide penumbra of Catholicism : the very broad margin of those who would not face persecution but were still at heart in favour of the ancestral religion.

The English Reformation was the most important European event between the conversion of the Roman Empire and modern times. It was the most important because upon it the unity or break-up of Christendom depended. It is of especial importance to Englishmen because it is by far the greatest event in the story of their country ; but it is of still greater importance to Europeans as a whole, because if England had not been torn away from the unity of Christendom that unity would be intact to this day. It was the loss of England which determined the whole affair. Because of that loss Europe ultimately fell into two camps, the Protestant culture on the one hand, and the Catholic culture on the other. On account of this division men grew weary of general conceptions; scepticism became first common, then universal. Sovereign nationalities ceased to admit any common bond, and therefore became at last the murderously self-destructive things they are to-day. It was through the Reformation that the dissolution of Europe came and that chaos of which we are now suffering the last, and perhaps mortal, effects.

But how can we say that the English Reformation was of such importance? After all, the revolt against unity, the effort to destroy Christendom, did not begin in England; it began (as might have been expected) in the Germanies, and in the non-Romanised part of the Germanies. Nor was England the battle-field of the Reformation. The battle-field of the Reformation was France. A whole lifetime of fighting in France decided for the rest of Europe that compromise on which Europe afterwards attempted—most insecurely—to live. The French religious wars did not establish Protestantism, on the contrary they saved the Catholic culture; but they went on so long and were so indecisive that they allowed the new religion to take root.

Again, no Englishman or group of Englishmen appeared as leaders of the reaction against Catholic morals, Catholic doctrine and the old European unity. Everything at the beginning of the English movement came late, everything was accidental. How, then, can we regard the English movement as being of such supreme importance?

For this reason: That the original upheaval was without form. The religious turmoil had been like a boiling-pot. Its prime quality was an unco-ordinated enthusiasm directed to no one end, but everywhere negative; an indignation against the corruption of the Church had been rising for more than a lifetime, indeed for more than a century. It at last overflowed, and the only common spirit in that revolution was a disgust with the papacy. Nothing so negative and so unorganised could possibly survive.

The princes, nobility and squires, large and small, the free cities, the distant little Scandinavian States, took the opportunity to loot the goods of the Church as did all manner of adventurers. The economic motive came in to give driving power to the reformers everywhere. But when the first blind fury had spent itself it would have been possible to compromise upon the economic revolution to which it had given rise. The zeal for making a recovery after the fever would have been sufficient to restore Christendom—had it not been for England; and it is tragic to remember that England was thrown upon the revolutionary side through no national movement, through no special national conditions, through nothing beyond a petty personal accident : the violence, in appetite and ambition, of an impulsive, unbalanced man, who happened also to be the whole English Government. Henry Tudor was King of England just at the moment when kings were reaching the maximum of their power : just at the moment when mediæval kingship was dying and the worship of personal kingship was being born.

England was an ancient Roman province. It inherited to the full the traditions of 1500 years. It was an integral part of Europe and of Christendom. When England went the whole structure reeled.

I say, therefore, that it is of the first moment, in our effort to understand the story of Europe, to grasp the real nature of the *English* transformation, since, but for that transformation, the unity of Europe would have been restored.

Unfortunately, the questions : What was the Reformation in England? What were the steps by which it proceeded? What was the nature of English character and thought at each stage of the great change? have never been answered worthily.

One might almost say they have never been answered at all. And the reason of this lamentable deflection of historical knowledge is that, when a united England was at last re-established, after a century and a half of kaleidoscopic change, that new Protestant England became so vigorous and so united that its literature, especially its writing of history, became engaged wholly upon the propagation of the new thing.

English letters in general and English historians in particular took up an attitude of what is called to-day ' propaganda '—anti-Catholic propaganda—and the new unity of the nation was such that this attitude was universal. Since the first generation of the eighteenth century the whole directing class in England, our teaching, our social spirit—all—has been a continuous plea for the anti-Catholic thesis. In particular there appeared a determination, partly conscious in a few but in the most of men only instinctive, to represent the English Reformation as being, from its origin, at once national and inevitable.

The modern Englishman, meaning by that term the Englishmen who made the great new expansion of England in commerce, in colonisation and the rest, the aristocratic England which became and has remained so great, propounded almost without exception a certain historical thesis which is false. This false thesis has taken deep roots and has acquired such a strength that it is now almost impossible to over-set it and to restore the true picture.

Our official history has taught by continual suggestion and by taking it as it were for granted that the English people were in some fashion naturally antagonistic to Catholicism. The confused revolt against the Church officials and their crystallised later-mediæval Church system of government, with its huge top-heavy income and its bureaucratic corruption, is represented by our official history as something which the English people were awaiting, and welcomed, when it came, as an emancipation from an unpopular faith.

Again, what was essentially a political, or at the most, a social ill-ease, is represented as being essentially a spiritual movement.

So much for the false motive power ascribed to the English Reformation.

Official falsehood equally misrepresents the successive steps by which Catholicism was ultimately driven out. We are given to understand that the architect of the whole affair was a highly popular, typically national monarch, Henry Tudor, a man of strong will and strong political sense as well; that with judgement suitable to the great occasion he gradually loosened the irksome bonds which had attached England to the general civilisation of Europe.

Of what followed his death, a further false picture is drawn. His eldest daughter, the legitimate Queen of England, Mary, is set out as opposing the natural tendency of Englishmen to deny their ancestral religion; as attempting to defend a failing cause by futile cruelty. His illegitimate daughter, Elizabeth, is represented as the idol of the nation, a woman who ruled with individual power and skill, piloting England on the course which England desired to follow, protecting the nation against the violent aggression of Spain and leaving her realm a great power at last, after having founded English predominance at sea.

The Catholic tradition, we are told, had sunk so low by the time of her death (in less than fifty years!) that it appealed only to a fast-disappearing minority, principally confined to a few remote landed families who were at issue with the mass of the nation. The long Stuart period, from the Gunpowder Plot to the expulsion of James II, eighty years later, is represented as an unnatural effort on the part of kings, who were not English in temper, to deflect the natural development of England, challenging the English instinct for parliamentary government (called 'constitutional') and ending in an insane attempt on the part of the last Stuart, James II, to impose upon the whole English people by force and fraud the Catholic system which they detested and which only a handful of them still accepted. Against so monstrous a provocation the English people rose in rebellion, driving out the tyrant who had conceived it and settling down into a formation which exactly suited their high destinies—substituting representative government for an irrational personal monarchy and giving full freedom to the instinctive Protestantism of the nation.

The whole of that official picture is false.

The truth, which it is the business of serious history to proclaim, is that the English Reformation was a very slow, laborious and difficult process, because it was established by force of wealth and arms *against* the traditions and *against* the inherited nature of English society. At every stage in the process our historians depict a state of affairs other than what was. They under-value—always in a large measure, often in a grotesquely large measure—the strength of the conservative resistance and, what is more important, the quality of that resistance. It is the business of true history to replace their official legend by a just estimate of the slow pace at which the change proceeded and of the gradual yet irregular advance of that process.

England did indeed become at last a new thing. The English Catholic past became after the generation 1688–1715 a foreign country to Englishmen. A new England had arrived and the old England was at last rapidly disappearing. But the great change had only come after a very long, difficult, uncertain and varying conflict.

In general, one may say that at each main landmark in the journey from European Catholic unity to national anti-Catholic unity, the remaining strength, value and even numbers of English Catholicism were far greater than official history allows, and it is our business to discover the right balance of the forces at work during the two lifetimes over which the transition extended. What we have to find out is not so much how many Englishmen could still heroically oppose the increasing attack on them at various dates, but how much England was still Catholic *in mind* at the beginning of the Governmental pressure against Catholicism in 1560; how much England was still Catholic *in mind* at the end of the first Cecil's effort about the time of Mary Queen of Scots' death and the consequent Armada; how much when the second Cecil had done his work and the turn of the tide following the Gunpowder Plot was gathering momentum; how much in the mid-seventeenth century during the wrestling between the money power and the Crown, the great London merchants and the Crown, the Puritan minority and the Crown; how much in the earlier years of the Restoration; how much at the time of the Popish Plot; how much at the terminal of all this when the Stuart dynasty fell and the work was concluded.

In order to arrive at the right solution of these difficult problems we have to consider three elements.

First of all we must estimate the real proportions, numerically, not so much of those who declared themselves openly on the one side or the other, as of a general anti-Catholic feeling on the one side and of traditional feeling more or less in sympathy with Catholicism on the other. These two categories divide the nation into much larger groups than the conventional and official ' Catholic ' and ' Protestant.'

B

Next we must satisfy ourselves on the *intensity* of the feeling on either side.

Thirdly, we must estimate the effect of power exercised through wealth and through office from the beginning to the end of the development : all executive power and most wealth were with the small anti-Catholic Minority from 1560 to 1570; with the larger anti-Catholic Minority of 1570–1580; with the rapidly growing anti-Catholic Minority of 1580–1600; and, after 1600, with what had become the anti-Catholic *Majority*, thenceforward.

Thus, in making our estimate, we have to appreciate that the real divisions of English society throughout the affair were not mere definite Catholicism, *still less definite Papalism*, on the one side, and definite Protestantism on the other. To think in those terms is to 'read history backwards' : to think of the past in terms of the present. To ask such questions as : How many Englishmen were Catholic at such and such a date ? How many were Protestant ? is to misstate the thing altogether. The real divisions of England up to the very moment when the Catholic element collapsed in 1689, a century and a half after the movement against Catholicism had begun, were, it would seem, as follows :

First, there was a body of strong anti-Catholicism making up in zeal, conviction and energy what it lacked in numbers. It began as a tiny minority : what are called abroad 'intellectuals.' It grew with time, but still remained a minority, did that nucleus of convinced, persistent and intense reaction against the Catholic Faith.

Next, there was from the beginning a large body impossible to define, but certainly for a whole lifetime more than half the nation, which was fairly indifferent to the purely religious question, with a left wing and a right wing of indifference : indifference with anti-

Catholic tendencies on the left, indifference with tendencies vaguely traditional and therefore vaguely Catholic on the right. Lastly, there was from the beginning and at the beginning a very large minority definitely awakening to the importance of preserving the Catholic spirit, if no more. But, within that large minority, there was a nucleus which was ready to make a definite pronouncement of full Catholic conviction at a risk. It was always small; and that part of the small nucleus which was ready to make the sacrifice of fortune (let alone of life) was, of course, smaller still.

Of these three elements the fortunes of the first, the anti-Catholic element, increased. It annexed more and more of the indifferents. It became more and more identified with national feeling.

At the other extreme, that dwindling minority which desired to restore the old religion grew more definite even as it declined in numbers; but, though it grew more definite, it felt, at heart, its prospects to be more and more doubtful.

There was still a chance, as late as 1688, for the establishment and retention of an organised, practising Catholic community, amounting to perhaps one-eighth or more than one-eighth of English people, when the combined bad policy and misfortune of the last Stuart reign led to the final catastrophe.

Had James II maintained his throne there would have lived on in England a body of organised Catholicism, strongly surviving; not indeed on the scale of the Dutch (where it was nearly half the nation), but at least sufficient to modify the nature of the State. Of rather more than a million English families, much more than a hundred thousand but less than two hundred thousand, were ready to rank themselves openly as Catholics when the fall of the active Monarchy ended everything. For after 1688 onwards, more and more rapidly, this at first considerable Catholic minority melted away like ice at the change of the seasons.

At the mid-eighteenth century, the critical date of '45, one comes across continual allusions to Catholic traditions in this family and that of Catholic sympathies with the fallen dynasty which sympathies were connected with the religion of the Pretenders. Men and women recall in their letters and diaries, in their sketches of biography, in their family anecdotes, the Catholicism of this or that member—a grandparent, an uncle or aunt, a cousin. They speak of them as relics, but not as relics of things dead.

Another long half lifetime, by, say, 1785 (the loss of the American colonies and the eve of the French Revolution) and English Catholicism may be said to have disappeared. It is estimated, apparently with justice, that by that time not one English family in a hundred had any knowledge of the Sacraments, of the Mass, or in general of the Catholic Faith. The Faith had become wholly alien and odd, as well as antipathetic, to all the English mind.

If we take then as our starting point the date 1559–60, when Cecil launched the policy which held the field for two long lifetimes (for over a century and a quarter), and, as the term of the affair, 1688–90, we can in that period of 130 years establish a few clear marking points at which to gauge the rate and the successive heights of the flood.

We have, of course, no general statistics, for it was an age in which statistics were not drawn up.

In the pages that follow will be found a close analysis of such figures as we possess; but, for a main outline, we have to content ourselves with the general statements of contemporaries, checked by probabilities, common sense and our general knowledge.

A little before the push begins during the rash experiment of the usurping Council (1546–53)—the nominal reign of little Edward VI—a man who had the best opportunity for judging, Paget, the man who had all the papers of the Council before him—reports from various parts of England, his own experiences and his own excellent judgement for a guide, the man who was at the centre of government—easily explains why Somerset and the rest failed and why the attempt at establishing a new religion, odious to the mass of the nation, though it had not broken down under the widespread and popular risings, could not win in spite of hired foreign mercenaries and artillery. He left it on record that barely *one in twelve* of the English people were upon the side of the Reformation. We know, of course, that even of that tiny fraction the greater part were in London.

When Mary took the throne in 1553 amid popular enthusiasm, England was what it had always been, fully Catholic. There is no evidence that the persecution, the very numerous burnings of the last three years before Elizabeth (a repression directed against what was felt to be rebellion and undertaken in spite of protest from the Emperor and his son, the Queen's husband) greatly affected opinion one way or the other. Common sense will tell us that the large measure of such violence and suffering had *some* effect—especially in London, where the executions were more numerous than elsewhere. Converts were made to the new opinions. Those already convinced in them were confirmed in their new zeal and faith. Particular cases (such as Hooper the popular Bishop of Gloucester) undoubtedly provoked strong local feeling. But England as a whole was not much less Catholic at the end of Mary's reign than at the beginning. The persecution had not touched the great bulk of the country towns. It had not been presented at all to the mass of the agricultural population which then composed the overwhelming majority of the nation. Besides this, the persecution, cruel though it was and unprecedented in scale, was a national protest against foreign interference—foreign interference of the oddities introduced by Cranmer (Swiss, German, French and other Reformers); interference of the Spaniard and his chaplains who tried to prevent the persecution altogether and to protect the heretics.

When Mary was dead, and Philip of Spain and William Cecil between them had put Elizabeth upon the throne, the popular mind was thoroughly bewildered. It is impossible to put the thing with precision, but probably the proportion of convinced Protestants (which virtually meant, in that day, convinced Calvinists) was still not much larger than one family in twelve. But what *had* changed in the violent official action and reaction of fourteen years was the security of the public mind.

The small but active and intense Protestant minority was now allied with the executive power. Those who had feared for their newly-acquired wealth, the loot of religion, were vastly relieved to remember that with the new administration under Cecil they were—after 1560— secure.

Mary had guaranteed them the possession of the loot and the Pope had reluctantly agreed; but they could not feel so safe under her as under the man who was now at the head of affairs.

The ramifications of the great economic revolution ran everywhere throughout society. There had been sale and re-sale of the looted endowments not only of monasteries, but of colleges, schools, hospitals and of every form of corporate property. Apart, of course, from the large fortunes, such as those of the Russells and the Cromwells, acquired by the sack of religion, there was a mass of minor interests. A large proportion of the squires had got some of the pickings, and there were in every market town, almost every village, speculators who had benefited by the economic upheaval.

Those who were indifferent to religion would naturally support the new Protestant establishment as making their new wealth more certainly secure, but even those who regretted the national religion of the past in which they had all been trained did not for the most part feel as strongly about it as they did about their new-found wealth. The mass of the people in the country-sides had been pushed backwards and forwards and what with the First Prayer Book, the Second Prayer Book, the preachers trimming their sails to each change of government, the popular restoration of the Mass under Queen Mary, then the unexpected and violent persecution of which rumours reached even the remote counties, then the appearance again in the Parish Church of a service in English—and so on, there was a thorough confusion.

Of that confusion William Cecil took full advantage. With the utmost skill he piloted his reform through the first ten years of the reign, till the abortive rebellion in the North gave him his chance. He was helped by a number of factors. At this date, after Elizabeth had been on the throne ten years, those who had grown up before the schism with Rome were old men; those who had grown up in the later years of Henry VIII, when last the Mass was still an unquestioned universal national habit, were already in late middle age; all those who had been boys under Queen Mary, with opinions unformed, had passed through their teens and early manhood under anti-Catholic direction. No one could keep a school or even act as private tutor unless he supported Cecil's religious policy. The populace thought of the Tudors as a national dynasty. The rightful heir to the throne of England, Mary Stuart, was doubly a foreigner, French and Scotch, and that helped to contrast her attachment to the old religion unfavourably with that of the new experiment. As the younger generation grew up and the elders died off, the nation began to fall into two divisions more clearly separate than before, but of a different texture. It was no longer a case of a small intense Protestant minority using its power against a slack but very large Catholic majority. It was rather a case of something like half the English, and that the younger half, beginning to think of themselves as national rather than as Protestant or Catholic.

Indeed, that was the chief work of William Cecil. He deflected that tendency to worship, which is in all of us, from the universal worship of the ancient Church to the particular worship of England. A shamefully romantic literature, grown up in the nineteenth century, has absurdly exaggerated the antagonism between national feeling on the one side and Catholicism on the other, but the antagonism was there and was growing. Had the wind veered on that July day of 1588 and favoured the landing of the Spaniards after the killing of Mary Stuart, it is morally certain that the Catholic rising which would have followed must have succeeded. It is almost equally certain that Elizabeth herself would have made terms; for she preferred the side of civilisation and order to the side of piracy and of rebellion, and she chafed at her subservient position. But after the Armada had failed things went more and more as William Cecil had originally intended them to go, and as his son Robert, whom he had trained and who had succeeded him, directed them.

When Robert Cecil put James Stuart on the throne after Elizabeth's death, one can fairly say that a good half of the nation, not only accepted, but was in real sympathy with, the new religious establishment, and of the other half only a few privileged people could live lives actively Catholic, however strong their family traditions and personal preferences. Every official force made for the gradual stifling of the old worship, and even for the extinction of its memory, yet the number who preferred the old tradition to the new experiment was still very large.

The pivotal date, *after* which there was certainly a growing anti-Catholic majority, is the Gunpowder Plot of 1605–6. Whether that plot were originated by Robert Cecil or only fostered by him, it at any rate exactly suited his policy and was the making of a new and really Protestant England.

By the time James's son, Charles I, was at issue with the squires in Parliament and the merchants of the City of London, those who were still in some degree of sympathy with the old religion were perhaps little more than one-third of the nation in mere numbers, while in spirit, initiative and organisation they could not compare with their opponents.

As for numbers, a good test is the officers of the two armies after the outbreak of the Civil War. We have it on contemporary estimate that two-fifths of the officers who died for Charles were professedly Catholic. The officers on both sides were drawn from much the same class, but there was a somewhat larger proportion of officers from the non-gentry on the parliamentary side, especially after the New Model had been formed, so it is better to call the Catholic proportion of gentry one-third than two-fifths. With the avowed Catholics forming one-third of the Royalist half—one-sixth of all the commissioned officers—they would represent with their estates a corresponding part of the nation as a whole. But a nation of which one-sixth openly professes and suffers heavily for a tradition contains at least as many who will run no risk but are in sympathy, stronger or weaker, with those who risk all. One-third of England was opposed to the Protestant spirit, sympathetic in various degrees with the older tradition, at the outbreak of the Civil War in 1642.

Meanwhile, there went on, for 160 years, an economic revolution which, on the material side, was the main cause of the great political change whereby England ultimately lost the Faith.

From 1536 to 1540 the great mass of collegiate property, monastic, academic, educational and charitable, was looted wholesale. At least one-fifth, perhaps more like one-third—at any rate something between one-fifth and one-third—of the surplus rental values of English land and buildings was seized by force from its former owners and taken over by the Government and later bestowed or sold cheap to a mass of speculators, favourites and landed families whose support the Crown needed. The endowment, not only of the monasteries, but of the colleges, the hospitals and of the schools was violently seized in a revolution on such a scale as had never been known before. Even the colleges of the universities were to have gone the way of the rest, when they were saved by Henry's death in 1547. After that date, for six years, there was a perfect orgy of further looting on the part of the irresponsible men who had seized upon the Government, led at first by the uncles of the wretched little diseased boy King, their favourites and their fellow-conspirators. The endowments of the innumerable little elementary schools up and down the country, often supported by the Chantries, went, and great parcels of the regular Church endowments as well—the incomes of sees, prebends, etc.

By the time the diseased lad died, a new landed class had arisen and the old landed class was gorged with the spoils of religion. The flood was checked under Mary but rose at her death and went on uninterruptedly under Elizabeth, during whose long reign of forty-three years more and more of what remained to steal was stolen.

The patrimony of the Crown was snatched piece-meal by successive favourites ; there was a continual conspiracy for despoiling the public to the advantage of private men. By the time Elizabeth died the Crown was ruined—and let it be remembered that it was to the personal advantage of every one of these robbers, from before the death of Henry VIII until after the death of Elizabeth, to ward against the return of the old religion.

On top of the general scramble for sudden wealth at the expense of religious and other corporations went the confiscation of individual lay estates, to the advantage of those whom the Cecils, now the main directors of the great change, favoured. The old nobility was impoverished to the advantage of new men. The Cecils themselves are a first-rate example of what happened. They began as inn-keepers ; the next generation were Civil Servants ; then, from a position of what we should call a few hundreds a year just at the middle of the sixteenth century, they became in one lifetime, in the early years of the seventeenth, one of the richest families in England, with a huge palace on the North Road, a town-house with swarms of servants, and two separate peerages and corresponding establishments for the elder and the younger son ; and the Cecils are but one main example out of dozens.

With the Civil Wars the thing continued. All Catholic Ireland was looted. About half her land was still in Catholic hands, that is in the hands of the original owners, when Cromwell's usurpation was beginning. By the time he died hardly a twentieth remained. A vast amount changed hands in England itself and in Scotland. Everyone who had supported the legitimate Government of Charles, and most of those who only sympathised with him too openly, were either ruined altogether or fined so heavily that they were crippled to the advantage of their opponents. William Cecil, the originator of the new policy, had very truly said that the instrument for the destruction of the old religion was the confiscation of wealth. He practised what he preached; and he and his son and their successors effected the transformation of England. Yet such was the tenacity of the ancient Faith that although the Sacraments were cut off and although Mass was unobtainable save in a few privileged places, although no Catholic might teach and every Catholic endowment was destroyed, one-eighth of the nation was still standing out openly for the ancestral religion after the ordeal had continued for 150 years— and at least another one-eighth must have secretly sympathised with tradition. It was not until 1688 that the final blow fell and that, thenceforward, the religion which had made England disappeared from English land.

It will be seen that my general conclusion corresponds with that of the valuable book for which I am writing this introduction; that is, the numerical position of active and acknowledged open Catholics in 1688 was about one-eighth of the population.

It will also be seen that I have suggested, I think without exaggeration, that if a violently persecuted minority could muster open adherents to the proportion of one-eighth there must have been at least an equal number in greater or less degree of sympathy with the ancestral religion.

One should always remember in writing a history that the characteristics of any date with which one is dealing are those of living men: human beings under the conditions common to all of us: sons and daughters remembering their parents, grandchildren remembering their grandparents, households filled as our own households are filled, with all manner of memories and relics of the past. The England of the Popish Plot was to the England of 1600 (even those who least understand the survival of Catholicism must admit that half England was then still Catholic in tone) much as we are to the early '70's, the full Victorian period when Parliament was still a great and active institution, and the Party system still had reality about it ; when such innovations as, let us say, teetotalism or woman suffrage were no more than the fads of a tiny minority ; when the traditions of the mass of Englishmen were still drawn from the country-sides, and when the position of the great landed families was unquestioned. There has been a vast change since then, yet the England of 1938 retains strong traditions of the England of 1870. So it was with the England of the later Stuarts : it retained a strong memory and hold of an earlier time.

The spiritual revolution of 1600–1700 was certainly far deeper and more violent in its effect than any modern change, but though the intensity of the thing is different the rhythm is much the same.

I may conclude by repeating what is perhaps the most convincing consideration of all, the fact that these presumed figures for the various stages of the Reformation correspond to what we should, *a priori*, have expected. The rate at which Catholic numbers declined, the pace and various material stages of the change are exactly what would be natural to the generations in which it took place. There is nothing violent nor unlikely in the supposition, which one may almost call a certainty, that the half of a population opposed to official power falls to a quarter in the course of a long lifetime. The younger men belong to the new idea and gradually forget the old traditions. There is nothing violent or odd in the conclusion that for one man who actively proclaimed himself adherent to the old and officially persecuted Church, there was at least one other man who secretly sympathised with it in some degree. The improbabilities are all on the other side. The official thesis still taught in our schools and universities, of an England already almost wholly anti-Catholic within a lifetime of the Reformation, of men giving up easily at command the habits and traditions of a thousand years is not credible. *That* thesis is indeed unhistorical and does indeed do violence to common sense.

H. BELLOC.

INTRODUCTION.

THE story which Father Robo here gives of his parish in penal times and subsequently in the decisive moment of the French immigration is particularly valuable for its account of the latter, to whom—I mean to the immigrant priests of the French Revolutionary period —we owe the revival of Catholicism in England to-day: to them and to the great Irish famine in the 19th century.

It is not perhaps sufficiently appreciated what a part the immigrant priests of more than 150 years ago played in the re-founding of the Faith in England. The vividness of the picture is obscured by the later effect of what has been called the Oxford Movement, and especially by the fame of Newman. For this there are many reasons, the first of which is, I suppose, the fact that no one likes to find in these days of extreme Nationalism an alien origin for anything which he supports. For English Catholics it is naturally more attractive to emphasise the influence (and very great it was) of those thoroughly national men who surrounded Newman, and of whom Newman was the chief, and through whom the more cultivated classes, at least, of England, and especially of the Church of England, were brought into touch with the Catholic past. Moreover, the effect of the French immigration was neither immediate nor on any considerable scale.

Nevertheless, it was the true seed whence the present development sprang. That development must not be exaggerated, either in its actual extent (we form, I believe, only some 7 per cent. of the population of Great Britain, and of that small body a very large proportion is either Irish in descent or with some Irish

iii.

connection). Nor is it too certain that our expansion as yet is greater than the general expansion of population in, say, the last 40 years. On that there is dispute. But what is certain is the point which Mr. Woodruff, the distinguished Editor of the *Tablet,* made so forcibly in an address given the other day: the fact that Catholicism is now a known and familiar thing in this country, where, not much more than 100 years ago, it was quite unfamiliar. As Mr. Woodruff put it, there is hardly anyone who counts in England to-day that has not some friend or relative, or at least contact, through which he can feel, however vaguely, what the Faith is.

If you would know why and how it was the French émigré priest that began the planting of the seed, you must dig out from some library and read two very remarkable books written by Digby Beste in the earlier part of the 19th century, long before the catholicising movement of Newman and Pusey and the rest began. The title of that section in these books which is capital to an understanding of the time, is " Priestly Absolution at Oxford," a half ironical title—ironical in the juxtaposition of the thing with the intensely anti-Catholic locality where the thing took place. The irony and the lightness of touch are typical of the author, one of the most delightful chroniclers that ever put light and delicate pen to work upon a mighty subject. In Digby Beste's work—now forgotten but over-due to be revived by those who care for the national history—he describes a sermon preached by him as a young Anglican clergyman from the pulpit of the University Church of St. Mary at Oxford. This sermon advocated the validity of sacerdotal, sacramental, Absolution after Confession to a priest *of the Church of England.* It had an immediate and very great effect, and it was with that sermon that everything began.

Some have called that novel effort at grafting Catholicism upon the Protestant tree " Laudian," but

iv.

the adjective is a misnomer. Laud was never of that mood, still less of that doctrine. There were still memories in his time, there was still usage, upon which a return to the Seven Sacraments might have been built. There was still a practice of private, but *not* sacramental Confession. More than that there was not under Laud. This sermon preached by young Digby Beste was the true starting point of the whole affair.

Now Digby Beste tells us in his account of this critical origin that the thing had been implanted in his mind by the French immigrant priesthood.

Like Newman, long after him, the young man at first thought to reconcile the Church of his baptism, which was his home, with that other thing which had grown so alien in English eyes. He would have understood and perhaps used the term "Anglo-Catholic." But Anglo-Catholic he could not be, and in due time, still young, he was reconciled. It is not the first case and will not be the last of forgotten origins. Does anyone know, for instance, to-day that "Members of Parliament" began not with Simon de Montfort, nor with any of the experiments immediately before his time, but with King John in 1204? It was King John who called together the first Knights of the Shire. So with that movement which ended with the re-establishment of organised Catholic worship in England, it began long before the date generally ascribed to it.

Yet in all the careful and most interesting analysis which Father Robo here gives of the 200 French priests who were received in Farnham as refugees from persecution in their country, we find no parallel to this Oxford episode. It seems to have been a thing by itself. But historically it is one of the most important things in the modern history of Europe. How important it was we shall not know till long hence, when the final fate of English Catholicism, so very nearly murdered, shall be decided.

v.

I have devoted the space at my disposal to that one point, which seems to me of such special value, and I trust that Father Robo will forgive my having so underlined it, although his most valuable work includes much else, as the reader may now see—the story of the modern parish, some pages upon penal times, and some on the "Second Spring," as it is called—a phrase generally reserved for the Oxford Movement in particular.

One incidental point of the highest historical interest is the value of money at the time of the immigration. The reader will find it from page 32 onwards. The value of money at different periods is essential to the understanding of history and is one of the most difficult things to establish. Father Robo's minute research gives us glimpses here and there which are of the most illuminating kind, notably the mention of two guineas (on page 34) as the stipend or pension received as livelihood in 1796—just over a shilling a day.

I must not continue my poor contribution to this most valuable publication lest I should exceed my function. But I hope it may be read as widely as it deserves.

H. BELLOC.

King's Land,
　Shipley, Horsham.
　　　November, 1938.

EDITOR'S PREFACE

IF there is one idea more deeply rooted than another in the modern world outside the Catholic
Church, it is the conception that some natural
antagonism exists between the Catholic system
and the conclusions, positive and negative, of the
human reason working independently upon the
universe in which it finds itself, and coming to
its own final judgments.

By an irony which perpetually appears in the
field of religious debate, that very faculty which
should enable us to perceive the absence of conflict is made the cause of conflict. In proportion
to the power of a man's reason can he distinguish
categories one from another: in proportion to
that power is he free from the error of confound-
ing ideas with words and of confusing totally
different principles because the formulæ for them
may happen to contain similar phrases.

The belief that there is a necessary conflict between the Catholic system and the human reason
is based upon two false conceptions which it is
the special task of the Catholic apologist to

7

dispel. The first is the conception that the Catholic system consists in a number of detached affirmations with no logical connection binding them — a mere agglomeration — each unit of which is either fantastically marvellous or insane because it reposes upon no real ground for conviction. The second is the conception that a truth can *only* be known in one of two ways — by deductive proof from an established general principle, or by the direct appreciation of the senses and inductions from such direct appreciation.

Now both these conceptions are false. The Catholic system is an organic whole far more consistent than any philosophy opposed to it, or neutral to it. A man may reject it, but he cannot reject it on the ground of its particularism; for if he does that, he shows himself ignorant of his subject matter. The Catholic system is not one of many; it is not to be chosen out of a heap of similar things all making similar claims; it is unique. Alone of any system propounded to the mind of man it bears two marks which render it thus a thing of itself amid the turmoil of human thought and speculation, in that it proceeds from the most general conceptions of all on and down to its last details, and that it claims divine and infallible authority. It is based upon a thorough examination of the last nature of things: beginning with the prime question, whether the purpose of things can be discovered at all, proceeding to the second, whether there be a God, and thence by successive steps to an examination of all that is necessary to be known for the higher end of man. But it does not *convince* by such a process. It convinces by the effect of a Personality, an authority manifest. Those conclusions which the Faith reaches in the processes of examination and propounds whether the hearer has examined them individually or no—a Personal God, human immortality, the Incarnation and all its consequences in the Church—are often separate from lesser experience; they are always (as are the foundation and implications of every science) intermixed with mystery—that is, with truths beyond, but not contrary to, reason. They are never of a kind which pure ·reason must reject.

And the second conception is false. It is not true that one cannot be sure of a thing save by deduction from a general principle, or by a direct appreciation through the senses. There is a third method, a method by which we recognise truth through a convergence of a vast number of processes of different kinds through what might be called, in a mathematical metaphor, *integration.*

You may know that a tree is an oak tree without having seen it, deducing this truth from an already ascertained certitude that a tree is present in such and such a place, and that in view of the evidence nothing but an oak tree could be there. Or you may be certain of that oak tree by an exact physical examination, noting carefully the contour of many leaves, the nature of the bark, a specimen in section of the wood. But you are not only *as* sure, you are *more* sure, that your oak tree is an oak tree when you see it as a whole, though you see it from a hundred yards away, where you cannot perceive the detail of the bark or of the leaves—and you are sure through the faculty of integration. You have received an indefinite number of converging evidences in shape, colour, situation, etc. With no process of deductive thought and no close series of analysed physical tests, you say the thing is an oak tree.

There are two propositions in connection with the truth of the Faith and its supposed conflict with reason, which propositions reason itself can distinguish—but rarely does so. The first is the proposition that the truth of a system or of a thing is established by reason; the second is the proposition that the truth of a system or a thing can *only* be established by reason. It is a characteristic confusion of many a modern mind that these totally variant statements are confounded one with another. If it be expected that the Faith shall be proved as a mathematical proposition is proved, then the expectation will be disappointed, and if anyone having the Faith be so foolish as to make the claim, he does the Faith an ill-service. But if, on the contrary, an opponent maintains that nothing is known or can be known save as truth dependent on mathematical proof is known, let him consider such truths as our recognition of personalities, our certitude in the external universe, the continuity of our individual moral responsibility—and any number of other certain facts which are not proved, but appreciated and only known by an essential quality in them conforming to what they should be. So it is with the Faith, which is held principally because it is found to conform to what the Divine Authority claims it should be.

H. BELLOC.

EDITOR'S PREFACE

Part of the universal misconception concerning the Catholic Church as seen by those outside it—a misconception which dominated the non-Catholic world of the 19th Century and is only now being set right—that the one department of human activity which might have been specially pointed to as the peculiar province of Catholicism has been imagined to be not so much in conflict with Catholicism, as neglected by it. I mean philosophy.

The peculiar function of the Catholic Church in the story of our civilisation has been to preserve the philosophic conquests of pagan antiquity and to expand them over an even greater range of *discovery* than the greatest of the ancients had commanded.

There is no one acquainted with the story of Europe who does not know this to be true. Yet the story of Europe in its main outlines has been so neglected through the effect of religious conflict that even this elementary historical truth still sounds novel in many ears.

It is to be noted that the function of the Catholic Church in this respect is not connected with the truth or falsehood of her claim to be a divine

vii

and infallible authority in matters of morals and doctrine.   A man might believe the very worst of the Catholic Church as a guide and teacher of men, or might be completely indifferent to her claim, or regard it as preposterous, and yet be necessarily acquainted through history with the plain historical truth that the Church was above all a promoter of philosophy.   Yet is that truth still insufficiently recognised.

Your average educated man, if he were told that the Catholic Church, the culture which it created and has hitherto maintained in Europe, had preserved the vestiges of architecture, and had caused, after centuries of conservation, a new great architecture to arise in the Middle Ages, would at once agree.   He is familiar by this time with the fact that the traditions of Christendom not only saved but expanded the architecture of the ancients; preserved it and transformed it.   If he were told that the culture of Christendom had done something of the same kind with letters, he would generally agree.   But when he is told that what is true of letters and architecture is especially true of the prime function of philosophy, the statement is still (too often) a strange one in his ears.

We have used in this connexion the word "discovery," in connexion with philosophy.   It needs a line of explanation; for the modern world has come to use the term "philosophy" to mean something very different from its true meaning. Philosophy signifies primarily the love of knowledge—ultimate knowledge upon the ultimate realities; and, by extension, it especially signifies *the solving of questions which the mind puts to itself relative to the most important subjects with which the mind can deal.* Thus this word "discovery" is especially applicable to the philosophic function—the action of the mind when it succeeds in philosophical research. For instance, one of the prime questions man asks himself is whether his personality be mortal or not. The answer given to such a question is the supposed solution of a problem, and if the answer is true it is a *discovery.* Or again, a process of reasoning which establishes the existence of a personal God is a *discovery.*

It is the discovery of a new piece of reality; the establishment of a new certitude in the place of guesswork. It is just as much discovery as is the discovery of a new district of the earth's surface —and infinitely more important.

Now because many of these questions have seemed at first sight insoluble, there has arisen, from the beginnings of philosophic discussion, a sort of imitation of philosophy which the later Greeks called "sophistry," and of which it is a fair definition to say that it is the art of making up systems which do not really solve problems and which are hardly intended to do so by their authors; which are, in a word, not discoveries, but merely guesses at the best, or at the worst a mass of verbiage. This kind of stuff, which antiquity early learned to separate from true philosophy (which is the search for reality and the definition of it when discovered) has flourished prodigiously, especially among the Germans, from the end of the 18th Century to the latter part of the 19th; and to it most modern educated men, outside the Catholic culture, still give the term philosophy to-day.

Now philosophy is not that at all. True philosophy is to such making-up-of-systems what research in physical science is to the old *a priori* assertions of a pre-scientific age.

For example, one of the prime questions which the mind puts to itself is whether Evil be of positive existence or no. A man spinning systems may answer by mere metaphors, such as "Evil is but the shadow of Good." Or by something little more than verbiage, such as, "Evil can only exist in the relation of things to themselves"; or again, by still emptier formulae, such as that "there are no ultimate contradictions; any two apparently contradictory things may be resolved into a higher unity." But such fogs do not belong to philosophy; they belong to sophistry. The philosopher is he who shall determine by a process of reason and observation combined whether or not positive evil exists. When he arrives at a true answer in this matter, he has made a discovery. Even if he arrive at a false answer, he has acted as a philosopher; for he has made an attempt at discovery. But if he does not give a clean answer at all, but only something which makes the matter more confused than ever, he is not a philosopher at all, but a sophist.

It is the glory of the Catholic Church to have insisted throughout her existence upon the treatment of the gravest questions in a philosophical manner, and especially to have developed since the 12th Century a vast scheme of exploration which has definitely achieved conquest upon conquest; discoveries of realities. The more the educated men of our time turn to the examination of that piece of cultural work, especially to its culminating point in St. Thomas, the more will they appreciate with how vast a matter they have to deal when they curiously approach the Faith. It is not a long time since one might say that St. Thomas was unknown outside the Catholic seminaries. Already to-day he is read even at Oxford (where not thirty years ago his name was a mere jest). In Paris to-day and in the whole university system of France there has been, as it were, a resurrection of the scholastic method. And so it should be; for men will find therein not the incomprehensible, the vague, nor the evading of questions in a mist of words, but research, discovery, and consequent rational and exact affirmation.

THE EDITOR.

INTRODUCTION

That it should be supposed there is a conflict between the Catholic Church and physical science is one of the most astonishing psychological phenomena of our time. It is in the nature of a legend, but a legend with no correspondence to reality. It is believed in with a firmness and devotion which makes one envy the faith of the believers, and yet not one of them could tell us the grounds of his belief.

However, the feeling is there; it is very strong; and it must be met with patience.

Like many other strong and highly unified emotions, it has a multiple source. It comes from the coalescence of several streams of experience, false and true. There is, for instance, the obvious fact that the Church in every epoch uses the language of that epoch, being a corporation of living men existent in this world. Therefore, in time, discovery (or retrogression in knowledge, for that matter) renders verbal statement imperfect. And that is true not only of the Church, but of any institution that lives for a long time. Before the discovery of America, a

9

man might well call the Atlantic "the ocean
bounding the world." Indeed, there was a
Mohammedan soldier who said exactly that
when he rode his horses into the surf on the
Moroccan coast. Before certain modern developments of mathematical speculation (and after
it), positive statement, as though final, of tri-
dimensional common geometry passed into the
metaphor of ecclesiastical as well as of laical talk.
Men said, "You might as well expect two parallel
lines to meet," or "Matter is impenetrable." The
language, though limited, was sound. A truth
expressed in each language remains true. But
the untrained mind is shocked by the contrast
in phraseology. That is one very puerile but
very natural origin for the supposed conflict. We
get, in any age, ecclesiastics talking the language
of that age, though that has nothing whatever
to do with doctrine. And to this must be added
the fact that *some* language must be talked, whatever the epoch and whatever the extent of knowledge, and that *all* language is metaphorical. For
instance, no one ever meant by "ascension into
heaven" the crude idea of going up for ever from
a plain; but you have to express the idea some-
how, and that is roughly the best way of
putting it.

Then there is the eternal Galileo incident,
which is irrelevant, but dramatic and striking.

Then with a mass of modern men, though only among the uncultured, there is the idea that physical science has discovered a great number of things of a metaphysical sort so that it can refute the metaphysics of a day before its own. Perhaps the crudest example of this misconception was afforded by a Dr. Barnes, Bishop of Birmingham, in England, who thought that modern chemistry had disproved the possibility of a resurrection of the body!

Then there is the mere fact that physical science has lately been advancing very rapidly, while true doctrine upon the only things that matter cannot of its nature "advance"; it can only develop from within, remaining always of the same substance and adding nothing to itself. A man may confusedly conceive that that which is moving in one manner and that which is moving in another must be in conflict, because their modes of being are diverse.

Then there is a very powerful factor—personally I think the most powerful—which proceeds from the misconception that the Catholic Church is a sort of extreme form of what is sometimes called "fundamentalism," and that, whereas most Protestants once did and now do not follow a literal interpretation of the Scriptures, *all* Catholics were bound to it and could never remain Catholic if they did not so remain bound.

But physical science—and for that matter common experience—perpetually shows Scriptural language to be allegory or metaphor. When a particular visual concept created by the text (for instance, precise locating the first man so many years ago, in such and such a precise place, and the making of him, as it were with hands, out of mud) is upset or weakened by physical discovery, the non-Catholic says, "I was wrong in my old visual concept"; and as his visual concept was all the faith he had, he loses his faith. *He imagines the Catholic to be similarly dependent upon a visual concept,* and he therefore naturally concludes that the Catholic must follow in his footsteps and lose his faith as well.

It is as though an Englishman were to think that the French language could only be artificially taught in classes, and, hearing of some French community where there were no schools, should conclude that the French language could not exist in that community; and that they therefore must, in the nature of things, talk English.

The truth is, of course, that Catholicism lies in the acceptation of doctrine, not in the visual concepts of the believer; that the Catholic Church proposes to the believer, not a series of pictures called up by his fancy in the realm of imagination, but in the realm of *thought*, a consistent scheme: an explanation of the nature, not of individual phenomena, but of the ultimate causes upon which all phenomena depend.

Now between two or more philosophical conceptions of the universe physical science can never decide. For it is the business of a philosophical conception of the universe to explain what contains phenomena or that without which phenomena would not be. You can never prove by phenomena that one philosophic system is more right than another.

For instance, the observation of mankind has told them for centuries that a stone falls when it is let free from a height. The Catholic Church explains the repetition of this phenomenon by saying that the universe is governed by an Almighty and Perfect Spirit infinite in His attributes, Which imposed its special characteristic upon every special form of matter. The atheist says, "No, these characteristics are present, but not through any conscious action; they are inherent in the unconscious mass." The so-called agnostic says that he will not decide between the two conceptions; in other words, that he has no philosophy, a position really impossible for any intelligent being to hold for five consecutive minutes, but one which many think they hold for as long as they refuse to give a verbal decision one way or the other—although their minds have long ago accepted one or the other solution, for every agnostic is at heart Theist or anti-Theist.

Now all that physical science can do is to add to the number of such phenomena. It cannot discover their ultimate cause. It can only discover sequences. If indeed the Catholic Church were to contain some doctrine whereupon physical observation could be brought to bear, and if that doctrine were found to be invariably opposed to the results of such physical observation, a quarrel would arise. But (singularly enough!) those who are most certain that such a conflict exists have hitherto failed to put their finger upon a single doctrine of the kind.

If the Church had said, for instance, "It is of faith that there never was perennial ice over the area of what is now Northern Britain," then the research of modern geology would present a conflict between dogma and physical science. But when has the Church said any such thing?

What is true is that there is a conflict between that materialist philosophy in the atmosphere of which physical science has been taught outside the Catholic Church, and the philosophy of the Catholic Church. But the philosophy in the atmosphere of which physical science has been taught outside the Catholic Church has nothing to do with physical science itself; and very lucky it is for science! For the philosophy in the atmosphere of which physical science has till recently been taught outside the Catholic Church is a philosophy already manifestly breaking down.

H. BELLOC.

EDITOR'S PREFACE

WHILE Christendom was united, two authorities, one primary, the other secondary, were put forward as the bases of Christian belief. The first was a living, traditional authority, that of the existent and continuous Church. Her personal voice, her interpretation of all problems, was the main foundation. But, apart from this, appeal was made universally and continuously, by the Church herself, to another authority, which was also a part of herself, yet had to be vouched for by herself. That authority was the canon of Holy Writ. Here one has to go very carefully, lest one should use any word that would conflict with sound doctrine and definition. It is matter for the expert theologian rather than for the layman. Scripture did not become Scripture by the authority of the Church; but it is the authority of the Church which decides what is Scripture and what is not.

When the breakdown of Christian unity took place in the sixteenth century, and a great part of Christendom was lost to the Catholic Church, of the two authorities one alone was left upstanding. To that one alone, therefore, men referred for their conclusions upon matters of final import: for the answers to the only questions which are really worth asking about human life and its conduct: the questions on the answers to which depend the ultimate fate of man (whether he be immortal; if so, to what end of happiness or unhappiness, and why).

Scripture remained, for the separated sects of Christendom, not only the sole, but the main authority. The fact that the Catholic Church claimed to interpret Scripture, to

[7]

314 Pope / *Church and the Bible*

define the limits between what was and what was not canonical, to include in practice and doctrine much that was not superficially obvious in a personal reading of Scripture, led to her being regarded in the Reformed Churches as the enemy of that very group of documents which she had presented to the world, upon which she continued to rely, and which she cites copiously after nearly two thousand years, and will continue to cite copiously as the reference for her doctrine and the roots of her being.

It was a strange perversion of history, but one historically understandable enough.

It is to-day, I suppose, much weakened. Your average educated man of to-day does not regard the Catholic Church as the enemy of the Bible, or as the gaoler of the Bible. He could not, if he had any reading. But this achievement in historical truth is a negative achievement. The complementary, positive achievement which remains to be secured is the pointing out of what the Bible means to the Catholic Church.

Ironically enough, it is the Catholic Church which (outside a comparatively small body of men who still base themselves on an exact literal interpretation of the English translation made three hundred years ago) is, in the modern world, the defender of Scriptural authority. Therefore is this the very moment in which the defence now thus left mainly to the Church should be understood by those outside the Church. As the Church was blamed for doing something more than merely reciting the naked words of the text, as she was blamed for proclaiming the Living Voice and Tradition, so now she is being blamed for supporting too much that very authority which she had been accused in the past of neglecting. It is always so with things central and true. They are attacked first from the east and then from the west.

[8]

At any rate it is of prime importance for the non-Catholic who takes an interest in these matters to know exactly how the Church stands herein; and the work of Father Hugh Pope, our principal English scholar and authority in these things, will sufficiently inform him.—*The Editor.*

[9]

316 Pope / *Church and the Bible*

EDITOR'S PREFACE

The modern world has a peculiar problem to deal with. When I say "peculiar," I am not perhaps quite just, for one should add that all very old civilizations have had something of the sort to face. Yet in a sense our problem *is* peculiar, because under the effects of the reformation we have come, over a large part of our culture, to a degree of intensity in the problem which has not been known either in other places or in other times.

That problem is the problem of the destitute.

Let us define our terms. We mean by the destitute human beings who are allowed no part in the normal economic functioning of society. A man who does not know where to turn for his next meal or lodging is obviously destitute. But he also is destitute essentially who does not know where he may turn for his meal or lodging, though still a living man, after some undefined moment. Everyone working under the competitive wage system is in this sense very truly destitute. The French Revolutionaries of the nineteenth century discovered an exact word for this kind of man. They call them the "disinherited."

Note here, at the beginning of any examination of the affair, however brief, a great philosophic quarrel. Has man a right to sufficiency and security?

The Catholic Church lays it down that he has. The Opposition to the Catholic Church lays it down that he has not: and therein lies the root difference. Our modern revolutionaries (such as the sincere and inflamed Communists) derive all the good in their system (which is bred by a hunger and thirst after justice) from Catholic morals. From Catholic morals also derive all those pallia-

3

tives of the odious, inhuman, unstable, and obviously doomed organization of modern industrial society. It is from the doctrine that a human being because he is a human being, because he is created in the image of God, because his soul is equal (in its rights) to any other soul, that, in the Catholic system, the presence of destitution, even as an exception, is immoral. It is because an adverse system began to arise four hundred years ago, with Calvin for its clearest exponent and directing genius, that, wherever that system has prevailed, destitution in the largest sense of the word (that is, the exile of most men from security and sufficiency) has been taken for granted.

For herein lies the peculiar mark of our unhappy times wheresoever industrial capitalism has been able to spread its tentacles. It is that the mass of men are in peril of destitution, and in the civic sense of the word are actually destitute. They are not secure of a sufficiency. They can but obtain the means of livelihood by a competition which is guaranteed unrestrained at every level; permitting wholesale dishonesty among those struggling to control the means of production, wholesale oppression by those who control the great mass to whom they dole out wages, and complete bewildering insecurity for all: for the rich in their ill-gotten and ephemeral industrial fortunes, juggled for in an unending gamble, for the bulk of citizens in their weekly and monthly wages, which may for each individual at any moment cease at the arbitrary bidding of another man.

There has been destitution at all times, and there will always be. There was never a nomadic tribe nor even a perfectly organized medieval parish in which some rebel or some idiot was not an outcast. But the special mark of our time is that the citizens are outcast in bulk. They are not deprived of livelihood in bulk, for if they were, the wealth of the rich would fail. The masses must be employed in producing. But they are deprived of a secure sufficiency. No economic arrangement determines that secure sufficiency for the great majority of citizens, as it is determined in free peasant societies even to-day, as it was determined everywhere in the middle ages.

Here, then, as everywhere, we come to that perpetual alternative. Either our civilization will return to Catholic morals or it will lose its essentials.

We are to-day passing through an ephemeral phase in which the citizen is called free, though deprived of economic freedom. The strain is becoming intolerable.

There is proposed for the relief of that strain the absurdity—generous in so many of its votaries, but still a grotesque inhuman absurdity—called Communism. That is, the relief of the strain by handing over our lives to the politicians or a clique, or a despot (I do not count the people calling themselves "socialists" for it should be clear to any thinking man that the only explicit socialism is communism, that if you pretend to be a socialist without being a communist you are a liar).

That solution of the strain we may readily dismiss. It is tomfoolery, like asking men to walk on their hands. It may be attempted, but if it is attempted, the attempt will be merely destructive, like all attempts to work against the nature of things.

The next solution of the strain is that mixture of private property and coöperation, of well-distributed wealth and of corporate safeguard against its reagglomeration, which would be the natural outcome of a renewed general Catholic culture: it is the ideal of the Guild, of the medieval manor, of all feudalism, and its object is the achievement of security and sufficiency for the mass of citizens.

This is what we shall have if the Catholic Church conquers in the temporal sphere.

If the Catholic Church does not conquer, if we return to Paganism, then the strain will be resolved by the reestablishment of that ancient and very stable institution called slavery. When we were all Pagans, slavery was normal, and when we become, or if we do become, Pagan again, slavery will be normal again. Not the slavery of an alien and inferior race, but the slavery of the mass of citizens compelled by social organization to work for the benefit of the few.

There is no other issue, save the acceptation of the Catholic culture.

ONDON makes upon the traveller an impression utterly different from that which any other of the capitals of Europe can produce.

THE sense of this difference is felt almost equally by one who arrives from a neighbouring country—from some province of Europe almost twin to our own, and by one who comes from the new countries to Europe and sees for the first time, and as a whole, the scheme of European civilisation. There is but one type of man to whom the individuality of London is less apparent, and that is the untravelled Englishman. An Englishman who has not travelled abroad, but who knows his modern England well, sees in London but one of the great towns which are the distinctive mark of his country to-day. It has indeed an atmosphere of its own—but so has every other. It is larger by far than the Manchester or the Liverpool or the Birmingham with which he may contrast it, but he feels this factor of difference to be mainly one of degree.

AT the very outset of any consideration of the City, we must first ask why this double point of view exists; why the Colonial, the American, the Frenchman, the German or the Italian, when he reaches London reaches something so absolutely new, and why to the untravelled Englishman that impression of peculiarity is lacking.

THE most obvious answer to such a question would seem to be that London, being an English town, an Englishman finds it ordinary enough, a foreigner extraordinary. Such an answer betrays an historical error. The growth of the great towns in every part of the United Kingdom (even to some extent in the South) has masked the peculiar character of London, and the interest of the query propounded above lies in the fact that it would apply to almost any period of the history of Christendom, and that long before the modern English industrial town was dreamt of, even in that not very distant past when no other English town was more than a market borough, London was enormous; it was more densely populated than any other northern or western centre of government in Europe, and possessed in the eyes of all who saw it for the first time a character and an individuality which then, as now, sharply separated it from the other great provincial capitals of that unity which had once been called the Roman Empire. London stood, in size, at least, and possibly in wealth, for many, many hundred years the second city of the West.

BUT not only the size nor only the commercial character of London has distinguished it. Its climate, its half maritime origins and functions, its inviolability as the capital of an island, have marked it always; and the recent hypertrophy by which it has swelled to an agglomeration almost exceeding the normal powers of government, is but a development (in most of its details at least) of the old spirit of the place. The type of tenure upon which London has been built can be traced in historical consecution from the old London to the new, the lack of plan, the extension along the main arteries of travel, the engulfing of neighbouring villages which remain fossilised, as it were, in the general mass of the town, the high local differentiation between one quarter and another, and the permanent mercantile life of the river, all these belong not only to modern London but to the London of the eighteenth and of the seventeenth centuries, and even, in some measure, of the sixteenth.   The prime element in the structure of the town from its very beginnings has been its combination of commercial port and national centre.   Many commercial ports have had an independent existence as city-states up and down Europe.   One Continental City has been at once the chief port of a nation and its commercial capital—Lisbon.   But the situation of Lisbon was never such as to concentrate upon it the whole energy of the nation in the way in which London concentrated the energy of England.

TO understand this supreme position of London in the island it is necessary to consider the geographical causes which have brought London into existence. Briefly, the City of London has always been and even now remains the chief nodal point of commercial communication in the territory of a nation commercial by genius and exactly so situated as to reap the greatest advantage open to that genius.

IT is evident that where two or more streams of commercial communication cross, there will a centre of commercial activity arise.   Such a point of crossing we call a nodal point, because it forms the knot uniting two or more separate lines of commercial energy.   Such a point forms a natural depôt.   There the merchant will seek to establish his counting-house, thither the producer will come for the exchange of his goods, and from such a vantage-ground the surrounding markets dependent upon single lines of communication can best be watched and contrasted.   London lay (as will presently be shown) from the moment when the advantages of its site were first seized, at the crossing-point of at least two great streams of travel and of exchange.   But there was more than this : it was also a point of trans-shipment where a great part of inland carriage, by river and road, was transferred to carriage by sea.   There was yet more to make of London the master nodal point not only of this island but of all north-west Europe ; its market commanded not only those various streams of commerce and travel whose channels are determined by geographical causes, but also those which are determined by racial and political ones.   In London met most naturally the export from Gaul and the export from that outer band of Christendom which spoke and speaks a mass of Teutonic dialects, and which has been more or less successfully won to our civilisation by the expansion of that civilisation in the form of religion after the fall of the Roman Empire.   The seaboard of the newly won eastern territories of the Dark and early Middle Ages communicated as naturally with London as did the seaboard of Gaul, and the fixing of the centre of Gallic civilisation in the North was as powerful in helping London to develop as was the expansion of German civilisation eastward from the Rhine along the shores of the Baltic.

LONDON, in a word, was in every way called to be a meeting-place, and especially a meeting-place of commerce.   Not only because it occupied the cross-roads of commerce within the island of Britain, but also because it was the place
10

where trans-shipment of goods was necessary, and further because it stood opposite the junction of what are conventionally called the Teutonic and the Latin peoples.

SUCH a centre once formed, inhabited and developed, becomes itself the cause of its own further development. It tends itself to create new lines of commercial energy radiating from itself as a centre, and when the original conditions which called it into being change (as they have changed in the case of London), when new political groupings and new factors in commercial geography make of what was once a favourable position an unfavourable one, a great commercial town well fixed can, for some time at least, maintain and increase its wealth and status in spite of new routes and conditions theoretically favourable to its rivals. So it has been with London ; the great Western trade over the Atlantic towards which it does not look, and for which it would seem, by position ill-suited, has been made to serve the purposes of the City ; the great trade with the East which arose somewhat earlier than that across the Atlantic, and for which the Western capital seemed peculiarly unfitted, was captured by its merchants and until lately almost monopolised by them. The future, and perhaps the near future, will show whether that somewhat artificial position can be maintained.

THAT London is primarily the nodal point in English commercial communication does not appear at first sight upon the map of modern England ; but when we consider the commercial conditions of the island throughout the centuries during which municipal life was founded in Britain, this nodal point can be seen very clearly.

SOUTHERN and Eastern Britain were for those centuries by far the wealthiest part of the whole island. The West and the North were mainly mountainous, and with certain exceptions (such as the Yorkshire and Cheshire Plains, important exceptions which also largely helped the development of London), they were, when agriculture formed the main source of wealth, poor and thinly populated. The formation in the dales of the West Riding, in the valleys of Durham and of Northumberland, in those of Lancashire and South Wales, of vast centres of population, is due to the industrial revolution ; to the use of coal and of the machinery upon which coal is dependent. But until quite modern times the wealth of England lay mainly to the south and east of a line drawn from the head of navigation upon the Severn (say from Worcester) to the estuary of the Humber. Of this territory again it was the southern part that was the best cultivated, the nearest to continental civilisation, upon the whole the best in climate and certainly the most fruitful. But that southern part, as a glance at the map will show, had for its main artery the waterway of the Thames. All primitive civilisation must make use of rivers as the main highway of commerce. The hard road capable of bearing traffic demands for its up-keep a reserve of wealth, a scheme of taxation, an untiring energy in government which are only to be found in periods of high material development. And not only is it true that primitive conditions favour the use of waterways for commerce, but, in all save the most exceptional circumstances, waterways when they are available afford the cheapest avenue of transit for

11

goods. When civilisation breaks down (as when Roman civilisation entered the Dark Ages), the use of waterways tends everywhere to replace the use of roads. Thus the local capitals of the Dark Ages, notably Paris, can trace their supremacy over the old official Roman centres largely to their command of carriage by water in several directions. And even when civilisation has extended to the utmost its forms of carriage by land, water carriage, wherever it is organised under a strong government for the use of the community, remains a serious competitor against land carriage.

THE River Thames, then, before the advent of the Romans and their roads, formed the principal highway east and west through the wealthiest part of Britain. But it did something more : in its lower reaches it separated that wealthy district into two unequal portions, which formed considerable fractions of the territory we are considering. Kent, which we may assume to have been, from its proximity to the continent, its soil and its long individual history, a district of capital importance, was cut off from what we now call East Anglia, and therefore from what the early history of Roman Britain teaches us to have been one of the chief centres of British life. From Kent to East Anglia there was no direct road; a labyrinth of muddy creeks and miles of impassable marshy foreshore divided the one from the other. Not only did the estuary thus divide one wealthy and important part of Britain from another, but it prevented the main road from the Straits of Dover (which formed the gate into the country) from passing directly northward towards the frontier, and later, when the Roman organisation was developed, towards the military capital at York. That great route which was the backbone of the Roman Empire, and which ran from the boundary of the African desert round the Mediterranean, through Gaul to the Wall and to the Irish Sea, could run in a direct line across Gaul as far as the Straits of Dover, but the Straits once passed, it could not proceed directly northward : it must find a crossing-place somewhere upon the estuary; and by a coincidence which has been all important in the history of London, it found that crossing-place at the spot where also maritime commerce entering the Thames could best establish an inland port. For it so happened that just where the marsh was narrowest (or rather cut off altogether) upon the northern shore by the advance of a low gravelly hill to the very edge of deep water, and just where opposite this spot on the northern shore a belt of muddy foreshore not too wide permitted the throwing of a causeway, there also men coming in from the North Sea by water could best land.

THE lower reaches of the estuary were too wide to afford safety for small craft. The upper reaches of it, though here and there upon the southern shore short belts of dry land came down to the water's edge, afforded no good place at which boats should lie and their navigators land : such an advantage was first found on the journey inland from the North Sea, when the traveller saw on his right as he went up the tide the dry steep bank upon which prehistoric London rose. From that bank to the comparatively narrow belt of marsh upon the south, London Bridge was thrown : a causeway united the bridge across the marsh to the higher land which the road from the Straits had been pursuing,

12

and once that bridge was thrown across the Thames the nodal point of London was established.

AT that point would cross the stream of travel and of commerce going from the Straits northward to the military capital at York, to the Irish Sea, to the Barbarian frontier upon the Solway or upon the Clyde, to the garrisons in the marches of Wales, to the wealthy cornlands of what was later East Anglia.

AT that point all those streams of commercial and political energy would cut across the old east and west highway of the Thames.

THE bridge forbade maritime commerce to proceed further upstream: yet the fact that it crossed over tidal water permitted the tide for many miles above it to be used for the trans-shipping up and down of goods proceeding inland or coming from inland to the sea.

THE port (with its depôts of merchandise, its opportunities for civil intercourse and its fixed market for exchange) once established, looked right at that pocket in the narrow seas where the Gallic and the Teutonic states were later to meet; it faced the mouth of the Rhine (the early artery of German commercial life), and it faced the teeming civilisation of the Low-lands which was destined to arise between the ninth and the sixteenth centuries; it further faced the territory whose capital importance in Europe was to be established by the Kings who were descended from the Counts of Paris, and who for eight hundred years made of north-eastern France the nucleus of Christendom.

LONDON BRIDGE thus made London all that London became; but the wanderer in modern London should always remember with reverence an older line of crossing even than is the crossing of the Thames at London Bridge, I mean the ford between Lambeth Palace and the Horseferry Road, for at low water a ford was and is to be found, following the line of that hideous and insecure suspension bridge which is to-day one of the curiosities of the town.

BEFORE ever London was more than a group of huts, perhaps before these huts arose, the old prehistoric road from the Straits of Dover to the North crossed the Thames, not from Southwark to the City, but from Lambeth to Westminster. And the reasons of this were, first that a man following the edge of dry land not submerged even at high tides, would be led on past Southwark westward; next that he would there find what was probably the first ford over the river, and lastly that on a line with this ford was a low gravel bank on the opposite shore, closely approaching the stream and suitable for landing.

A CURIOUS vestige of this line of route, remaining for us in the midst of modern London, is the line of the Edgware Road. That great Roman Way was built upon the straightening of the prehistoric British track which led from the valley of the Thames to the north and west. Even if we knew nothing of the ford at Lambeth it would be remarkable that the Roman road to the north and west from London should not start straight from one of the City gates (as does every other Roman road), but branch out from the great western road at the point now marked by the Marble Arch; and the explanation of this anomaly is that the prehistoric British track coming from the Thames here crossed the Roman road to Staines and the west. The southern portion of that track, the

D

portion between Oxford Street and the river, has for the most part been lost; the first section of it remains in the Horseferry Road, but the rest of the lane going as it must have done through Buckingham Palace Gardens, following the high ground through the western extremity of the Green Park and then along the edge of Hyde Park to the Marble Arch, has left no continuous topographical mark upon modern London. It is recovered again in the line of the Edgware Road.

THE mention of that Roman Way affords an opportunity to the reader for considering the striking manner in which the Roman roads still visibly converge upon London.

IN the neighbourhood of no other provincial city of the Empire, not in that of Lincoln (which is an important junction) nor in that of Paris, nor in that of Lyons, can this be so clearly seen as in the neighbourhood of London: the only parallel to it throughout all the municipal scheme of Roman civilisation is in the case of Rome itself.

CONSIDER how there converge upon London Bridge and the southern water gate of the City at least two of the great roads from the south; the military road from Chichester and Portsmouth, which follows more or less the series of broad modern streets through Balham to the Borough, and the great main road from the Straits of Dover, which still passes through Southwark in the shape of the Old Kent Road. Consider also how the great road to the eastern districts, to Colchester, etc., goes out by the Eastern Gate, Aldgate, and is still visible in the Mile End Road, how the North Road, the Ermin Street, the road to Lincoln and to York, goes out through the North Gate of the City, Bishopsgate, and is still traceable in the great North Road. Consider how the roads to the west begin in the main artery of Holborn, branching at the Marble Arch northward to Chester, and continuing in the other limb of the fork to the crossing of the Thames at Staines, and so to Silchester and the south and west. The site of London is the hub of a wheel whose spokes are the great Roman roads radiating from it and still used as modern streets and highways.

SUCH are the geographical and political causes which made London possible and necessary, and such were the effects of the town, once established, upon communications.

WHEN all this is grasped it will be easily understood how this square mile proved so much the largest of the Roman cities in Britain, how even in the first century the chief of Roman historians has alluded to its vast concourse of merchants, how (without reasonable doubt) we may assume it to have repelled the pirates at the beginning of the Dark Ages, and how throughout Saxon and Norman times, it presumably remained (in spite of the meagreness of its record) what it had always been, the second city of the West.

WHEN records become at once clear, detailed and numerous, and when the united life of England is governed (from the thirteenth century onwards) from the neighbourhood of London, this character in the City is no longer one of conjecture, but one of historical certainty. With the possible exception of the one generation when Paris went through its sudden expansion in the last years of Philip Augustus and the first part of the reign of St. Louis, London has
14

permanently maintained its superiority of extent and population. And, as has been observed, it is remarkable that the new commercial importance of the Western seaboard since the Renaissance, the vast expansion of the Americas, even the re-opening of the Mediterranean highway by the French canal across the Isthmus of Suez, has so far not diminished but increased the standing, the wealth and the population of the City in proportion to the other great capitals of Europe. Commercially, one port would seem to be its rival in the immediate future: the port of Antwerp; but the many reasons that lead one to such a conclusion would make too long a digression in such an essay as this.

*   *   *   *   *   *   *

THE supremacy of London led, from some very early time, to the legends which (though, like all legends, they were but partially believed even in the moment of their greatest vitality) reflected the impression which the City made. There was the vast Celtic legend of King Lud; the characteristic university legend of the founding of the City by Brutus, son of Priam, making it a sort of second Rome, and the claim that London was " New Troy." To these legends should be added one of those statements of the Middle Ages with regard to the origin of the Christian religion, which have no support from documents and which are yet so curiously tenacious in tradition that they are worthy of respect: I mean the presence of St. Paul in Britain. On documentary evidence we have no more than the one phrase of St. Clement, in which it is said that St. Paul visited "the ends of the West," but that expression would have exactly corresponded to Britain in the first century in which it was written. At any rate the story of St. Paul's journey makes London, as the legend of its foundation by Brutus does, a sort of counterweight against Rome, for upon the basis of that myth or tradition the great cathedral of London was dedicated to St. Paul.

I HAVE said that there stood in the early Middle Ages, and perhaps earlier still, a persistent conception of London as a distant counterweight to Rome, the capital of all Christendom.

THIS conception found expression, not only in the dedication, but in the character of Old St. Paul's, for when the revolution of the human mind in the century of the Crusades—which was marked by so many triumphant changes— stamped Europe with the Gothic, the Gothic cathedral which replaced that of Ethelred was designed to exceed, in size at least, anything else of its kind in Europe. Its spire was higher than any other then standing; in length it surpassed every other metropolitan church, and the curious can still note upon the floor of St. Peter's at Rome, the mark showing the length of Old St. Paul's and proving it to surpass in magnitude any of its rivals.

IT was a building characteristically English, depending for the effect of vastness upon its length, upon its spire for an external effect of height, with the square east end of English Gothic, and the Great English perpendicular light occupying that east end at the end of the Middle Ages.

WESTMINSTER stood twin with London from the thirteenth century, and in

15

the huge agglomeration that we know, Westminster and the City still stand side by side with separate histories and certainly a very separate atmosphere and character. Nor is there any better example of the peculiar position of London in England and in Europe than the way in which a government was carried on for five hundred years at the very gates of London and yet not within the City. True, the tendency of royalty to avoid the heart of the capital was seen throughout Europe ; the Crown always at least escapes from the chief city, whether from Westminster to Windsor or from the Louvre (once just outside the walls of Paris) to Versailles, or to Vatican Hill beyond the Tiber, or to the Escorial : nay, Madrid itself was a sort of escape from Toledo. But it is characteristic of the position of London and of the English monarchy that the courts did not sit nor were parliaments held within the walls of the City, but always in this ecclesiastical and royal suburb.

WESTMINSTER, whose name has endured through seven centuries associated with the conception of English government, sprang like so many of its parallels, from the civilising zeal of monasticism, for when Roman civilisation broke down, and just at the moment when culture, whether of the mind or of the soul, seemed doomed to gradual extinction, there rose in the midst of Europe the conception of those ardent and laborious communities, celibate, organised at once for high production and low consumption, and therefore the maximum of accumulation, very hives for the storing of capital in a time when the creation of new capital was almost unknown in civil life, and secure retreats for documents and tradition. The monastic institution undoubtedly saved both the soil of Europe from dereliction and its mind from a complete decay, and the origin of that institution is coincident with the crisis through which Rome passed from the clear light of the Empire into the Dark Ages.

IN other countries, notably in Gaul and in Ireland, the task of monasticism was easier than in Britain. In Britain civilisation had been so swept by the pirate invasions that the reconquest of the mind and of the soil was arduous ; but here, as elsewhere, monasticism established itself in the wake of the missionaries and was successful. And just as outside Paris, to cultivate the fields which a decline of knowledge and perpetual warfare might have overwhelmed, was founded over Roman Ruins the great Abbey later dedicated to St. Germanus, so, just outside London and on the river also, was founded over Roman Ruins the great monastery dedicated to St. Peter.

ITS origins are obscure and perhaps mythical ; they stretch back to the very beginnings of the re-civilisation of Britain, to the seventh century ; and the spot chosen for that foundation, the "*locus terribilis*," the Island of Thorns so chosen, was the next patch of gravel upstream from the City and the bridge of London : the patch of gravel to which was directed the ancient ford of the prehistoric road we have noticed and over which that prehistoric road went north and west through the length of the island.

ITS fortunes through the Dark Ages were the fortunes of any one of the great monasteries. It was almost autonomous, it governed its village, it cultivated its territory, it was a sanctuary and a place of peculiar sanctity to
16

the general people and to the Crown. When all Europe stirred under the beginnings of the Middle Ages, in the midst of the reform of the Church under Gregory VII., of the Norman expansion and of all that preceded the creative effort of the Crusaders, Westminster was re-established by Edward the Confessor. The limits of its jurisdiction were those which still mark the limits of the City of Westminster. It extended eastward to the boundaries of the City of London, northward to the great military way, as it was called, of Oxford Street ; southward it was bounded by the river, westward by an artificial line including much of what is now Kensington. The first century after the Conquest probably saw its position defined, as everything was made more strict and legal by the vigorous Norman mind. There the Conqueror was crowned, there Edward the Confessor's shrine was established, there in the next generation the plans for the new royal palace were established and their execution begun, notably the great hall was traced out. But the chief change in the national function of Westminster occurred when, under the reign of Henry II., royal jurisdiction gradually came to be established within its boundaries. London was never in a strict and legal sense the capital of England, though it was always the commercial centre of England. But Westminster may be called the administrative capital of the island from the moment when the Royal Courts began to sit in Westminster Hall.

THE Abbey is the proof of what that central authority thought of Westminster, and of how the kingship incarnated itself in the royal village. The thirteenth century in its noblest expression remains there a very rare exception to the general ruin which the dissolution of the monasteries brought upon such monuments of the national tradition. Bermondsey has gone, Chertsey has gone, and every other suburban foundation except the Abbey. When the monasteries had been sacked and destroyed, the Great Fire came to complete the obliteration so far as London was concerned, and those buildings which, being of secular foundation, remained, especially the great Cathedral of St. Paul's, were lost. Westminster remains, and we must be grateful to whatever motive it was, policy, or avarice, or family pride, or mere delay, that saved this one witness to the spirit of mediæval London. There is no other. In Westminster, where the King's Court was already firmly established, the thirteenth century saw another growth. Somewhat tardily, if we compare it with its forerunners upon the Continent, the English Parliament there arose. And before the Middle Ages were over, St. Stephen's Chapel in the King's Palace had become the common meeting place of the Knights of the Shire and of the Burgesses, summoned to grant taxes to the King, and ultimately admitted to take some share in the legislation which the King, with his great prelates and abbots round him (and the less numerous lay nobility), inaugurated.

THE last of this chapel disappeared in the fire of 1834, which destroyed the old Houses of Parliament. Its site has been taken by the present "St. Stephen's Hall," which leads into the central lobby between the modern House of Lords and House of Commons. But the crypt chapel beneath St. Stephen's Chapel, nearly contemporary with and in part an imitation of the crypt of

E   17

St. Chapelle in Paris, remains, though dreadfully disfigured by modern superficial additions.

* * * * * * *

THE uniting of Westminster to the City along the high gravel bank of the Strand was the first expansion of London. The line of wealthy houses built along the Strand on the spoils of religion, formed the first of the long streets which London has since regularly thrown out along its main avenues of egress, and by which it has maintained its perpetual growth. For the growth of London has been from the sixteenth century to the present day, and still continues, a growth along the chief roads which lead out in all directions from the town. The wanderer who walks in the neighbourhood of modern London will often note the way in which, between one such great arm of expansion and another, wedges of pure country intervene. Thus a man is virtually in the town or its suburbs all the way to Epsom along the Worthing Road, and far past Croydon upon the Brighton Road. But the wedge between these two divergent highways is full of fields and woods still almost untouched by the builder; and this is true of the space between any two of the great roads leading out of London. So it was in the beginnings of the expansion of the town. Two generations after the first houses were built continuously along the Strand, and two generations after the long line of buildings and of gardens stretched out along Holborn as far as St. Giles' Green and the Tottenham Court Road, the wedge between, traversed by Drury Lane, was occupied by green fields, the Long Acre and the rest, upon which no one had thought of building. The process has been continuous from that day to our own.

IF it be asked why London has during the last four hundred years followed this peculiar type of expansion, a type hardly to be recognised in continental cities, but common enough in the modern great towns of England, the answer is not far to seek. The accident of English political development—a wealthy oligarchy slowly established upon the Reformation, spending the ancient endowment of religion, and welding the nation into a perfect homogeneity within the security of an island—has spared London and other English cities the necessity of defence. Save for one passing moment during the Civil Wars—a crisis which had no lasting military effect—London has, since the Middle Ages, had no necessity for fortifications. Cities which have it in their whole tradition to live within a wall and a military ring of defence, expand as a tree expands, outward, in circles. So Rome expanded; so Timgad; so Paris even at the present day expands. But if a city be not so bound, communications will naturally determine its development, and especially the main lines of communication. Men will build first along the great roads leading outwards, and it is this plan which is followed in the increase of nearly every modern city where the tradition of civilisation is commercial rather than military.

IN this connection there may be noted the curious way in which London engulfs village after village, creeping round it as a flood of lava might creep round a temple or a walled enclosure. The villages which the expansion of

18

London thus encloses are never at once destroyed. Some remain almost intact for generations, some for centuries.

CHELSEA is of this kind ; though less definite in boundaries. Kensington is of this kind ; and in its way Clapham still remains of this kind. If the future expansion of the City shall engulf Hampstead and Highgate, as it has engulfed Islington, for instance, we shall find the phenomenon repeated ; and such are the conditions, and especially the great size of London, that in nearly every case we find the same social results following upon the capture of these outlying villages. The old houses, their gardens, and sometimes their family traditions as well, remain almost untouched. Outside of them, upon what were the open fields of the village, the poorer districts are built. Chelsea is completely isolated by such a belt, and any one going from Hampstead into town, or from Highgate, will have noticed how an intervening layer of what was once waste land, now occupied by industrial buildings or poorer residences, cuts off the old-established suburb from the City.

THE end of such historical origins, and of such an expansion, is the London we know, and the mind turns from considering why and how London has come into being, to look at the town as it stands : probably the most amazing collection of men dependent upon an organisation they cannot control : probably the largest agglomeration of men living under municipal, and therefore artificial conditions, which could be found in the history of the world : certainly the largest of which we have direct evidence.

IT is large, not only in the numbers of those who dwell helplessly within it, but also, and perhaps especially, in the immense area which it covers ; and unique in the lack of central control, which partly the size of that area, partly the nature of its development, but most of all the genius of the nation of which it is the capital, have decreed for it. Paris, if its closely-built suburbs be added to the official unit of the city, numbers half the population of London. It is close on three millions ; London is close on six. But Paris could be put under martial law under one authority, could possibly still be besieged, could perhaps still be organised for one united revolt, is in every respect one thing. London—and this is at the root of every problem which the more serious contemplate when they think of the City, and which the merely observant must curiously note—London is not one thing. It would starve together if its food-supply were interfered with, it would decline together if its commercial opportunity dwindled ; but it can never act together. No common enthusiasm can move it, no common enregimentation can direct its efforts.

NOT that London lacks a common atmosphere and a common spirit ; it possesses both to an extraordinary degree. It does not indeed breed a breed of men. For the myriads of Romans, of Parisians, of Marseillese, of Hamburgers and the rest, London can show no parallel. Its breeding-grounds are in the slums and obscure, lacking any civic tradition ; its middle class, which might produce a tradition, is perhaps the least prolific in Europe ; it has no resident aristocracy ; it is merely used by the plutocracy of the moment as a place of leisure, of enjoyment, and of control. Yet the spiritual unity it evinces strikes every foreigner and

19

possesses every native observer. It possesses him strongly though it eludes the pen, whether of the traveller or of the native. But if that general atmosphere be indefinable (as it is), and even if its description eludes the pen (as I have said it does), yet is it possible to note certain aspects of it, and the summary of those aspects gives some hint of the permanent spirit of London.

THUS the skies conspire with the English temperament to give to all that is of the London kind something cosy and domestic. From the other great English cities men fly with the more zeal in proportion as they are the more wealthy. Manchester, Leeds, and Birmingham are deserted by such as can afford to desert them when the peculiar work of those cities is not in hand. Upon holidays (Sundays, for instance) or before or after the offices of the merchants and the money-lenders are closed, the centres of the great English towns lie dead. But London remains, throughout all her expansion and change, above all a place of residence. This happens not to be true of the commercial part of the City; but even that is an accident, and up to the very edges of that commercial part, to some extent within its boundaries, the residential instinct of London presses. The town has a roof and is a stay-at-home town, and in its vast area so many little local centres have arisen that a man can hardly tell whither he is to fly if he desires to escape the pressure of the town, or rather those who most desire to escape that pressure often escape it best by seeking the heart of its oldest quarters.

THIS spirit it is which has given to London alone out of all European capitals a character which not even modern building has been able to destroy, the character of a city of small homes. Nothing is more remarkable to the foreigner (and his astonishment has been expressed a hundred times in European literature) than the miles of low roofs above and beside which a man passes as he comes by train from the Channel ports into London. In spite of all the anomaly of English land tenure, and in spite of the servile and hopelessly precarious conditions of English labour, these roofs cover homes. No other capital in Europe shows that passion.

ANOTHER character which may be arbitrarily noted is the effect upon London of its smoke and cloud. These are not wholly produced by modern industrial conditions. The mists of the Thames estuary, the murkiness of the North Sea fog, were there long before London arose. But between them all the forces which have produced the London sky have made something which all Londoners know, and which no one who has never seen London has ever seen. Among other things it produced the visions of Turner. How many there are who, if they recall their childhood, will chiefly remember the particular tone of London clouds, especially at evening.

*   *   *   *   *   *   *

THIS London, the spirit of which is so united, has no famous citadel or dominating hill from which it may be seized at once, and the circumstance of its air and contours seems to forbid one vision of it.

I WOULD, nevertheless, advise any one who desires an impression as rare as

20

it is permanent, to sit up some Saturday night in the neighbourhood of the Spaniards, in June let us say, having chosen fine weather, and watch the dawn over London. He will be surprised. A Sunday morning after a spell of south-westerly gales of wet weather, followed by the beginning of a fine day, shows you the heights upon the Surrey side almost as clear cut as in a southern continental landscape. Hampstead Heath has been so protected by the law that to the northward building, though it exists, is masked by belts of trees, and one looks down as it were from the edge of an inviolate countryside, down on to the immensity of the town. It is with difficulty and without curiosity that a man can pick out in that view such and such a shapeless monument, such and such a site, or possibly if he be keen-eyed, hints of the distant shipping below the Pool. What he sees is more wonderful than a view the points of which can easily be determined ; he sees a sort of dead lake of men under the empty and silent morning, a hollow land into which have flowed, almost in spite of their own wills, these millions, packed as water is packed, and level as water is level. It lies there, defenceless, thinking nothing and asleep.

I HAVE watched it so perhaps half a dozen times in my life upon Sunday mornings so chosen. The memory is profound.

FOREWORD

THE interest of the Calas Case does not lie in the crude (and imaginary) elements of an obvious melodrama. No one worth listening to now believes that a man clearly innocent was put to death by wicked enemies. Nor does it lie in the violent emotions of the time, though the contemplation of these is a much more respectable subject of interest than a mere legend of supposed martyrdom. It lies rather in the example it gives of historical method and the opportunity for historical analysis. It is one of those questions which will presumably remain debated for a very long time without any fixed conclusion being arrived at. The continued discussion of the Calas Case is a model of that contrast in the use of evidence with which all those who engage in history are concerned.

Briefly, it is a model of the way in which historical evidence turns upon psychological judgment, of the way in which our acceptation of a witness's credibility, or of the greater value of one piece of his testimony over another, turns on our judgment of men.

The first rule to be put before anyone who has to read history, let alone to write it, it this : all historical evidence is a matter of psychology : all evidence whatsoever depends for its judgment upon our knowledge of the mind of man in general and of the mind of man in that

13

particular society where the disputed event took place, and of the minds of individuals concerned.

It is sometimes advanced that evidence from material circumstance does not fall under this rule. But it does. Footprints are taken, they are found to correspond with a particular footgear. But how are you to judge whether there was fraud ? A thing asserted to have happened on a Friday cannot have happened on the Wednesday preceding that Friday, therefore a document dated on the Wednesday does not apply. But can you judge whether the document were rightly dated ? A tomb seems certainly of the twelfth century from the particular character of its sculpture, coupled with the overlying remains of later human handiwork. May not the sculpture have been copied and the overlying matter replaced ?

In every enquiry of whatever sort, from distant historical enquiry which is the most general and the most useful, to some particular enquiry in a contemporary court of justice, all depends upon what you believe of the human mind and of what you know of its action under particular surroundings.

In the Calas Case we have gone through all the cycle of a typical modern historical myth. First of all there was the horrible persecution and death of an honest Huguenot, innocent of that crime for which he stood accused, and condemned by monsters of iniquity. Then came the reaction ; a detailed examination suggested a doubt of Calas' innocence, and this doubt went on growing greater and greater ; the guilt of Calas was roundly affirmed ; counter-affirmations of his innocence, at first contemptuously brushing aside the growing mass of criticism, then showing indignation against it, at last condescending to rather more serious examination of the opponent, next succeeded. Then came the phase of an even ding-dong battle leaving all in doubt. That is the stage in which we still remain to-day. I doubt whether we shall soon advance from it to any final certitude.

Meanwhile the Calas Case shows us to perfection how a myth may take root to the corruption of history. Its later discussion has happily also shown how myth may be undermined ; but it has equally shown that historical certitude is a thing of varying degrees and that the destruction of a myth is not equivalent to the construction of its opposite.

The Calas myth in its original form was very simple and its author was Voltaire, whose principal object was the ridiculing and degrading of the established Church of his country.

The son of Calas was discovered dead. His father was accused of the murder. This father, though occasionally conforming to Catholicism in early life, was of Huguenot stock. The son inclined to Catholicism. The official tribunals were attached to the State religion. The populace was, in the city where the tragedy took place (Toulouse), inflamed against the Huguenots. Therefore (said the Myth) the father was monstrously accused of the murder of his own dear son and barbarously put to death for a crime he never committed. His memory was triumphantly rehabilitated by the efforts of a number of impartial men devoted to justice and his innocence was thus secured for all time.

Such was the Calas Myth and it would not hold water. At the first serious, critical examination its weakness was bound to appear.

336   Chassaigne / *Calas Case*

The main facts now established are these. A weak violent man, at loggerheads with his eldest son, who was something of a wastrel, whom he could not control, and who seemed a traitor to the family religion, was accused of murdering that son ; the circumstances and circumstantial evidence told heavily in favour of such an accusation. The young man was found strangled, and yet with the marks of strangulation carefully concealed. He was found in the house of his parents ; there was evidence that the father had already threatened him in fits of passion, and when the family were accused they lied right and left.

Those are the broad lines of the affair. Then comes in a mass of particular detail. The father said the lad had hanged himself in a particular fashion which proved manifestly impossible. The first depositions of the witnesses were different from their later ones. The members of the family contradicted themselves at every turn. No one can deny that on mere probabilities the probability is for the death of the young man at the hands of someone in the house, and again, probably, at the hands of his unstable father.

Against this you must set the undoubted prejudice of opinion and of the official courts, the abnormal character of the deed and, (much the strongest point of all), the steadfast maintenance of his innocence, made by the supposed culprit under torture, in the extremity of the breaking of his limbs upon the wheel, and even as he lay dying after that dreadful execution.

To such an over-brief summary innumerable exceptions may be taken on either side. A mass of detail remains to us. I have myself read it at intervals during the last twenty years pretty thoroughly and I did so particularly in Toulouse, believing as I do that it is of capital importance in history to recover the atmosphere of a place. I went through the matter as closely as I could while staying there in the year 1911. I now, nineteen years after, consult the pages for which I am writing this preface, and there find a new theory, neither that of the myth nor that of the religious motive of the father, nor indeed, as the last pages of the book will show, a complete conclusion. The matter is still left in doubt.

It may seem a futile summing-up to say that I am glad it should be so. It is not so futile as it looks. I am glad that even now after so exhaustive a sifting of the facts possible, probable and certain, throughout a period of three human lifetimes and expecially during our own generation under the critical method of exact reference and vast documentation, myth should be destroyed. And I take it that the old Calas myth has indeed been knocked on the head as thoroughly as the Nag's Head myth in the story of the English Church, or the " Forgery " myth in the matter of the false Decretals.

There are many other historical myths, some hundreds of them, awaiting their medicine. May it be duly applied.

Meanwhile new myths arise day by day. I have myself lived, for my sins, through the Dreyfus myth in both its forms. I have heard highly educated, competent French officers affirming, at one moment, that Esterhazy was incapable of any base action ; and I have heard dons of the University of Oxford affirming with hysterical passion, in a matter of which they knew nothing, upon technical evidence as remote from them as is bimetallism from a negro chief, and given in a language which not

B

one in ten of them could read with ease, that a man of
whose whole circumstance and society they knew nothing
whatsoever was an injured martyr.

The myths will continue to sprout like asparagus in
spring. It is our duty to cut it and eat it. In the matter
of the Calas myth the dish has been prepared and consumed and the future of it is fairly certain. We know
where we stand, and we stand in doubt. The evidence is
heavily against Calas, save in the matter of his heroic
death : but that death leaves all uncertain.

H. BELLOC.

KING'S LAND, SHIPLEY,
  HORSHAM.

PREFACE

Miss Pitter has in this book done the best thing that a poet can do, or indeed any writer—and that is, to challenge variety. The more manners one has, the more subjects one deals with, the better for one's Muse in verse or prose.

But the two peculiar gifts which make Miss Pitter's verse what it is and ensure its permanence are as clearly present here as in the earlier poems. Those two gifts are a perfect ear and exact epithet. How those two ever get combined is incomprehensible—one would think it was never possible—but when the combination does appear then you have verse of that classic sort which is founded and secure of its own future.

I take it that the poem in this collection which might be made the title for the whole (it is in my judgment the best, but I cannot pretend to be a critic save of manner and to some extent in the matter of discovery) is the second, that on page five, 'The Kitten's Eclogue'. I saw it first when it appeared in THE NEW ENGLISH WEEKLY, *spelt in the old seventeenth-century fashion with redundant e's, and I confess I regret to see it transmuted into modern spelling. I shall never forget the impression it made upon me when* **first** *it thus appeared. I*

vii

had already learned to admire Miss Pitter's verse of the Elegiac and Tragic mode (and particularly the noble 'Persephone'); I did not know her power in the Comic.

I could wish to be younger in order to mark the moment when talent of this very high level reaches its reward in public fame. It must come. But the day in which we live, having no standards and having apparently forgotten what verse is—and, indeed, what the art of writing is—may keep us waiting some time.

However, I don't feel that that matters much, for stuff which is clearly permanent can wait as long as it likes. The obvious truth that the other kind of stuff washes away like mud, and that automatically the earth is purged of it, is the one consolation we have for living in the chaos we do.

HILAIRE BELLOC

viii

INTRODUCTION

SOME two or three years ago I was asked in the United States to broadcast a few words on my own trade of writing—what I thought of it and why I disliked it.

I understand that this broadcast was heard by a very large number—some millions it seems. Now in the course of this broadcast I gave as the best writer of English now alive, Mr. P. G. Wodehouse.

It was not only a very sincere but a reasonable and well thought out pronouncement. Yet I got a vast number of communications asking me what I exactly meant. Not that those who had heard me doubted Mr. Wodehouse's genius. They had given proof of their perception of that genius by according him the very wide circulation which he enjoys on that side of the Atlantic, as I am glad to say he does elsewhere. No; their puzzlement was why I should call the author who was supreme in that particular line of country the " best " writer of our time: the best living writer of *English*: why I should have called him, as I did call him, " The head of my profession ".

I cannot do better in such a brief introduction as this than take that episode as my text and explain why and how Mr. Wodehouse occupies this position.

Writing is a craft, like any other: playing the violin, skating, batting at cricket, billiards, wood-carving—anything

v

you like; and mastership in any craft is attainment of the end to which that craft is devoted. A craftsman is excellent in his craft according to his degree of attainment towards its end, and his use of the means towards that end. Now the end of writing is the production in the reader's mind of a certain image and a certain emotion. And the means towards that end are the use of words in any particular language; and the complete use of that medium is the choosing of the right words and the putting of them into the right order. It is *this* which Mr. Wodehouse does better, in the English language, than anyone else alive; or at any rate than anyone else whom I have read for many years past.

His object is comedy in the most modern sense of that word: that is, his object is to present the laughable, and he does this with such mastery and skill that he nearly always approaches, and often reaches, perfection.

It is a test of power in this craft of writing that its object shall be attained by some method which the reader cannot directly perceive. To write prose so that your search for effect appears on the surface is to write bad prose. To write prose so that you get your effects by unusual words, deliberately chosen for their oddity, is to write bad prose. To write prose so that the reader thinks more of the construction than of the image conveyed is to write bad prose. So to write is not necessarily to write the worst prose nor even very bad prose, but it is to miss perfection.

There are various ways in which you may test the truth of what I here say about this master in my own craft of writing. One is to attempt an imitation. You will find you cannot do it. In all the various departments of his skill Mr. Wodehouse is unique for simplicity and exactitude, which is as much as to say that he is unique for an avoidance of all frills. He gets the full effect, bang! One may say of him as the traveller in the story, hearing Shakespeare for the first time, said of Hamlet: " Doesn't he pull it off? " Or again one may consider his inimitable use of parallelism. The use of parallelism is one of the special marks of leadership in English. For it has become one of the chief marks of English prose in its most sharp-edged form. Now in parallelism Mr. Wodehouse is again supreme. There is no one like him in this department. One may say of him what he might say of his own Jeeves, " There is none like you, none ". Whether one quotes a single phrase such as " quaking like a jelly in a high wind " (for the effect of an aunt upon a young nephew), or of the laugh of another lady and its effect upon another young man: " it was like cavalry clattering over a tin bridge "; or any one out of a hundred examples, it is always the same success. Mr. Wodehouse has done the trick. In every case the parallelism has enhanced to the utmost the value of the thing described. It appears not only in phrases, but in the use of one single metaphorical word, and especially in the use of passing vernacular slang.

Then you may consider the situations: the construction. Properly this does not concern the excellence of the writer as such. It is the art of the playwright more than of the prose-writer pure and simple. But observe how admirably it is used in these hands! The situation, the climax, general and particular, the interplay of character and circumstance are as exact as such arrangements can be. They produce the full effect and are always complete.

There is yet another perfection which I note in him. It is one which most moderns, I think, would not regard as a perfection at all—Well! I differ from them. It is the repeated use of one set of characters. The English country house and its setting, the aged absent-minded earl, the young ladies and gentlemen with too much leisure or too little, too much money, or (contrariwise) embarrassment—all these form one set of recurrent figures, one set of " property " scenes. Another is New York with its special characters and special situations —particularly the suddenly enriched and the vagaries of their young, more human than their mothers.

There is the club of the young, idle, and very-much-to-be-liked young Englishmen of the wealthier sort, the pageant of the Drones (and, by the way, talking of clubs, what more exact bullseye has ever been hit by any marksman than the casual remark about the man being shown all the sights of London, " ending up with Bucks "?) Then there are the immortal, vivid glimpses of suburban life, for example the glorious adventures of the uncle who breaks loose once a year and showers gold upon the young man who jellies eels and his devoted would-be spouse: a lovely pair of lovers, as vivid as a strong transparency concentrated on one small screen—yet not a dozen adjectives between them.

Everything this author has seen he has observed; everything he has observed he has engraved; but, what is more remarkable than observation (which is common to many), or even than the record of observation (which is, though rare in any excellent degree, yet fairly well known) is the presentation of the thing observed so that it rises almost violently before the eye to which it is presented. That is everywhere, in every style, in every manner of subject the very heart of prose; not only of imaginative prose but of all prose.

Those great masters of prose whom the foolish think dull possess that power, as may be proved by the way in which whatever they have written is retained in the memory of the reader. To quote an instance of which I am fond and which is little known: Newman's chapters on "The Arians of the Fourth Century".

Now my fellow-worshippers at this shrine which Mr. Wodehouse has raised to the glory of his country, that is, of English letters, may rightly complain that praise of a man's craftsmanship is arid praise. When you say that Brou (which I suppose is the finest sculpture in Europe) leaves you breathless, you do not want to add any long technical discussion of how the figures were modelled or how the chisel worked upon that stone. Let me end therefore with something that is not a mere hymn of praise to Mr. Wodehouse's style (which I repeat and still maintain to be the summit of his achievement); let me end with something about him which is intensely national—I mean the creation of one more figure in that long gallery of living figures which makes up the glory of English fiction.

For the English people, more than any other, have created in their literature living men and women rather than types—and Mr. Wodehouse has created Jeeves.

He has created others, but in his creation of Jeeves he has done something which may respectfully be compared to the work of the Almighty in Michael Angelo's painting. He has formed a man filled with the breath of life. It is probable that the race of butlers will die even sooner than other modern species. They rose to meet a need.

They played a national rôle triumphantly. That rôle is now near extinction and they are ready to depart. You may say that Jeeves is not exactly a butler, but he is of the same rare divine metal from which butlers are made. He leads among those other butlers of Mr. Wodehouse's invention and indeed he leads all the gentlemen's gentlemen of the world. I should like the foreigner or posterity (much the same thing) to steep themselves in the living image of Jeeves and thus comprehend what the English character in action may achieve. Talk of efficiency!

I have just said that those of whom Jeeves is the prototype or the God are perhaps doomed, and this leads me to the last question which one always asks of all first-rate writing: will Mr. Wodehouse's work endure?

Pray note that literary work does not necessarily endure through its excellence. What is called " immortality " (whereas nothing mortal is immortal) is conferred upon a man's writing by external circumstances as much as by internal worth. I can show you whole societies of men for whom Keats would be meaningless and I know dozens of English men well versed in the French language who find Racine merely dull. Whether the now famous P. G. Wodehouse will remain upon that level for as many generations as he deserves, depends, alas, upon what happens to England. For my part I would like to make it a test of that very thing—" What happens to England."

If in, say, 50 years Jeeves and any other of that great company—but in particular Jeeves—shall have faded, then what we have so long called England will no longer be.

H. BELLOC.

About this book

Hilaire Belloc's Prefaces was designed by Loyola University Press. All type-setting except the facsimile prefaces was done in its composing room in Bodoni Book, 10 and 12 point.

It was printed by Photopress, Inc., on Warren's 60-pound English Finish paper and bound by The Engdahl Company.